Innovative Qualitative Methodologies
in Multilingual Literacy Development Research

Research Methods in Applied Linguistics (RMAL)

ISSN 2590-096X

The *Research Methods in Applied Linguistics* (RMAL) series publishes authoritative general guides and in-depth explorations of central research methodology concerns in the entire field of Applied Linguistics. The hallmark of the series is the contribution to stimulating and advancing professional methodological debates in the domain. Books published in the series (both authored and edited volumes) will be key resources for applied linguists (including established researchers and newcomers to the field) and an invaluable source for research methodology courses.

Main directions for the volumes in the series include (but are not limited to): Comprehensive introductions to research methods in Applied Linguistics (authoritative, introductions to domain-non specific methodologies); In-depth explorations of central methodological considerations and developments in specific areas of Applied Linguistics (authoritative treatments of domain-specific methodologies); Critical analyses that develop, expand, or challenge existing and/or novel methodological frameworks; In-depth reflections on central considerations in employing specific methodologies and/or addressing specific questions and problems in Applied Linguistics research; Authoritative accounts that foster improved understandings of the behind the scenes, inside story of the research process in Applied Linguistics.

For an overview of all books published in this series, please see *benjamins.com/catalog/rmal*

Editor

Rosa M. Manchón
University of Murcia

Volume 11

Innovative Qualitative Methodologies in Multilingual Literacy Development Research
Amplifying voices from immigrant, transnational, and refugee communities
Edited by Amanda K. Kibler and Fares J. Karam

Innovative Qualitative Methodologies in Multilingual Literacy Development Research

Amplifying voices from immigrant, transnational, and refugee communities

Edited by

Amanda K. Kibler
Oregon State University

Fares J. Karam
University of Nevada, Reno

John Benjamins Publishing Company

Amsterdam / Philadelphia

TM The paper used in this publication meets the minimum requirements of
the American National Standard for Information Sciences – Permanence
of Paper for Printed Library Materials, ANSI z39.48-1984.

DOI 10.1075/rmal.11

Cataloging-in-Publication Data available from Library of Congress:
LCCN 2024061210 (PRINT) / 2024061211 (E-BOOK)

ISBN 978 90 272 1980 0 (HB)
ISBN 978 90 272 1975 6 (PB)
ISBN 978 90 272 4493 2 (E-BOOK)

John Benjamins Publishing Company · https://benjamins.com

Table of contents

List of contributors

Melissa Adams Corral is an Assistant Professor of Mathematics Education at the University of Texas — Río Grande Valley. She takes a community organizing stance in her work developing methodologies. Her research draws attention to the knowledge and educational experiences of Latinx children from multilingual communities.

Fátima Andrade Martínez is a PhD candidate in the University of California, Santa Barbara Department of Education. Fátima's work focuses on undocumented students' experiences in higher education institutions.

Diana J. Arya is an Associate Professor and Faculty Director in Education at the University of California, Santa Barbara. Within the framework of Community Based Literacies (CBL), Diana leads explorations with a K-20 multilingual community who collaboratively engage in researching, knowledge building, and communicating about local issues and interests.

Maneka Deanna Brooks is Dean and Professor at Portland State University's College of Education. An equity-focused leader, her research explores bilingualism, adolescent literacy, and course placement. By reimagining traditional practices, Dr. Brooks advocates for just, inclusive learning environments, emphasizing the transformative role of education in society.

M. Sidury Christiansen is an Associate Professor of Applied Linguistics at the University of Texas at San Antonio. Her research explores the intersection between digital literacy and language ideologies, identities and cultures among multilingual populations. She engages in long-term ethnographic and self-reflexive research in online and offline environments.

Liv T. Dávila is an Associate Professor at the University of Illinois at Urbana-Champaign. Her research engages with applied linguistics, literacy studies, and educational anthropology to analyze how students' languages and literacies shape and are shaped by learning contexts, as well as global phenomena including migration, racism and racialization.

Sarah Gallo is an Associate Professor of Language Education and Urban Social Justice Education at Rutgers University. Her research has brought attention to the ways that undocumentedness shapes the educational and languaging lives of elementary school-aged children, their families, and their teachers in Mexico and the United States.

María Paula Ghiso is a Professor of Literacy Education and Chair of the Department of Curriculum and Teaching at Teachers College, Columbia University. Her scholarship investigates literacy in multilingual and transnational contexts and community-based research methodologies. The latter is the subject of her co-authored book, *Methods for Community-Based Research*.

Fares J. Karam is an Associate Professor of Teaching English to Speakers of Other Languages (TESOL) in the College of Education and Human Development at the University of Nevada, Reno. His scholarship focuses on the language and literacy development of students from immigrant and refugee backgrounds in addition to TESOL teacher education.

Amanda K. Kibler is a Professor in the College of Education at Oregon State University. Her scholarship focuses on the interactional and ecological contexts through which multilingual children and adolescents from immigrant backgrounds develop language and literacy expertise, as well as the ways in which teachers collaborate and use inquiry to facilitate these processes.

Jinhee Kim is an Associate Professor in the Department of Elementary and Early Childhood Education at Kennesaw State University. Her research areas include Asian/Asian American children, highly mobile children such as children experiencing homelessness in teacher education, notions of home in the school curriculum, and culturally sustaining research methods.

Hsiao-Chin Kuo is an Associate Professor of Literacy Education at Northeastern Illinois University. Dr. Kuo teaches teacher preparation classes to both pre- and in-service teachers, with a special focus on supporting culturally and linguistically diverse learners. Her research interests include multimodal literacies, school-home-community partnerships, and multimodal/visual art-based research.

Lizeth Lizarraga is a Ph.D. student in the Education Policy and Planning program at the University of Texas at Austin. Her research interests focus on educational equity and opportunity issues for culturally and linguistically diverse students in the K-12 education system. Lizeth is particularly interested in Latinx family access, collaboration, and advocacy regarding special education.

Andrew Maul is an Associate Professor in the Department of Education at the University of California, Santa Barbara. Andrew's work focuses on the conceptual foundations of research methodology in the human sciences, and in particular on the theory and practice of educational and psychological measurement.

Jim McKinley, SFHEA, is a Professor of Applied Linguistics at University College London. He has taught in higher education in the UK, Japan, Australia, and Uganda, as well as US schools. His research targets implications of internationalization for academic writing and higher education studies. He is an Editor-in-Chief of the journal *System*.

Sohyun Meacham is an Associate Professor in the Department of Curriculum and Instruction at the University of Northern Iowa. Her research interests center around children's meaning-making processes and teachers' dialogic intelligence to enhance these processes in classrooms. She advocates for diversity and social justice using multicultural children's literature in teacher education.

Valerie Meier is the Assistant Director of the McEnroe Reading and Language Arts Clinic at the University of California, Santa Barbara. Within the framework of Community Based Literacies, Valerie supports literacy programs that provide space for younger and older co-learners to share their interests, creativity, experiences, and multilingual expertise.

Rachel Salas is an Associate Professor of Literacy Studies at the University of Nevada, Reno, where she investigates intersections of STEM, literacy, language, and race in education. Her research focuses on enhancing the disciplinary literacy skills of marginalized students through robotics. She founded the Wolf Pack Bots/Lobos Robóticos program and collaborates with diverse communities through robotics-based educational initiatives.

Sanela Sprečić, a doctoral student at Western Michigan University in Education and Human Development (ESL focus), holds a Master's in Educational Leadership. With 27 years of experience, she leads the EL Program at Kentwood Public Schools. A 2021–2022 ESEA Distinguished Schools Award recipient, her interests include instruction and program improvements.

Amy Stornaiuolo is an Associate Professor of Literacy Education at the University of Pennsylvania. Her research investigates people's digital literacy practices, drawing on digital methods to trace literacies on the move across formal and informal cross-cultural spaces and broader socio-technical systems.

Zhongfeng Tian is an Assistant Professor of Bilingual Education at Rutgers University — Newark. His research interests include translanguaging, TESOL, bilingual education, and teacher education, utilizing participatory qualitative and self-reflexive methods. He also serves on the editorial boards of *TESOL Quarterly* and the *International Multilingual Research Journal*.

Su-Jeong Wee is an Associate Professor in the Department of Child and Family Studies at California State University, Los Angeles. Focusing on children's early childhood development, she critically analyze children's multicultural picturebooks, emphasizing the experiences of minoritized populations, intersectionality, cultures, diversity, and social justice.

CHAPTER 1

Introduction: Innovative paths in researching multilingual literacy development

Rethinking data, theory, and positionality

Amanda K. Kibler & Fares J. Karam
Oregon State University | University of Nevada, Reno

In this introductory chapter to the volume, *Innovative Qualitative Methodologies in Multilingual Literacy Development Research: Amplifying Voices from Immigrant, Transnational, and Refugee Communities*, we situate the key aims of the collection in the context of conceptual innovations in multilingualism, literacy, and equity. To unlock the full potential of these recent developments, innovative rethinking of methodological approaches is needed to keep pushing the boundaries of our understanding of multilingual literacy development and to further our ethical commitments to humanizing research. We describe selected recent empirical studies in which qualitative literacy researchers have begun to "rethink" data, theory, and positionality in their work before presenting an overview of the contributions in this volume.

Keywords: qualitative research, literacy, multilingual, methodology, innovation, equity

Introduction

Qualitative research focused on multilingualism and literacy development has proliferated in recent decades, reflecting exciting developments in theory and methodology that have brought important insights into the literate lives and experiences of multilingual children and adults from immigrant, transnational, and refugee backgrounds. However, scholars working in these areas span several different disciplinary fields with their own scholarly emphases, traditions, and publication venues. This volume draws together interdisciplinary and diverse scholarship on this topic in a single volume, and does so in ways that foreground

https://doi.org/10.1075/rmal.11.01kib

the importance of engaging in equitable research practices that serve to promote systemic change. As such, the studies contained in this volume highlight methodological innovations in qualitative research that are used to:

1. investigate the development of varied multilingual literacy practices that include diverse modalities, sociopolitical and racialized spaces, and materialities; and
2. explore these practices among diverse members of immigrant, transnational, and refugee communities in multiple contexts, including online/virtual and in-person settings across home, school, and community spaces.

We begin by first providing a brief overview of significant recent conceptual developments in multilingual literacy studies before then turning to the third purpose of our volume: documenting how methodological innovation can inform critical and equity-oriented research and instructional practices. We then explore the current scholarly landscape on qualitative data, theory, and positionality, the three areas to which our volume's chapters contribute.

Resituating concepts in multilingual literacy development

Recent decades have seen significant and ongoing developments in understanding multilingualism and literacy, as well as who multilingual learners are and the settings in which they learn. Here we provide a brief overview of some of these developments to situate the qualitative methodological innovations presented in our volume.

We utilize the term "multilingual" in this volume in an overarching and inclusive sense to emphasize multiple languages in use, but we do so with the knowledge that conceptualizations of language have evolved considerably over time and continue to do so. In general, early notions that emphasized "native-like" control over two or more distinct, autonomous languages (e.g., Bloomfield, 1933) have shifted to varied recognitions of the ways in which language repertoires are varied, dynamic, and interconnected. Terms including polylingualism, metrolingualism, plurilingualism, codeswitching, code-mixing, code-meshing, translanguaging, and translingualism reflect what Marshall and Moore (2018) describe as a "panoply of lingualisms", currently used to conceptualize how multilingual language resources are used by individuals and communities or societies. There are important differences among these perspectives, and although a review of the nuances of each term is outside the scope of this introduction, it is important to recognize that Applied Linguistics and literacy scholars have increasingly come to agree upon: (1) an overarching multilingual turn in the field that holistically acknowledges all languages in multilingual individuals' repertoires rather than considering solely the additional language(s) being developed; (2) a recognition that named languages are — to a greater or lesser degree, depending on the scholar — sociopolitical idealizations more than linguistic realities; (3) an understanding that language users each have unique repertoires for meaning-making that cross a range of linguistic boundaries and that change over time and by context; and (4) an acknowledgement that these ideas have important implications for pedagogy. Many readers of Applied Linguistics and literacy research are familiar with a surge of interest in and ongoing debates about translanguaging in relation to other understandings of multilingualism (e.g., García & Wei, 2014; Leung & Valdés, 2019; MacSwan, 2017, 2020, 2022; Otheguy et al., 2015, 2019). These and other disciplinary conversations about defining multilingualism remain contested and actively evolving aspects of the field. Authors in this volume take a variety of perspectives on defining language, which have important implications for the research they have undertaken.

The term "literacy" has similarly been the subject of re/interpretation by a range of scholars over time. In the 1990s and early 2000s, scholars began to actively explore literacies as social practices, and ones that are situated in dynamics of power, marginalization, and resistance (Barton & Hamilton, 2000; New London Group, 1996; Street, 2003). This perspective has continued to flourish in explorations of multiliteracies (e.g., Cope & Kalantzis, 2023), among other topics, and has been joined by a similar "panoply" of literacies that scholars have used to further explore the varied conditions under which individuals and communities create and interpret a range of texts that are not only written but also oral, digital, and multimodal.

These conceptualizations vary widely. For example, they include living literacies, which emphasize "the ways that meaning is made as people conduct everyday activities" (Rowsell & Pahl, 2020, p. 1). Some scholars have instead explored literacies in terms of the disciplinary contexts or practices in which they are situated (e.g., Coyle & Roca DeLarios, 2023; Shanahan & Shanahan, 2017), while others have emphasized literacies' multimodality (e.g., Jewitt, 2008; Kendrick, 2016; Hawkins & Mori, 2018) and the nuances of technology as individuals engage in digital literacies (e.g., Illomäki et al., 2023; see also Mirra & Garcia, 2020). Other scholars have sought post-humanist approaches to literacy, with attention to materiality (Hackett et al., 2020), embodiment (Gonzalez-Ibarra & Saavedra, 2021), and affect (Truman et al., 2020), among other concepts. Yet others have sought to better understand relationships between literacy and equity through attention to critical literacies (e.g., Bacon, 2017) and racial literacies (Chávez-Moreno, 2022). Other types of literacies that are particularly relevant to multilinguals include: transliteracies (Stornaiuolo et al, 2017), literacies of refuge (de Los

Ríos & Molina, 2020), cosmopolitan literacies (Hull & Stornaiuolo, 2014), transcripting literacies (Androutsopoulos, 2020; Wei et al., 2020), and literacies across timespace (Compton-Lilly & Halverson, 2014) and transmodalities (Hawkins & Mori, 2018), among others.

As this brief overview attests, conceptual developments in multilingualism and literacy have brought about new frameworks to the study of individuals and communities from immigrant, transnational, and refugee backgrounds. To unlock the full potential of the recent innovations and conceptual developments described above, a need arises for parallel innovations and creative rethinking of methodological approaches that provide additional tools to expand the boundaries of equitable research in multilingual literacy development.

Resituating equity in multilingual literacy development

In an age of resurgent nationalism and increasing xenophobic sentiments against migrant communities, it is important to better understand the complex settings in which multilingual learners from immigrant, transnational, and refugee backgrounds develop literacies across languages. Often subsumed under various bureaucratic labels, an increasingly diverse and multilingual population of learners across the globe continues to challenge our perceptions of literacies, and of what it means to read words and worlds (Freire, 1985).

In the context of conceptual developments, we as researchers must also address why we do the research that we do, and in this volume we emphasize how innovative methodologies can inform critical and equity-oriented research and instructional practices aimed at supporting multilinguals' literacy development. Thus, the third and final goal of our volume is to highlight how scholars use innovative qualitative research methodologies to document or support social and/or systemic change.

If we better understand the literacies undertaken across modalities, sociopolitical and racialized spaces, materialities, landscapes, and timespaces, it becomes possible to document multilinguals' engagement with various literacy practices that constitute forms of resistance, innovation, and hope in countering dominant and dehumanizing narratives that further marginalize this diverse population of learners. Methodologies that allow for explorations of such literacy contexts and practices in ethical and humanizing (Paris & Winn, 2014) ways can allow scholars not only to "study" multilingual learners' development but also to learn from their border-crossing and trans/multilingual literacy practices in order to enact social and systemic change.

Resituating research on multilingual literacy development

The conceptual and equity-oriented developments above have important methodological implications for research. Although such implications could be conceptualized in many ways, here we divide them into three main areas in which qualitative literacy researchers have begun to "rethink" their work: data, theory, and positionality. We explore selected recent empirical studies that address these areas to situate the methodological innovations presented in this volume. There are also powerful connections among these three areas of rethinking, which we discuss below.

Rethinking data

Although often treated unproblematically, the nature of data in qualitative research has been an ongoing subject of inquiry and critique. Writing from a post-qualitative methods perspective, St. Pierre (2013) explained why data need to be rethought:

> Data appear, come into being, exist (or not) in a particular ontological, epistemological, and methodological structure. The meaning and function of data depend on the meaning and function of a constellation of other concepts with which it is imbricated, for example, the concepts [of] reality, evidence, warrants, claims, reason, knowledge, and, of course, truth.   (p. 223)

St. Pierre described positivist perspectives as typically treating data as "given" (p. 224), objects that exist and carry meaning independent of how they are gathered and interpreted and by whom (although for positivist challenges to this approach from the philosophy of science, see Leonelli, 2015). Interpretive qualitative researchers tend to reject this proposition, instead understanding data as constructed by both researchers and those whom they study, thus becoming "interpretations piled on interpretations" (p. 224). However, according to St. Pierre (2013), even interpretive researchers often fail to acknowledge the theory-laden nature of data and instead employ positivist approaches to the analysis of data. While most innovative qualitative researchers have not "give[n] up data along with the conventional humanist qualitative inquiry in which it appears" (2013, p. 226), as St. Pierre describes having done, these critiques provide an important basis for rethinking data in qualitative research on multilingual literacy development.

The recent qualitative studies described below demonstrate how scholars are reconceptualizing data in ways that provide opportunities for more authentic and profound engagement in critical and equity-oriented research. For example, research that includes or focuses on multimodal data not only reflects our increasingly digital world: it also recognizes a broader array of literacy practices and resources for meaning making in which multilingual learners might have or gain expertise. Additionally, literacy research that attends to lived experiences across time and space help capture the ways in which both learners and their literacy practices are "on the move" and challenge geographic, conceptual, and institutional boundaries for languages and literacies, which Hawkins and Mori (2018) describe as the consideration of "trans" perspectives in Applied Linguistics research. In this sense, rethinking data is one way of amplifying voices of multilinguals from immigrant and refugee-backgrounds.

As researchers address new conceptualizations of multilingualism and literacy, they have reconsidered what "counts" as data in their studies. For many, this means moving beyond the written word and into multimodality. Arts-based visual methodologies allow for collection and analysis of new kinds of artifacts from both teachers (Ibrahim, 2022) and students, and pedagogical approaches such as language mapping (D'warte, 2014) and storyboarding (Ayoub & Omidire, 2021) can be analyzed in new ways as literacy practices and opportunities to better understand participants' experiences.

Reflecting literacy scholars' attention to 21st century technological developments, methodologies also consider a range of digital, virtual, and other multimodal literacy data. These often include attention to digital multimodal composing and storytelling (e.g., Vu et al., 2019; see also Kessler, 2024, and Zhang et al., 2023, for overviews of the field), and imply new types of data sources. Such data include screen capture and video observations, student design interviews, and multimodal products (e.g., Smith et al., 2020) as well as wearable technology, video diaries, and photography (see Yi et al., 2022 for a methodological review related to digital literacies). Ehret and Hollet (2014) have also called attention to including the "real virtualities" (p. 428) of embodiment and affect that occur as people engage in multimodal literacies together, not just a digital product itself. Such data require theoretical frameworks that account for the dynamic and multimodal nature of multilingualism and literacy, which are addressed further in "rethinking theory."

Material and embodied literacies outside of the digital world also imply a consideration of new data, ranging from gestures to artifacts. Baker and Scott (2016), for example, drew upon researchers' interview notes written during interviews conducted in American Sign language in a longitudinal case study of the K12 educational pathway of a deaf Latina student. Studies also draw upon artifactual literacies (Pahl & Rowsell, 2010) as a lens to underscore the role of material artifacts in multilingual literacy development. For example, Karam et al. (2021) documented how two Syrian refugee-background parents used artifacts to evoke counternarratives that challenge stereotypical representations of Muslim refugee-background families. Along similar lines, McNeill (2022) described the role of an artifactual literacy project in supporting the literacy development of emergent bilinguals and honoring their cultural heritage and religious traditions.

Related to notions of "living literacies" in everyday worlds, qualitative literacy research that purposefully moves beyond traditional school-related literacy practices likewise broadens our considerations of data. For Vieira (2016), this meant considering the sending of remittances by immigrants to their home counties as literacy practices worthy of exploration. Both Kim and Park (2020) and Iida and Chamcharatsri (2022) considered poetry as data in their explorations of translanguaging and poetic inquiry, respectively. In other instances, data have included covert literacy practices that are not privileged in classroom spaces (Kiramba, 2017) or even refusals to participate in school-related literacy practices (Truman et al., 2020).

Other innovations in rethinking data focus not only on the data themselves but on when and how it is collected and analyzed. For example, longitudinal data collection has a long history in Applied Linguistics and literacy research, but its recent uses are innovative in capturing how participants themselves develop, struggle, and adapt as contexts for literacy change. With the increasing pace of change, capturing these fleeting moments are important to understand literacy development, and in transnational and border-crossing settings, data move both over time and across physical and digital locations (e.g., Kibler, 2019; Kim, 2014; Little, 2024). Relatedly, rethinking data also encourages us to view literacy data as interconnected in new ways. Purcell Gates et al.'s (2011) proposal of a methodology for cross-case analysis and Compton-Lily et al.'s (2019) use of meta-ethnography suggest ways in which literacy data can be contextually situated but also able to be synthesized to gain larger insights into literacy practices and development.

Rethinking data has important connections to other aspects of innovative qualitative research. For example, rethinking data implies rethinking the ways in which it is analyzed. In addition to more explicit approaches to "thinking with theory" (Jackson & Mazzei, 2012; St. Pierre & Jackson, 2014), qualitative researchers have also drawn upon concepts from Deleuze and others to emphasize "connections rather than oppositions, movement rather than categorization, becoming rather than being" (St. Pierre, 2013, p. 226: see also Masny, 2013). From a different perspective, Arlander (2017) argued that in arts-based research, the role of research data, methods, and outputs or results can be "interchangeable, mixed, or hybridized" (p. 181) as artworks are developed and interpreted. Another important implication of rethinking data relates to positionality. As St. Pierre (2013) notes, an emphasis on connection, movement, and becoming implies new ways of conceptualizing researchers themselves: "We are not separate from the world.

Being in every sense is entangled, connected, indefinite, impersonal, shifting into different multiplicities and assemblages" (p. 226). As a result, our roles — including the ways in which we integrate an emphasis on equity into our work — are inextricable from the data we collect and interpret, including the ways we draw upon theory, to which we turn next.

Rethinking theory

The role of theory in educational research has often been perceived as problematic, ambiguous, and sometimes in tension with practice (e.g., Carr, 2005; Thomas, 2007). Freire (1985) described this "tension which exists between theory and practice, between authority and freedom, and perhaps between yesterday and today" (p. 177) to highlight the imbalance in power dynamics between theory and practice. Scholars also note a schism between theory and practice, and many have addressed this topic in TESOL, Applied Linguistics, and literacy studies, inviting scholars to bridge that rift and establish more concrete connections between the two (e.g., Cook, 2015; Handsfield, 2015; Kramsch, 2015; Rose, 2019).

From a researcher's perspective, theory is often described as the "orienting lens" (Creswell, 2013, p. 62) through which they can start making sense of their data and interpreting their findings. In a recent corpus-based analysis of the role of theory in quantitative and qualitative second language learning research produced between 2013–2019 in four top tier journals, Gao et al. (2022) found that while both quantitative and qualitative researchers used theory frequently, "qualitative researchers seemed more ready to both align themselves with the stances that the theories took and adjusted the theories to new contexts" (p. 12), showing flexibility in adapting theories to their particular research settings and using theory to both interpret and give legitimacy to their findings.

Within that frame, it is important to note how theory is not only "applied" to a certain context or set of participants, but it is also (re)shaped through interaction with overlapping local and transnational settings and experiences. One dimension of an ethical approach to qualitative research emphasized in this volume is to allow space for a dialogue between participants' agentive voices and the theories that the qualitative researcher is using as a lens. To build on the "orienting lens" (Creswell, 2013, p. 62) metaphor, the researcher no longer only *applies* the theory to participants' experiences but is also open to rethinking theory through the prism of participants' dynamic and ever-changing literacies and languages.

In short, rethinking theory does not only mean using it as a lens to better understand research findings. Indeed, literacy scholars use theory to highlight mechanisms whereby participants resist unjust conditions and engage in resistance literacies (Stewart & Babino, 2022), or (re)position themselves in ways that challenge dehumanizing and stereotypical representations of multilingual learners, drawing on various theories to achieve this goal. Abril-Gonzalez (2020) utilizes the concepts of *nepantla*, and a pedagogy of acompañamiento (accompaniment) to highlight a Mexican multilingual teen's identity as a *nepantlera* artist, and Moses and Kelly (2017) draw upon identity theory (among others) to show how a group of "struggling" multilingual first graders repositioned themselves as competent readers.

Other scholars expand theoretical horizons in literacy research by drawing on non-Western theories and approaches. In second language writing, McKinley (2022) calls for a more globalized approach as an innovative means to reconceptualize argumentative writing that has long been analyzed and perceived through the lens of Western deductive methods. Recent studies in literacy increasingly draw on non-Western theories, adopting Anzalduan concepts and notions of acompañamiento (e.g., Abril-Gonzalez's, 2020) and Afrocentric approaches and methodologies such as Sankofa (Wynter-Hoyte & Smith, 2020) and Kijiji-Mji-Jiji-Majuu (KMJM) (Wandera, 2020).

Other researchers use theories in an innovative manner to analyze their data. For instance, Lee et al. (2020) used affect theory as both theory and method to analyze the narratives of Latino immigrant youth. Others combine theoretical frameworks with analytical tools to sharpen their data analysis procedures and better interpret the data. For example, Rowe adopts social literacies (Street, 1995) as a theoretical lens in combination with a microethnogarphic (Bloome et al. 2010) analytic approach to better understand how a teacher promoted rationales for biliterate composing in a second-grade classroom. Along similar lines, Kim and Park (2020) adopt a translingual (e.g., Canagarajah, 2017) lens to highlight the potential of Sijo (Korean poetry) and poetry writing in general as a means to enact meaningful literacy instruction.

Overall, literacy scholars have gone beyond using theory as a mere "orienting lens" (Creswell, 2013, p.62) to center or better interpret findings. The examples described above show how researchers have engaged in rethinking theory as a means to allow new literacies and stories to emerge and to create spaces for multilingual participants to claim new identities and positionalities. Obviously, positionality is another important aspect of conducting qualitative research on multilingual literacy development that we turn to in the following section.

Rethinking positionality

A rethinking of qualitative research would be incomplete without explicit attention to researchers themselves. A researcher's positioning — including both their worldview and their situatedness in relation to a given research topic and context — are shaped by the varied values, beliefs, and multiple identities researchers hold

(Holmes, 2020). Investigating this positioning is "an exercise in deep reflexivity throughout the research process" (Martin et al., 2022, p. v), rather than an afterthought at the end of a study. It is this ongoing reflexivity that informs positionality: as Holmes (2020) explains, "self-reflection and a reflexive approach are both a necessary prerequisite and an ongoing process for the researcher to be able to identify, construct, critique, and articulate their positionality" (p. 2). Secules et al. (2021) noted that positionality is far more profound than an understanding of methodological limitations, an approach to minimize bias, or a measure of research quality. Rather, it impacts all facets of a study, including the research topic, epistemology, ontology, methodology, relation to participants, and communication.

Although positionality statements found in research reports are a manifestation of this exploration, such "products" should not be confused with the extensive process of reflexivity, which has the potential to lead to more transparent, ethical, and socially just research (de los Ríos & Patel, 2023; Martin et al., 2022; Sybing, 2022) through attention to the inherently political and power-laden nature of research. In this sense, positionality is "an important tool for reflecting on and dislocating privilege, particularly when working on equity research" (Secules et al., 2021).

Such reflexivity is complex for several reasons. In one sense, positionality is deeply relational and as a result is inherently fluid, changing over time during a study as relationships evolve (Fasavalu & Reynolds, 2019). Researchers themselves are also shaped by their work as they engage in it (Palangas et al., 2017), further underscoring the dynamic nature of positionality. Engaging in reflexivity can also be challenging because many power asymmetries between researchers and participants may be unspoken but nonetheless have notable impacts on data gathering, as shown by Deliovsky (2017) in relation to race and gender. And neither the process of reflexivity nor the negotiation and articulation of positionality can be reduced to checklists or sets of universal criteria, given their inherently contextual and nuanced nature (Martin et al., 2022). Finally, writing about positionality is meant to reveal power relations, but it can often simply reinstate researchers' authority. Such statements — including discussions of insider/outsider positionality — can purposefully or inadvertently imply that researchers are uniquely able to discern identities, relations, and their impacts in situations in which they are embedded (van Wingerden, 2022). Alternatives seek to explore the complexities of positionality without attempting to resolve them, such as Fine and Weis' (1998) lengthy exploration of the ethical dilemmas with which they grappled throughout their study and which remained unresolved in many ways. From a similar perspective, van Wingerden (2022) argues for a "more modest way of embodying researcher positionality" (p. 14) that explores the complexities of "being there" in a research context, "being moved" emotionally through this work, and "being vulnerable" as people and as researchers (p. 1).

While positionality statements have become almost a staple of qualitative research studies, scholars examining multilingual literacy development have approached describing and accounting for their positionalities in multiple ways and adopted various methodological approaches with respect to positionality. Some address the nuances of the outsider/insider status of the researcher pertaining to a certain research context or when working with certain populations. For example, Owodally (2011) described how her positionality as a Muslim woman and a parent whose children attended a Sunni madrassah (Muslim religious school) facilitated her recruitment process using a snowballing technique (e.g., the chairperson of the school board connected her with a textbook writer) and facilitated access to two research sites in Mauritius for observations. Being a Muslim woman (and wearing a hijab) made it easier to interview men within the context of these madrassahs as "it would have been considered odd and inappropriate for me, a woman, to engage in conversation with the men at the madrassahs" (p. 142). Another perspective comes from Jang (2017) who examines his own positionality as an Asian male and consequently his perceived legitimacy as a qualified literacy researcher and educator in the United States. He shares some of his lived experiences as a multilingual early career scholar to construct a counter-story that challenges stereotypical perceptions of Asian international researchers and doctoral students.

Other scholars share with us the influence of their outsider status on their research. For example, Ruecker's (2017) research took him to the U.S. — Mexico border (a context he was unfamiliar with) to examine the experiences of Latina/o students transitioning from high school to community college or university. Ruecker shared how "we as researchers change and are changed by the settings we visit" (p. 55) and presented specific strategies on how to negotiate outsider positionality as a white urban researcher in a predominantly Latina/o rural community by making connections to unfamiliar research contexts (e.g. learning local languages and building collaborative relationships). Apart from an insider or outsider positionality, some scholars describe an in-between state where they negotiate both positionalities. For example, Karam (2021) documented how two Syrian refugee-background parents negotiated writing a bilingual multimodal bedtime story for their children. Although the author was born and raised in an Arabic country bordering Syria and experienced displacement himself (providing him with an insider lens), he also acknowledged differences between Lebanon and Syria (e.g., in the Arabic dialects and cultural traditions) and emphasized how experiences of displacement are far from monolithic.

Researchers also describe how their positionalities have motivated or influenced the research work they do. For example, García-Fernandez (2023) explained how her "Deaf Chicana consciousness awakening has led me to propose a new theoretical framework, Deaf-Latinx Critical Theory (Deaf-LatCrit)" (p.72) to give voice to Deaf-Latinx individuals and their families. Kedley (2022) shared how their language, gender, and sexuality led the researcher to examine how they were read (or misread) by LGBTI community members in Honduras.

Other researchers pay close attention to reflexivity and joint construction of data. Poveda et al. (2020) reflexively turned to liminal spaces in their research context. Through reflexive analysis of their positionalities, the authors rethink what counts as legitimate data sources whereby negotiations to establish a research collaboration within the context of bilingual English-Spanish programs in Spain become rich data sites. Their findings suggest that how participants (including teachers, administrators, and parents) negotiated or framed access to their classrooms or linguistic practices helped the researchers better understand participants' language ideologies and processes of commodifying English within that research context. Hunt et al.'s (2016) examination of a bilingual writers' workshop in a fourth grade classroom described how the teacher facilitating the workshop "challenged the traditional qualitative frame of data *collection* as she actively participated in data *generation*" (p.400). For example, in one instance, the teacher turned to the camera and asked the researcher if they wanted insight into what the students were doing, prompting students to recall past events and turn the observation into an informal interview on the spot. Furthermore, scholars have adopted different methodological approaches with attention to positionality. Some, for example, have engaged in autoethnography (e.g., Wargo, 2020; also see Keles, 2022 for a review of autoethnographic research in Applied Linguistics) or participatory research (e.g., Burns & McPherson, 2017; West & Crookes, 2017).

Overall, literacy scholars continue to seek innovative ways to rethink positionality. Such efforts cannot be separated from ethical considerations that accompany methodological innovations in literacy research. The following outline of studies will highlight how the chapters in this volume engage with innovative research designs and methodologies that are anchored in ethical and equitable approaches of conducting qualitative research.

Overview of chapters in the volume

Authors in this volume present innovative ways to rethink data, theory, and positionality in qualitative research examining multilingual literacy development.

In Part 1, authors focus on data in relation to qualitative meta-synthesis (Brooks), ethnetnography (Karam & Kibler), and multimodal artworks (Kuo & Sprečić). In the first chapter, *Rethinking qualitative meta-syntheses in literacy studies: Critical questions*, Maneka Brooks critically examines how qualitative meta-syntheses are conducted through drawing upon a previously published meta-synthesis of students' experiences within the context of reading intervention courses. The chapter presents qualitative researchers with specific guidelines on how to rethink meta-synthesis methodology through critical analysis of original research to support a more just representation of linguistically minoritized students.

The next chapter, *An ethnetnography of (non)belonging: The transliterate practices of a Muslim refugee-background mother*, by Fares J. Karam and Amanda K. Kibler, presents ethnetnography as a methodological innovation that combines traditional ethnographic methods with netnographic methods (focusing on participants' online interactions). The researchers define ethnetnography as "a form of qualitative research that combines both ethnographic and netnographic approaches to collect and analyze data with the purpose of examining the experiences of (transnational) individuals across multiple languages, spaces, temporalities, and modalities." (p. 56) They discuss theoretical assumptions underlying an ethnetnographic methodology and present practical and ethical guidelines of conducting an ethnetnography through sharing their own work that examines a Muslim refugee-background mother's resettlement experiences.

The final chapter in this section, *Communicating selves: Immigrant, emergent multilingual students' voices and agency through their multimodal artworks*, by Hsiao-Chin Kuo and Sanela Sprečić, employs critical multimodal analysis with various multimodal data sources to amplify the identities and sense of agency of students from immigrant backgrounds. More specifically, the chapter highlights participants' artwork and sketches to emphasize how monomodal and monolingual research approaches can unintentionally present an incomplete picture of multilingual students' identities and transnational experiences.

Part 1 concludes with a commentary by Amy Stornaiuolo, who calls out the importance of rethinking data in a "postdigital" world. Stornaiuolo reflects upon how the authors in this section explore the ethical and practical challenges involved in identifying and gathering data in multimodal and multilingual contexts, how they work to expand what counts as data, and how they provide unique insights into researcher positionality. Stornaiuolo further calls for future research into the complex systems behind digital platforms we often take for granted, and into the ways we can move further beyond distinctions between online and offline spaces.

The chapters in Part 2 call upon us to rethink theory in qualitative research on multilingual literacy with play-based family literacy and *suda* (Kim et al.), Anzalduan theory within the context of a robotics program (Salas & Lizárraga Dueñas), and transborder literacies of (in)visibility (Adams Corral & Gallo). In the first chapter of Part 2, *Korean American children's voices in translanguaging play-based family literacy (PBFL) through the Suda (수다) approach*, Jinhee Kim, Su-Jeong Wee, and Sohyun Meacham present suda as an innovative and culturally responsive tool to collect and analyze data. They define suda as "a type of conversation similar to small talk, but it entails a significant length of time with several emergent stories in Korean culture" (p.102). To demonstrate how to rethink theory and methods through suda, they draw upon their own children's play-based family literacy practices at home and share implications on the benefits of suda as a culturally responsive theoretical frame within the context of early childhood multilingual development.

The second chapter in Part 2 is titled *Bridging language and STEM: Using an Anzalduan framework to center Latinx elementary and middle school students' understanding of robotics*, by Rachel G. Salas and Lizeth I. Lizárraga Dueñas. The authors rethink Anzalduan theory through incorporating Deleuze and Guattari's (1980/1987) characteristics of a minor literature as an additional lens to better understand how a group of Latinx students use the imagery of the mestiza body to bridge their understanding of STEM topics to real-world experiences and make connections to their own identities, languages, and experiences.

The third chapter in Part 2, by Melissa Adams Corral and Sarah Gallo, is titled *Families' literacies of (in)visibilty: Methodological approaches to understanding precarity without culpability*. This chapter presents transborder literacies of (in)visibility as an innovative theoretical framework that can help us rethink what counts as reading and writing, centering the rich and often invisible literacies of transborder families and providing researchers with the chance to reconsider their own literacies as well.

In the commentary that concludes Part 2, Jim McKinley takes an ecological approach to explore how the three aforementioned chapters in Part 2 rethink theory in their studies of multilinguals' literacy development. McKinley notes that these innovative uses of theory align well with multilingual learners' sociocultural realities and with expanded notions of literacy. McKinley argues that such theoretical rethinking can support more culturally-sustaining and participant-centered research through considering the transformative potential of innovative uses of theory.

Part 3 focuses on interrogating research practices through new explorations of positionality in qualitative research on multilingual literacy development. Such explorations include embodied reflexivity (Dávila), the dialogic void (Arya et al.), and critical collaborative autoethnography (Christiansen & Tian). The first chapter in this section is titled *Embodied reflexivity and researching the literacy practices of an adolescent multilingual refugee who is d/Deaf/Hard-of-Hearing*, by Liv Dávila. The chapter invites us to rethink positionality as embodied and consider affective, spatial, and corporeal dimensions of reflexivity. To demonstrate, Dávila draws upon her ethnographic research with an adolescent multilingual refugee student who was diagnosed with a severe hearing impairment. She defines and presents examples of embodied reflexivity as it applies to her positioning within the context of her research, sharing specific guidelines for incorporating embodied reflexivity in research on multilingual literacy.

The next chapter is by Diana J. Arya, Fátima Andrade Martínez, Valerie Meier, and Andrew Maul. The chapter, titled *Exploring the 'void' of silent/ced knowledge and expertise of multilingual learners*, adopts the *dialogic void* as a means of uncovering silences in educational spaces. The chapter describes how researchers' positionalities and identities can be important factors in shaping or obscuring observations and representations of multilingual learners in English-dominant classroom contexts.

The final chapter in Part 3, by M. Sidury Christiansen, and Zhongfeng Tian, is titled *Critical collaborative autoethnography*. The authors draw upon their own experiences in navigating academic publishing and engaging with critical collaborative autoethnography as a means to decolonize academic writing and center non-Western perspectives in academia. They also share specific lessons that they learned through this process that can help shift our thinking from "individual positionality to relationality — a more dynamic understanding of the relationships and interactions that shape one's research" (p. 248).

The commentary for Part 3 is provided by María Paula Ghiso, who emphasizes the importance of rethinking positionality as part of a broader emphasis on collaborative research approaches that challenge extractivist approaches and disrupt traditional relationships between researchers and participants. Ghiso emphasizes the importance of positionalities of relation and community accountability in exploring innovative qualitative literacy research.

The volume closes with a concluding chapter by the Editors in which we argue for the importance of responsive, inclusive, and ecological epistemologies in guiding researchers engaged in critical and equity-oriented qualitative research. We close with implications for qualitative literacy researchers.

Overall, each chapter in this volume presents a unique innovation in qualitative methodology, inviting us to rethink data, theory, and positionality in researching multilingual literacy development and centering ethical approaches that amplify the voices of participants from immigrant, transnational, and refugee backgrounds.

References

Abril-Gonzalez, P. (2020). Accompanying a nepantlera border artist's empathy: One Mexican teen's testimonios of healing, empowerment, and transformation. *Journal of Adolescent & Adult Literacy, 64*(3), 271–280.

Androutsopoulos, J. (2020). Trans-scripting as a multilingual practice: The case of Hellenised English. *International Journal of Multilingualism, 17*(3), 286–308.

Arlander, A. (2017). Data, material, remains. In M. Koro-Ljungberg, T. Löytönen, & M. Tesar (Eds.), *Disrupting data in qualitative inquiry: Entanglements with the post-critical and post-anthropocentric* (pp. 173–184). Peter Lang.

Ayoub, A., & Omidire, M. F. (2021). Storyboards as a qualitative method of exploring learners' experience with the use of a multilingual support strategy. *International Journal of Qualitative Methods, 20.*

Bacon, C. K. (2017). Multilanguage, multipurpose: A literature review, synthesis, and framework for critical literacies in English language teaching. *Journal of Literacy Research, 49*(3), 424–453.

Baker, S., & Scott, J. (2016). Sociocultural and academic considerations for school-age d/deaf and hard of hearing multilingual learners: A case study of a deaf Latina. *American Annals of the Deaf 161*(1), 43–55.

Barton, D., & Hamilton, M. (2000). Literacy practices. In D. Barton, M. Hamilton, & R. Ivanič (Eds.), *Situated literacies: Reading and writing in context* (pp. 7–15). Routledge.

Bloome, D., Power Carter, S., Christian, B. M., Otto, S., & Shuart-Faris, N. (2010). *Discourse analysis and the study of classroom language and literacy events: A microethnographic perspective.* Routledge.

Bloomfield, L. (1933). *Language.* Holt, Rinehart and Winston.

Burns, A., & McPherson, P. (2017). Action research as iterative design: Implications for English language education research. In S. A. Mirhosseini (Ed.), *Reflections on qualitative research in language and literacy education* (pp. 105-120). Springer.

Canagarajah, A. S. (2017). Introduction: The nexus of migration and language: The emergence of a disciplinary space. In S. A. Canagarajah (Ed.), *The Routledge handbook of migration and language* (pp. 1–28). Routledge.

Carr, D. (2005). *Making sense of education: An introduction to the philosophy and theory of education and teaching.* Routledge.

Chávez-Moreno, L. C. (2022). Critiquing racial literacy: Presenting a continuum of racial literacies. *Educational Researcher, 51*(7), 481–488.

Compton-Lilly, C., & Halverson, E. (Eds.). (2014). *Time and space in literacy research.* Routledge.

Compton-Lilly, C. F., Rogers, R. L., & Lewis Ellison, T. (2019). A meta-ethnography of family literacy scholarship: Ways with metaphors and silence. *Reading Research Quarterly*, 55(2), 271–289.

Cook, G. (2015). Birds out of dinosaurs: The death and life of applied linguistics. *Applied Linguistics*, 36, 425–433.

Cope, B. & Kalantzis, M. (2023). Multiliteracies: A literature review. In C. G. Zapata, M. Kalantzis, & B. Cope (Eds.), *Multiliteracies in international educational contexts*. Routledge.

Coyle, Y., & Roca de Larios, J. (2023). Exploring children's L2 disciplinary literacy through a multimodal science project in a CLIL context. *TESOL Quarterly*,58(2), 628–663.

Creswell, J. W., & Creswell, J. D. (2018). *Research design: Qualitative, quantitative, and mixed methods approaches*. (5th ed.) Sage.

de los Ríos, C. V., & Molina, A. (2020). Literacies of refuge: "Pidiendo posada" as ritual of justice. *Journal of Literacy Research*, 52(1), 32–54.

de los Ríos, C. V., & Patel, L. (2023). Positions, positionality, and relationality in educational research. *International Journal of Qualitative Studies in Education*, 1–12.

Deliovsky, K. (2017). Whiteness in the qualitative research setting: Critical skepticism, radical reflexivity and anti-racist feminism. *Journal of Critical Race Inquiry*, 4(1), 1–24.

D'warte, J. (2014). Exploring linguistic repertoires: Multiple language use and multimodal literacy activity in five classrooms. *The Australian Journal of Language and Literacy*, 37(1), 21–30.

Ehret, C., & Hollett, T. (2014). Embodied composition in real virtualities: Adolescents' literacy practices and felt experiences moving with digital, mobile devices in school. *Research in the Teaching of English*, 48(4), 428–452. http://www.jstor.org/stable/24398691.

Fasavalu, T. I., & Reynolds, M. (2019). Relational positionality and a learning disposition: Shifting the conversation. *The International Education Journal: Comparative Perspectives*, 18(2), 11–25. https://openjournals.library.sydney.edu.au/index.php/IEJ

Freire, P. (1985). *The politics of education. Culture, power, and liberation*. Macmillan.

Gao, J., Pham, Q. H. P., & Polio, C. (2022). The role of theory in quantitative and qualitative second language learning research: A corpus-based analysis. *Research Methods in Applied Linguistics*, 1(2), 100006.

García, O., & Li Wei. (2014). *Translanguaging, bilingualism, and bilingual education*. Palgrave Macmillan.

García-Fernández, C. (2023) Shattering deaf and hearing dualism through a Deaf-Latinx epistemology lens, *International Journal of Qualitative Studies in Education*, 36(1), 72-86.

González Ybarra, M., & Saavedra, C. M. (2021). Excavating embodied literacies through a Chicana/Latina feminist framework. *Journal of Literacy Research*, 53(1), 100–121.

Hackett, A., MacLure, M., & Pahl, K. (2020). Literacy and language as material practices: Re-thinking social inequality in young children's literacies. *Journal of Early Childhood Literacy*, 20(1), 3–12.

Handsfield, L. J. (2015). *Literacy theory as practice: Connecting theory and instruction in K–12 classrooms*. Teachers College Press.

Hawkins, M. R., & Mori, J. (2018). considering 'trans-' perspectives in language theories and practices, *Applied Linguistics*, 39(1), 1–8.

Holmes, A. G. D. (2020). Researcher positionality – A consideration of its influence and place in qualitative research – A new researcher guide. *Shanlax International Journal of Education*, 8(4), 1–10.

Hull, G. A., & Stornaiuolo, A. (2014). Cosmopolitan literacies, social networks, and "proper distance": Striving to understand in a global world. *Curriculum Inquiry*, 44(1), 15–44.

Hunt, C. S., Crumpler, T. P., & Handsfield, L. J. (2016). "Do you want an idea of what they're doing?" Transgressive data generation and analysis within a bilingual writers workshop. *International Journal of Qualitative Studies in Education*, 29(3), 399–425.

Ibrahim, N. C. (2022). Visual and artefactual approaches in engaging teachers with multilingualism: Creating DLCs in pre-service teacher education. *Languages*, 7(2), 152.

Iida, A., & Chamcharatsri, B. (2022) Emotions in second language poetry writing: A poetic inquiry into Japanese EFL students' language learning experiences. *Innovation in Language Learning and Teaching*, 16(1), 53–66.

Ilomäki, L., Lakkala, M., Kallunki, V., Mundy, D., Romero, M., Romeu, T., & Gouseti, A. (2023). Critical digital literacies at school level: A systematic review. *Review of Education*, 11(3).

Jackson, A. Y., & Mazzei, L. A. (2012). *Thinking with theory in qualitative research: Viewing data across multiple perspectives*. Routledge.

Jewitt, C. (2008). Multimodality and literacy in school classrooms. *Review of Research in Education*, 32(1), 241–267.

Karam, F. J. (2021). Writing the story of Sabadullah: Transnational literacies of two refugee-background parents. In D. Warriner (Ed.), *Refugee education across the lifespan: Mapping experiences of language learning and use* (pp. 231–250). Springer.

Karam, F. J., Oikonomidoy, E., & Kibler, A. K. (2021). Artifactual literacies and TESOL: Narratives of a Syrian refugee-background family. *TESOL Quarterly*, 55(2), 510–535.

Kedley, K. E. (2022) The illegible and illiterate researcher in Honduras: Research in a transnational setting as a queer from the Global North, *International Journal of Qualitative Studies in Education*, 35(9), 1007-1021,

Keles, U. (2022). Autoethnography as a recent methodology in applied linguistics: A methodological review. *The Qualitative Report*, 27(2), 448–474.

Kendrick, M. (2016). *Literacy and multimodality across global sites*. Routledge.

Kessler, M. (2024). *Digital multimodal composing: Connecting theory, research, and practice in second language acquisition*. Multilingual Matters.

Kibler, A. K. (2019). *Longitudinal interactional histories: Bilingual and biliterate journeys of Mexican immigrant-origin youth*. Palgrave Macmillan.

Kim, M. S. (2014). The multi-literacy development of a young trilingual child: Four leading literacy activities from birth to age six. *European Early Childhood Education Research Journal*, 22(2), 154–168.

Kim, K. M., & Park, G. (2020). "It is more expressive for me": A translingual approach to meaningful literacy instruction through sijo poetry. *TESOL Quarterly*, 54(2), 281–309.

Kiramba, L. K. (2017). Multilingual literacies: Invisible representation of literacy in a rural classroom. *Journal of Adolescent & Adult Literacy*, 61(3), 267–277.

Kramsch, C. (2015). Applied linguistics: A theory of the practice. *Applied Linguistics*, 36, 454–465.

doi Lee, C. C., Falter, M. M., & Schoonover, N. R. (2021). Encountering the affective in Latino immigrant youth narratives. *Reading Research Quarterly*, 56(2), 273–292.

doi Leonelli, S. (2015). What counts as scientific data? A relational framework. *Philosophy of Science*, 82(5), 810–821.

doi Leung, C., & Valdés, G. (2019). Translanguaging and the transdisciplinary framework for language teaching and learning in a multilingual world. *The Modern Language Journal*, 103(2), 348–370. http://www.jstor.org/stable/45172005.

doi Little, S. (2024). Rivers of multilingual reading: exploring biliteracy experiences among 8–13-year old heritage language readers. *Journal of Multilingual and Multicultural Development*, 45(2), 323–336.

doi MacSwan, J. (2017). A multilingual perspective on translanguaging. *American Educational Research Journal*, 54(1), 167–201.

doi MacSwan, J. (2020). Translanguaging, language ontology, and civil rights. *World Englishes*, 39(2), 321–333.

MacSwan, J. (Ed.). (2022). *Multilingual perspectives on translanguaging*. Multilingual Matters.

doi Marshall, S., & Moore, D. (2018). Plurilingualism amid the panoply of lingualisms: Addressing critiques and misconceptions in education. *International Journal of Multilingualism*, 15(1), 19–34.

doi Martin, J. P., Desing, R., & Borrego, M. (2022). Positionality statements are just the tip of the iceberg: Moving towards a reflexive process. *Journal of Women and Minorities in Science and Engineering*, 28(4), v–vii.

doi Masny, D. (2013). Rhizoanalytic pathways in qualitative research. *Qualitative Inquiry*, 19(5), 339–348.

doi McKinley, J. (2022). An argument for globalized L2 writing methodological innovation. *Journal of Second Language Writing*, 58.

doi McNeill, E. (2022). Exploring global religious traditions through artifactual literacy projects, *English Teaching: Practice & Critique*, 21(3).

doi Mirra, N., & Garcia, A. (2020). In search of the meaning and purpose of 21st-century literacy learning: A critical review of research and practice. *Reading Research Quarterly*, 56(3), 463–496.

doi Moses, L., & Kelly, L. B. (2017). The development of positive literate identities among emerging bilingual and monolingual first graders. *Journal of Literacy Research*, 49(3), 393–423.

doi New London Group. (1996). A pedagogy of multiliteracies: Designing social futures. *Harvard Educational Review*, 66(1), 60–93.

doi Otheguy, R., García, O., & Reid, W. (2015). Clarifying translanguaging and deconstructing named languages: A perspective from linguistics. *Applied Linguistics Review*, 6(3), 281–307.

doi Otheguy, R., García, O., & Reid, W. (2019). A translanguaging view of the linguistic system of bilinguals. *Applied Linguistics Review*, 10(4), 625–651.

Pahl, K., & Rowsell, J. (2010). *Artifactual literacies: Every object tells a story*. Teachers College Press.

doi Palaganas, E., Sanchez, M., Molintas, Ma. V., & Caricativo, R. (2017). Reflexivity in qualitative research: A journey of learning. *The Qualitative Report*, 22(2), 426–438.

doi   Paris, D., & Winn, M. T. (2014). *Humanizing research: Decolonizing qualitative inquiry with youth and communities*. Sage.

doi   Poveda, D., Giampapa, F., & Relaño-Pastor, A. M. (2020). Gatekeeping the interactional order: field access and linguistic ideologies in Content and Language Integrated Learning–type bilingual education programs in Spanish secondary schools. *Qualitative Research*, 20(6), 854–873.

doi   Purcell-Gates, V., Perry, K. H., & Briseño, A. (2011). Analyzing literacy practice: Grounded theory to model. *Research in the Teaching of English*, 45(4), 439–458. http://www.jstor.org/stable/23050582.

doi   Rose, H. (2019). Dismantling the ivory tower in TESOL: A renewed call for teaching-informed research. *TESOL Quarterly*, 53(3), 895–905.

Rowsell, J., & Pahl, K. (2020). What is living literacies? In K. Pahl, J. Rowsell, D. Collier, S. Pool, Z. Rasool, & T. Trzecak (Eds.), *Living literacies: Literacy for social change* (p. 1–16). The MIT Press.

doi   Ruecker, T. (2017). Stranger in a strange land: Conducting qualitative literacy research across contexts. In S. A. Mirhosseini (Ed.), *Reflections on qualitative research in language and literacy education* (pp. 45-57). Springer.

doi   Secules, S., McCall, C., Mejia, J. A., Beebe, C., Masters, A. S., L. Sánchez-Peña, M., & Svyantek, M. (2021). Positionality practices and dimensions of impact on equity research: A collaborative inquiry and call to the community. *Journal of Engineering Education*, 110(1), 19–43.

doi   Shanahan, C., & Shanahan, T. (2017). Disciplinary literacy. In D. Fischer & D. Lapp (Eds.), *Handbook of research on teaching the language arts*. Routledge.

doi   Smith, B. E., Pacheco, M. B., & Khorosheva, M. (2020). Emergent bilingual students and digital multimodal composition: A systematic review of research in secondary classrooms. *Reading Research Quarterly*, 56(1), 33–52.

doi   Stewart, M. A., & Babino, A. (2022). Enacting resistance literacies through languaging and advocacy: Intergenerational testimonios to inform literacy research and instruction. *Literacy Research and Instruction*, 61(4), 361–382.

doi   Stornaiuolo, A., Smith, A., & Phillips, N. C. (2017). Developing a transliteracies framework for a connected world. *Journal of Literacy Research*, 49(1), 68–91.

doi   St. Pierre, E. A. (2013). The appearance of data. *Cultural Studies ↔ Critical Methodologies*, 13(4), 223–227.

doi   St. Pierre, E. A., & Jackson, A. Y. (2014). Qualitative data analysis after coding. *Qualitative Inquiry*, 20(6), 715–719.

doi   Street, B. (2003). What's "new" in new literacy studies? Critical approaches to literacy in theory and practice. *Current Issues in Comparative Education*, 5(2), 77–91.

doi   Sybing, R. (2022). Dead reckoning: A framework for analyzing positionality statements in ethnographic research reporting. *Written Communication*, 39(4), 757–789.

Thomas, G. (2007). *Education and theory*. McGraw-Hill Education.

doi   Truman, S. E., Hackett, A., Pahl, K., McLean Davies, L., & Escott, H. (2020). The capaciousness of no: Affective refusals as literacy practices. *Reading Research Quarterly*, 56(2), 223–236.

doi   Van Wingerden, E. (2022). Unmastering research: Positionality and intercorporeal vulnerability in international studies. *International Political Sociology*, 16(2).

doi Vieira, K. (2016). Writing remittances: Migration-driven literacy learning in a Brazilian homeland. *Research in the Teaching of English*, 50(4), 422–449. http://www.jstor.org /stable/24889943.

doi Vu, V., Warschauer, M., & Yim, S. (2019). Digital storytelling: A district initiative for academic literacy improvement. *Journal of Adolescent & Adult Literacy*, 63(3), 257–267.

doi Wandera, D. B. (2020). Resisting Epistemic blackout: Illustrating Afrocentric methodology in a Kenyan classroom. *Reading Research Quarterly*, 55(4), 643–662.

doi Wargo, J. M. (2020). Between an iPhone and a safe space: tracing desire in connective (auto)ethnographic research with LGBTQ youth, International Journal of *Qualitative Studies in Education*, 33(5,) 508-523.

doi Wei, L., Tsang, A., Wong, N., & Lok, P. (2020). *Kongish Daily*: Researching translanguaging creativity and subversiveness. *International Journal of Multilingualism*, 17(3), 309–335.

doi West, G. B., & Crookes, G. (2017). Critical practitioner research in language education under difficult circumstances. In S. A. Mirhosseini (Ed.), *Reflections on qualitative research in language and literacy education* (pp. 139-155). Springer.

doi Wynter-Hoyte, K., & Smith, M. (2020). "Hey, Black child. Do you know who you are?" Using African diaspora literacy to humanize Blackness in early childhood education. *Journal of Literacy Research*, 52(4), 406–431.

doi Yi, Y., Cho, S., & Jang, J. (2022). Methodological innovations in examining digital literacies in Applied Linguistics research. *TESOL Quarterly*, 56(3), 1052–1062.

doi Zhang, M., Akoto, M., & Li, M. (2023). Digital multimodal composing in post-secondary L2 settings: a review of the empirical landscape. *Computer Assisted Language Learning*, 36(4), 694–721.

PART 1

Challenges and affordances of qualitative methodological approaches

Rethinking "data" in qualitative research on multilingual literacy

CHAPTER 2

Rethinking qualitative meta-syntheses in literacy studies
Critical questions

Maneka Deanna Brooks
College of Education, Portland State University

This chapter presents a critical examination of qualitative meta-synthesis in literacy research, emphasizing its role in amplifying student voices and uncovering overlooked aspects of educational practices. Drawing from a previously published meta-synthesis on adolescent experiences in reading intervention courses (RICs), the chapter reveals challenges in applying findings to linguistically diverse students due to inconsistencies in data representations of multilingualism. The chapter underscores the potential of attentive data analysis and proposes two critical question sets to vet studies to ensure nuanced representations of linguistic diversity. By advocating for thorough analyses in original research and refining meta-synthesis methodology, the chapter underscores the significance of addressing multilingual students' experiences in literacy education.

Keywords: meta-synthesis, English learners, adolescents, literacy education, reading intervention

Introduction

Within the study of literacy, scholars have relied on a variety of approaches to synthesize research. Popular methods of research synthesis include meta-analyses, integrative reviews, and meta-ethnographies. In recent decades, qualitative meta-synthesis has been more frequently used in both education broadly and within the field of literacy studies (Au, 2007; Compton-Lilly et al., 2021). "A qualitative metasynthesis is an analysis and interpretation of the findings of a selected pool of studies" (Berry & Thunder, 2012, p. 43). Qualitative meta-synthesis provides a counterbalance to more popular and frequently used ways of synthesizing quantitative research, like meta-analysis. It builds upon the assets of interpretive synthesis to inform research, practice, and policymaking. Of particular importance

https://doi.org/10.1075/rmal.11.02bro

for this chapter, meta-synthesis allows researchers to construct meaning about a broad body of research and identify lacunae within areas of study.

This chapter has as its origins a meta-synthesis of adolescent experiences in reading intervention courses (RICs) that I conducted with Katherine Frankel and Julie Learned (Frankel et al., 2021). The guiding research question of that meta-synthesis was: How do students experience and perceive RICs? Within this study, we defined RICs as compulsory, yearlong courses that supplement content-area classes with the goal of improving adolescents' reading. We found that youths' own varied conceptualizations of themselves as literate beings, combined with the extent to which they viewed their RICs as relevant, agentive, and facilitative of relationships, mediated their experiences and perceptions of RICs. In addition, students across studies described placement policies and practices as confusing, frustrating, and embarrassing. As a part of conducting, publishing, and sharing this study, I witnessed the power of this type of qualitative research to amplify student voice. We were able to bring together 20 years of research in a single meaningful document. This meta-synthesis was able to attend to specific topics, like students' perspectives of course placement, that had been overlooked in popular and highly cited meta-analyses (Boulay et al., 2015; Edmonds et al., 2009).

As a scholar whose work is on the intersection of bilingualism and adolescent literacy, I encountered a fissure when I used our Frankel et al.'s (2021) meta-synthesis with high school teachers who served students identified as English learners (ELs) in their RICs. They were often curious as to the specific experiences and perceptions of students identified as ELs. However, I could not talk about our overall findings with relationship to this specific group of students. This fact was troubling because from professional experience and reviewing the research, I knew that this student population was frequently served in RICs. For instance, research has documented the varied roles RICs play in the educational trajectories of multilingual adolescents who are identified as ELs (e.g., Brooks, 2018, 2022; Callahan, 2006; Kim, 2017; Wu & Coady, 2010). This experience pushed me to conduct a second meta-synthesis that specifically focused on the experiences of high school students classified as ELs. The research question that initially informed this second meta-synthesis was: How do multilingual EL-identified students experience and perceive RICs?

Unfortunately, I halted my efforts to complete the second meta-synthesis during the initial stages of mining the larger corpus of studies for the experiences of high school students classified as ELs. I was hindered by researchers' inconsistent description of the students' official English language acquisition status (e.g., "English only", "English learner", "Former English learner"). The inconsistent use of these bureaucratic labels made specific topics related to multilingual students less salient within a general meta-synthesis of RICs and prevented the development of a meta-synthesis specifically on EL students in RICs. Instead, I shifted my focus to examine how researchers describe the official English language acquisition status and the linguistic backgrounds of students within the pool of studies that I had identified for the second meta-synthesis. As a result, this chapter's contribution to rethinking data in qualitative literacy research with and for multilingual students provides meta-synthesists with two critical question sets to ask of each study that is vetted for inclusion.

The critical question sets outlined and examined within this chapter are necessary because analyzing the corresponding patterns prior to engaging in metasynthesis allows for deeper understanding of the subpopulations that are present within the data. This practice will help to avoid overgeneralizations that can be detrimental. Moreover, it also highlights the consequence of original studies providing the same kind of critical analysis. Linguistic diversity is part and parcel of all schooling contexts and must be described with the requisite importance. Through detailing this additional focus for vetting articles for inclusion, this chapter intends to offer a novel contribution to meta-synthesis methodology for multilingual students.

Overview of the study and its findings

This section of the chapter centers on my thwarted attempt to complete a second EL-focused meta-synthesis, which evolved into an examination of how researchers describe participants' official English language acquisition status and their overall linguistic backgrounds. Prior to focusing on the resulting critical question sets that guided this analysis, it is important to set the groundwork for understanding why both official English language acquisition status and overall linguistic backgrounds are essential considerations for a literacy studies-focused meta-synthesis.

Official English language acquisition status, like "English learner" (EL) or "English only" (EO), are bureaucratic classifications that influence the overall trajectory of adolescents. For adolescents identified as monolingual English speakers, or EO, their performance on assessments of English literacy do not impact their official English language status. Regardless of the literacy practices in which they engage, they will be institutionally identified as *English proficient*. This official English language acquisition status does not prevent their English literacy practices from being stigmatized by schools or cause their linguistic abilities to be maligned (e.g., Baker-Bell, 2020; McMurtry, 2021). On the other side of the spectrum, English literacy plays a unique role in the lives of students who are identified by the United States school system as ELs. Their performance on standardized assessments of English literacy impact whether they remain in the EL classification (Hernandez, 2017; Umansky & Dumont, 2021). Moreover, the EL category impacts multiple aspects of multilingual youths' lives. It can shape to which classes they have access, the teaching methods to which they are exposed, and how educators and administrators understand their abilities (Abril-Gonzales & Shannon, 2021; Cabral, 2023).

Given the unique role of English literacy assessment in the lives of students identified as ELs, it is essential to understand the nature of their literacy instructional experiences within formal schooling. One of the common instructional environments for adolescent students identified as ELs are RICs. Drawing on my earlier work, I define RICs as *seemingly* compulsory, yearlong courses that supplement content-area classes with the goal of improving adolescents' reading (Frankel et al., 2021). In this chapter, I added the term "seemingly" because that is often how they are presented to youths and their families; however, they are not a part of the required graduation curriculum. Moreover, their supplementary nature is notable because they do not replace English language arts courses. For multilingual youths who are identified as ELs, there are two types of RICs in which they could be placed. EL-unique RICs are those which are solely for students with the EL label (e.g., Brooks, 2022; Callahan, 2006; Wu & Coady, 2010). On the other hand, EL-inclusive RICs are those which include students from a variety of official English language statuses (Brooks & Rodela, 2018; Frankel, 2016).

The focus on multilingual EL-identified adolescents' experiences and perspectives of EL-inclusive RICs is essential through a literacy-as-a-social practice theoretical lens (Street, 1998). Literacy is not conceptualized as a decontextualized skill that is taught and learned in isolation (e.g., Larson et al., 2021; Linares, 2021). Researchers must contend with the context because it impacts how individuals and their reading practices are perceived, the external resources available to engage in reading, and how reading and reading instruction is conceptualized and enacted (Vasudevan & Campano, 2009). EL-inclusive high school RICs are the instructional context that defined the scope of this meta-synthesis. It is important to note that there is not one singular way in which RICs are implemented or designed (Frankel et al., 2021). They are envisioned as being needed to account for some kind of difficulty youths are experiencing with reading. Whether this deficit is interpreted as being conceptualized as being remediable through an out-of-the box intervention program or re-mediated through restructuring the literacy learning environment, RICs are situated within the assumption that students assigned to them are somehow deficient (Learned et al., 2022; Learned, 2016).

Setting the stage for meta-synthesis research

Compton-Lilly et al. (2021) describe five steps that any synthesis of qualitative research should entail: (1) identifying an appropriate epistemological orientation; (2) identifying an appropriate purpose; (3) searching for relevant literature; (4) evaluating, interpreting, and distilling evidence from selected articles; and (5) communicating with audiences. Descriptions of best practices for meta-synthesis follow much of the same criteria; however, the way in which they are articulated and defined can look differently. For instance, Hoon (2013, p.529) discussed eight steps that characterized their meta-synthesis protocol: framing the research question, locating relevant research, specifying inclusion criteria, extracting and coding data, analyzing on a case-specific level, synthesizing on a cross-study level, building theory from meta-synthesis, and discussing results and implications. The methods of our initial meta-synthesis (Frankel et al., 2021) reflected common criteria that was consistent across several studies (e.g., Finlayson & Dixon, 2008; Sandelowski & Barroso, 2007).

We developed an author team composed of researchers with expertise in both qualitative research and RICs. Katherine Frankel, Julie Learned, and I used search engines and hand searches of journals to identify a body of peer-reviewed research published between 2000 and 2020 that (1) focused on secondary (grades 6–12) RICs in the United States and (2) included data related to students' experiences and perspectives. Then, using an appraisal tool that was informed by Berry and Thunder (2012), we appraised identified studies to ensure that our data set included reputable scholarly work. Table 1 illustrates the appraisal tool and the characteristics which we used to identify 21 articles that formed the initial data set for the Frankel et al. (2021) meta-synthesis.

Every aspect covered by the appraisal tool that we created is not characteristic of all meta-synthesis work. For instance, Compton-Lilly et al. (2021) do not include a discussion of how to analyze the quality of the research methods in articles in the metric for inclusion. However, they ask other questions that are important, like examining how language of publication and origin of studies can bias the pools upon which various types of research synthesis are constructed. Within this chapter, I diverge from the initial Frankel et al.'s (2021) meta-synthesis to insert two critical question sets to the vetting of literacy studies for meta-synthesis specifically, and integrative reviews of qualitative research more broadly. I added two sets of critical questions about how researchers represent student language background. The purpose of asking these questions is two-fold. Analyzing patterns prior to engaging in meta-synthesis allows for deeper understanding of the subpopulations that are present within the data and helps avoid overgeneralizations that can be detrimental. Moreover, it is also to highlight the impor-

Table 1. Appraisal tool as published in Frankel et al. (2021)

Criteria	Possible points	Points given
1. Research Problem, Purpose, and/or Question	2	
a. Problem is stated clearly and related to the research literature		
b. There is a clear statement of research purpose and/or question(s)		
2. Conceptual/Theoretical Framework	2	
a. There is a clear statement of the theoretical underpinnings of the work		
b. These underpinnings clearly inform the methods, findings, and interpretations		
3. Method: Data Collection and Analysis	6	
a. Study (or portion of study) is methodologically qualitative		
b. Selection and description of participants is included		
c. Researcher shows an awareness of their influence on the study (describes experiences and/or assumptions with which the researcher entered the research)		
d. Data collection procedures are fully described		
e. Data analysis process is clear with examples		
f. Techniques for credibility and trustworthiness are addressed		
4. Findings	4	
a. Interpretations are substantiated with data		
b. Overall findings address the purpose of the study		
c. Ideas (themes, categories, concepts, etc.) are precise, well developed, and linked to each other.		
d. Results offer new information, insights, or perspectives		
5. Discussion & Implications	2	
a. Discussion of interpretations and significant findings are linked to purpose, theoretical underpinnings, and research questions		
b. Implications include recommendations for theory, research, policy, and/or practice		
Total points	16	

High overall standards of quality and credibility = 11–16 points
Moderate overall standards of quality and credibility = 5–10 points
Low overall standards of quality and credibility = 0–4 points

tance of original studies providing this type of information. The focus of these critical question sets reflects the fact that inconsistent use of these bureaucratic language learner labels made specific topics related to multilingual students less salient within a general meta-synthesis of RICs and prevented the development of a meta-synthesis specifically on EL-identified students in RICs.

Round 1: EL-identified high school students

The original set of articles for Frankel et al. (2021) included research that focused solely on middle school students, high school students, or a mixed population of both groups. However, the second meta-synthesis was interested in answering a revised narrower research question with this study: How do multilingual EL-identified high school students experience and perceive EL-inclusive RICs? Therefore, I removed the four studies that focused solely on middle school. Unfortunately, I also removed two studies with populations of middle and high school students due to a lack of detail in the findings. There was either very little data about high school students or it was unclear the grade level of students whose experiences and perceptions were being reported. As a result, the set of studies that would be analyzed for the second meta-synthesis was reduced from 21 to 15 articles.

Round 2: Language background analysis

After reading through the 15 articles to make sense of the linguistic backgrounds, I recognized that questions about language background that should be added to the appraisal tool should fall into two categories: official bureaucratic classifications and language background descriptions. This moment is when I decided to move from completing the second meta-synthesis to examining the two critical question sets. The first question set examines how the student is identified through the lens of the school system. The second question set captures what information is shared about the language background of the student themselves. Research with students identified as ELs illustrates that official English language acquisition status does not necessarily accurately describe their language backgrounds; students can be labeled EO or EL and exhibit a wide range of linguistic practices (e.g., Catalano et al., 2020; Flores et al., 2020; Kiramba & Oloo, 2023). Therefore, understanding multilingual students' experiences of literacy instruction should entail going beyond bureaucratic labels.

Bureaucratic classifications. The first set of questions centers around the official English language acquisition status of students: Are there descriptions of bureaucratic classifications in relation to language(s)? How are they presented? Where in the study are they presented? It is important to attend to how the question set goes beyond merely mentioning official English language acquisition status but also gives contextual information about how it is presented and used.

As discussed above, students' official English language acquisition status, which is a type of bureaucratic classification, impacts many aspects of how they experience school. However, only seven of the 15 studies analyzed shared EL identification of students. Moreover, these seven studies did not discuss these labels

Table 2. Information about participants' official English language acquisition status

Author name	Year	Are there descriptions of bureaucratic classifications in relation to language(s)?	How are they presented?	Where are they presented?
Brooks & Rodela	2018	Yes	Included official bureaucratic identities of all students in a table along with other academic information. It is possible to connect label to a specific student.	Method section
Cantrell et al.	2017	No		
Cantrell & Rintamaa	2020	No		
Frankel	2016	Yes	Identified one focal student by bureaucratic EL label.	Method section
Gerber et al.	2014	Somewhat	Described EL population of school. It is not possible to connect label to participants within classroom.	Method section
Ginsberg	2020	No		
Goering & Baker	2010	Yes	Described EL population of classroom. It is not possible to connect label to participants within classroom.	Method section
Greenleaf et al.	2001	Yes	Described EL status of school. Identified one student as former EL.	Findings
Harmon et al.	2016		In a table with other information about students, identified specific students as ESL. No other descriptions of EL classification of other students.	Method section
Houchen	2013	No		
Learned	2016	No		
Masterson	2020	No		
Paterson & Elliot	2006	Yes	Described one student as taking ESL courses. It is not possible to connect label to participants within classroom.	Introduction
Sarroub & Pernicek	2016	Yes	Described the fact that parents opted one of focal students out of EL services. Did not describe remaining students.	Findings
Skerrett	2012	No		

in the same way. Three studies did not talk about the linguistic bureaucratic classification of the participants. Gerber et al. (2014) described the EL classification of the entire school with no specific reference to the participants. Two studies (Goering & Baker, 2010; Paterson & Eliot, 2006) described the number of EL-identified students in the classroom but did not identify to which students the label could be applied. These broad approaches to discussing the EL label meant that a reader could know that students were present yet could not identify any information about EL-identified students' particular experiences of instruction.

While the paragraph above described how researchers used the EL label, it is important to note that the first set of questions was not solely limited to the EL label. It specifically asked if there were any bureaucratic classifications related to language. All students within the U.S. school system are given a label related to English language acquisition (e.g., EO, Former EL). Sarroub and Pernicek (2016) noted that one of their participants' parents opted out of EL services and Greenleaf et al. (2001) identified one of the participants as a former EL. However, of the 15 studies, only one provided descriptions for all students in the classroom. Brooks and Rodela (2018, see Table 3) used the term "official English language acquisition status" and captured the range of classifications within the classroom. Through engaging in this type of descriptive practice, Brooks and Rodela made visible students formerly identified as ELs and denaturalized the EO classification. This offers important interpretative information for the meta-synthesis that follows; however, this practice was not common within the broader pool of studies.

Table 3. Descriptive headings from Brooks and Rodela (2018)

Student Name	Years in Read 180	Grade Entered Brookville District	Official English Language Acquisition Status

Language background. While descriptions of students' official English language acquisition statuses are important for the original purpose of this second meta-synthesis and important knowledge in general for research, researchers should not be limited by these labels in how they discuss the linguistic backgrounds of students. The way in which labels are created can offer a limited understanding of students' language histories and abilities that are reflective of particular understandings of how language is taught and learned (Kibler & Valdés, 2016; Valdés, 2020). Therefore, information outside of the official labels can provide much needed insight into the literacy development of multilingual students. The second critical question set reflects this context: Are any other indications of learners' multilingualism provided? How are they presented? Where are they presented? For the ease of reading information across tables, I also included a column that indicates whether or not the article was identified in Table 3 as describing students' linguistic bureaucratic classifications. Table 4 shares the results of analyzing these studies for information about students' language backgrounds and statuses.

Table 4. Information about language background and official English language acquisition status

Author name	Year	Are any other indications of learners' multilingualism provided?	How are they presented?	Where are they presented?	Referenced linguistic bureaucratic classifications
Brooks & Rodela	2018	Yes	The authors described the language (s) used within their households.	Method section	Yes
Cantrell et al.	2017	No			No
Cantrell & Rintamaa	2020	No			No
Frankel	2016	Yes	Described one of student's first languages.	Method section	Yes
Gerber et al.	2014	No			Somewhat
Ginsberg	2020	No			No
Goering & Baker	2010	No			Yes
Greenleaf et al.	2001	Somewhat	Described language back-ground of one focal student.	Findings	Yes
Harmon et al.	2016	No			Yes
Houchen	2013	No			No
Learned	2016	Yes	Table with home languages of all students.	Method section	No
Masterson	2020	Yes	Mentioned that one of the students is bilingual. Did not describe language background of remaining students.	Method section	No
Paterson & Elliot	2006	No			Yes
Sarroub & Pernicek	2016	Yes	Described one student as "English as a second language student". Did not describe remaining students.	Method section	Yes
Skerrett	2012	Yes	Described the language use and history of focal student.	Findings	No

Four studies included both reference to official English language status and other descriptions of multilingual language backgrounds. For the purposes of explication, Frankel's (2016) case study of two students described one of the focal students in the following manner: "Radi was Palestinian, and Arabic was his first language. Northern High identified him as an English learner and as eligible for free lunch" (p.505). This provides more information about Radi than his EL classification. Frankel provides information about his first language and his ethnic background. Four authors provided descriptions of students' linguistic backgrounds without referencing their official English language acquisition statuses. For example, Skerrett (2012) described Angelica's (the focal participant) at-home experiences with Spanish language literacy and Angelica's mother's desire for her child's Spanish language maintenance. This provides a more robust conceptualization of a student's linguistic background than what was provided in many other studies. In a unique move that was distinct from other studies of multiple students who were identified as monolingual and multilingual, Learned (2016) described the language backgrounds of all students.

Methodological discussion: Rethinking data for more equitable research

When I initially set out on the project to engage in a second qualitative meta-synthesis about the perspectives and experiences of multilingual EL-identified high school students in EL-inclusive RICs, I thought that it would contribute to re-thinking data on multiple levels. I assumed that the primary contribution would be to understanding what counts as data for research about multilingual high school students who are labeled as ELs. While qualitative meta-synthesis has found its use in many aspects of research, I thought that its use in understanding the literacy practices of multilingual youth in institutional spaces that were charged with their remediation would be essential to equity focused conversations. It would have provided a targeted research-based analysis of a body of research that would allow practitioners and policymakers to focus on a little understood aspect of this populations' literacy instruction: how students themselves experience and think about those interventions. The need for research in this area is particularly palpable given the existence of adolescent literacy research that speaks to the significance of these outcomes (Deroo & Watson, 2020; Seltzer, 2020). Specifically, it would contribute to the better understanding of the educational pathways of EL-identified students who are in EL-inclusive RICs. It is important to understand what these classes that characterize the education of high school ELs look like in practice. These broader questions regarding EL-identified youth in RICs remained unanswered because of a lack of explicit discussion of bureaucratic labels and inconsistent description of students' language backgrounds.

Nevertheless, I was able to pivot the focus of the chapter by adding two sets of questions to the original appraisal tool that we adapted in Frankel et al. (2021) to analyze the original data set. These two sets of questions (Figure 1) encourage researchers to critically rethink "data" within meta-synthesis in the field of literacy studies. They have implications for RIC-specific research and literacy research involving multilingual students more broadly.

Critical Question Set 1: Are there descriptions of bureaucratic classifications in relation to language(s)? How are they presented? Where in the study are they presented?

Critical Question Set 2: Are any other indications of learners' multilingualism provided? How are they presented? Where are they presented?

Figure 1. Critical question sets

Researchers from all backgrounds who engage in research in RICs should describe and address official the English language acquisition statuses of all those students enrolled in RICs and the specific participants of their research. This type of explicit discussion of bureaucratic labels allows research to illustrate how the institutional labeling impacts students' daily lives. It shines a light on who is educated within these stigmatized spaces. This awareness is particularly important because stigmatized educational spaces, like RICs, are often where those who are negatively impacted by bureaucratic and social labels are educated (e.g., Kangas & Cook, 2020; Martínez et al., 2022). Moreover, acknowledging these labels facilitates the examination of how they function within the processes and practices of marginalized instructional spaces. It is necessary to engage with bureaucratic language labels to understand issues of equity.

Absence of bureaucratic label

RIC research focuses on a context of instruction within schools in which students are deliberately placed. Although there is little research that explicitly focuses on placement decisions (Brook & Rodela [2018] is among few exceptions), studies show us that placement both within RICs and across different contexts of secondary school is not a neutral process. Issues of institutional labels, race, socioeconomic statuses, and other categories play a role in who gets placed and remains in RICs. For instance, Frankel (2016) illustrated how a white female student leveraged positive relationships and social capital to exit her RIC. She did this without actually improving on the criteria identified by the teacher. Similarly, Learned

(2016) documented the way even positive reading test scores were not sufficient to exit a Black male student from RIC. He was kept in the course because of teachers' feelings about the impossibility of changing the broader master schedule. Being explicit about who is in RICs is an essential part of qualitative research because it allows us to understand individuals and groups' experiences of the courses. For instance, we cannot know about the role that EL label has on placement in RICs if the label itself is never mentioned.

The trouble with bureaucratic labels like EL is that they are not neutral. Situated within linguistic bureaucratic labels are ideologies about language, language learning, youths themselves, their abilities, and their communities (García, 2009; Kibler & Valdés, 2016). It is for this reason that researchers call attention to look beyond the EL label to conceptualize how students are understood, taught, and treated in multiple aspects of schooling (e.g., Brooks, 2018; Martínez, 2018). Given these concerns, some researchers may shy away from using the official English language acquisition status to signify that students are more than how they are identified by the school system. Very often, researchers who hold this orientation are likely to describe students' multilingualism but purposefully avoid using the official label. This orientation to understanding language and youths is admirable. It reflects a commitment to push back against a system which can be seen as conflating youth with diverse linguistic backgrounds, achievements, and development needs.

Yet, the failure to explicitly name the official English language acquisition status of students is not beneficial for equity-focused research. Firstly, it does not facilitate differentiating the experiences of multilingual students who are labeled EL and those who are not. Qualitative research in this area suggests that it is important to examine the ways being a multilingual individual with or without EL label entails both distinct and intersecting experiences (e.g., Catalano et al., 2020). Nevertheless, there are other ways to register a theoretical disagreement with the conceptualization that are embedded within the policy driven EL labeling. For instance, Glick and Walqui (2020) drew on Valdés' (2018) wording to identify the students at the center of their chapter as "bureaucratically labeled long-term English learners." In this, they recognize how the labeling of a student as a "long-term" learner of English is not one and the same as a student's identity. Yet, it does not overlook the power of the long-term English learner label on their educational trajectory. Glick and Walqui's chapter both recognizes the impact of bureaucratic labeling and foregrounds instruction that builds upon youths' robust linguistic practices.

Another way in which labels were present and absent included identifying ELs within the classroom context, but then not identifying to which student the label was applied. Detail around English language acquisition status is necessary to better contextualize what is happening in the context of the research. In more egregious cases, there were descriptions of percentages of ELs at school, but not within the focal classroom. In these ways, the traces of information about linguistic bureaucratic classifications in the data are not sufficient to be clear about who is being talked about. The lack of clarity and consistency meant that existing research on EL-inclusive RICs could shed light on the experiences and perceptions of multilingual EL-identified high school students. However, researchers' lack of connecting labels to students meant that these contributions were hidden.

Still other researchers did not describe the official English language acquisition status of any of the students within the research. For example, Cantrell and Rintamaa (2020, p. 301) described the population of focus in their study in the following manner:

> In each school, participants were one male and one female from each intervention teacher's classroom (eight students total). All students were White. They were randomly selected (stratified by gender) from the full sample of students in the intervention classes who also had returned parental consent forms to participate in interviews. Five of the eight students received free or reduced lunch. School enrollments were 301, 430, 456, and 803 students. Three smaller schools included between 1.4% and 3.3% of students who were from ethnic minority groups. The larger school included 10.6% of students from ethnic minority groups. In two of the schools, approximately 40% of students qualified for the free and reduced lunch program. In the other two schools, approximately 70% of students qualified.

While using the context clues, one could assume that with such small percentages of ethnic minority students, there were few students identified as ELs and the students who were selected for this study were monolingual English speakers. This information would be based on assumptions. In today's schooling context, discussion of institutional language labels, special education labels, ethnoracial labels, and gender labels should all be basic parts of conducting qualitative research. While I use Cantrell & Rintamaa (2020) as an example, they are not the only individuals in the study who did this. Yet, their thorough approach to other aspects of describing participants made this absence more evident.

Absence of descriptions of language background

Discussing language backgrounds outside of the trappings of institutional labels is important because it allows for a level of description of linguistic diversity that is not accounted for by the school system. For instance, it acknowledges that there are people who may be considered monolingual English speakers, but whose speech is understood as non-normative for other reasons. Yet, within current policy contexts these students, the linguistic abilities they bring into the school and their experiences of language ideologies are erased. Bureaucratic classifications do not even provide us with insight into the different language histories of students. Students with the same label can have two very distinct life histories. The failure to attend to students' linguistic backgrounds minimizes differences in life histories. It also hides the experience of those who may be multilingual but whose official English language acquisition status may not indicate this background.

Examining whether researchers are robust in discussing the language backgrounds of students may seem unnecessary if the context of the research does not specifically focus on language. As a qualitative researcher, it can be difficult to find space to incorporate all the necessary detail into a study, and this seems like it is just adding unnecessary detail. However, descriptions of the language backgrounds of students do not necessarily have to occupy space. For instance, Learned (2016) used a single table to illustrate the language backgrounds of all students, which allowed students to describe their own linguistic repertoires. It shared that the languages of one of the focal students, Aziza, were Wolof and English. Moreover, this table included other information pertinent to the study like gender, ethnoracial identity, different standardized reading test scores, GPA, number of days suspended, and whether they were enrolled in school at the end of the year. In a very straightforward manner, Learned shared information about the language background of each student.

In studies that choose to attend to the multilingualism of their participants more specifically, the description of language background allows them to draw on different theoretical orientations in engaging research. Researchers do not have to stick to the conceptualization of focus on proficiency in English as defined by standardized assessments. In recent decades, there has been a strong contribution of theoretical and practical work within the study of bilingualism that has gone beyond the boundaries of policy classifications when discussing the language background of students (e.g., Leung & Valdés, 2019; May, 2014). Scholars with more social, critical, and multilingual perspectives have brought differing perspectives to the forefront of scholarship. However, these perspectives on students' language backgrounds were not evident within the qualitative research reviewed on RICs. Even a scholar like myself, who draws upon critical perspectives on bilingualism in other research, left this perspective outside of the discussion of my own research that was included within this review (Brooks & Rodela, 2018). As a result, the absence of greater attention to the language background of students misses the potential to have important discussions about the intersection between linguistic diversity and reading intervention.

Implications for qualitative research on multilingual literacy development

Meta-syntheses are an important contribution to research broadly and specifically in relation to multilingual students because they can impact theory, policymaking, and practice. They draw upon the unique properties that qualitative research brings to a topic and permit it to be used in a way that makes its findings accessible on a larger scale. If meta-synthesis research is to be used in this manner, then there needs to be clarity as to which participants are the focus of the research. Moreover, it is necessary to attend to what the findings of a meta-synthesis are saying about the various groups of students that form the communities served by this work. Therefore, within this section on implications I will address two overarching themes: the implications of meta-synthesis of RICs for multilingual students, and the power of meta-synthesis for literacy studies of multilingual students more broadly.

Critical question sets

The two sets of critical questions that I have put forth in this chapter are intended to offer a guiding light to both meta-synthesists and qualitative researchers generally (see Figure 1). Specifically, they encourage the type of reflection that is necessary to engage in literacy research that centers the literacy development of multilingual students. They do this by asking how the multilingualism of students is described both within and outside of the realm of institutional labeling. This type of descriptive analysis is necessary to move past broad generalizations about multilingual students towards nuanced representations of their linguistic lives. While I developed these critical question sets in relation to a topic that is specifically tied to multilingual students, these questions should not be limited to solely this work. It is central to the work of all those who study literacy. These two question sets ensure that meta-synthesis will attend to the linguistic background of who is within the classroom when moving forward with interpretations. However, and I argue more importantly, they can be used to guide researchers in ensuring that they attend to important dynamics that govern the literacy learning environments of multilingual students — even if that is not the stated focus of the paper. Multilingual students form part of every classroom space and environment, whether or not they have an official label applied to them. As a result, the critical question sets are important for a broad range of literacy studies.

I contend that these critical question sets are not only relevant for meta-syntheses; but that they would be useful in all literacy studies involving students. As such, these questions also create a forum for researchers to take a more critical lens within their primary studies. The necessity of this lens was evident throughout this chapter. Specifically, the previous section illustrates what is lost in the absence of discussion of bureaucratic labeling. Critically rethinking data within the context of this chapter extends beyond including the critical question sets within meta-synthesis. Rather, it requires that qualitative researchers ask these questions as they attend to how they conduct their primary studies. Therefore, I offer these critical question sets as tools to be used when reviewing journal articles for publication within the broad fields that come together to include literacy studies. Through asking these questions prior to publication, the data sets that qualitative meta-synthesists use will be more nuanced. This practice will push much needed conversation about labeling of multilingual students to the center of discussion within literacy studies.

Attending to the method section

The previous discussion highlighted the implications of proposed critical questions sets for rethinking data within meta-syntheses for multilingual students. However, there is another important implication for how data is identified within meta-syntheses that is relevant: the location of data within primary studies. While it is common practice within meta-synthesis research to examine and interpret the findings of primary studies (Compton-Lilly et al., 2021; Sandelowski & Barroso, 2007), the location of information within studies about language background and where the information is likely to be placed makes it necessary to use the Method section as part of data analysis. Tables 2 and 4 illustrate how the Method section is a predominant location for important information to be shared with a reader. The dogma that only findings can be used as interpretive data can prevent researchers from using this necessary information. In the process of publishing our first meta-synthesis (Frankel et al., 2021), we were instructed to not include any information solely found in the Method section for publication. If I had followed a similar line of thinking for this exploration, this chapter would contain very little information about bureaucratic classifications and students' language backgrounds. Within current practices for writing journal articles, key information about participants is presented within the Method section. Therefore, I contend that robust meta-syntheses will also include data from Method sections, as they are necessary to understand the participant population and broader sociocultural contexts. Critical interpretive data analysis requires these types of contextual understandings to be forefront. Within strong research, methods and findings are interconnected and being represented in the methods section does not necessarily diminish significance of the information presented.

Using critical question sets, this chapter provided a forum for researchers to critically rethink data within meta-syntheses. The topics addressed through the question sets are fundamental to judging the quality of research and interpreting findings. Moreover, the particular focus of the question sets on the ideas and conceptualizations that impact the educational trajectory of multilingual students makes it particularly relevant for this book. However, I want to close this chapter by noting that the ways of critically rethinking data are not limited to language. Firstly, linguistic bureaucratic categories and linguistic descriptions do not operate in isolation from other socially significant categories. For example, in this book Karam and Kibler highlight the significance of the refugee categorization and Davila's chapter calls attention to that of d/Deaf label. Therefore, these questions are also an invitation to discuss the other bureaucratic and socially significant categories that shape the lives of young people within schools. However, the ways of thinking that are emblematic of these question sets extend to a mindset that is relevant for all meta-synthesists and qualitative researchers.

References

Note. References with an asterisk are those that have been included in this chapter's analysis.

Abril-Gonzalez, P., & Shannon, S. M. (2021). English language development jaulas: Latinx students' critiques of ELD through confinement and resistance testimonios. *Bilingual Research Journal*, 44(4), 426–443.

Au, W. (2007). High-stakes testing and curricular control: A qualitative metasynthesis. *Educational Researcher*, 36(5), 258–267.

Baker-Bell, A. (2020). Dismantling anti-black linguistic racism in English language arts classrooms: Toward an anti-racist black language pedagogy. *Theory into Practice*, 59(1), 8–21.

Berry, R., & Thunder, K. (2012). Mathematics education at Teachers College. *Journal of Mathematics Education at Teachers College*, 3(1), 43–55.

Boulay, B., Goodson, B., Frye, M., Blocklin, M., & Price, C. (2015). *Summary of research generated by Striving Readers on the effectiveness of interventions for struggling adolescent readers (NCEE 2016- 4001)*. National Center for Education Evaluation and Regional Assistance, Institute of Education Sciences, U.S. Department of Education. https://files.eric.ed.gov/fulltext/ED560732.pdf

Brooks, M. D. (2018). Pushing past myths: Designing instruction for long-term English learners. *TESOL Quarterly*, 52(1), 221–233.

Brooks, M. D. (2022). What does it mean? EL-identified adolescents' interpretations of testing and course placement. *TESOL Quarterly*, 56(4), 1218–1241.

*Brooks M. D., & Rodela, K. C. (2018). Why am I in reading intervention? A dual analysis of entry and exit criteria. *The High School Journal*, 102(1), 72–93.

Callahan, R. M. (2006). The intersection of accountability and language: Can reading intervention replace English language development? *Bilingual Research Journal*, 30(1), 1–21.

doi Cabral, B. (2023). Linguistic confinement: Rethinking the racialized interplay between educational language learning and carcerality. *Race Ethnicity and Education*, 26(3), 277–297.

doi *Cantrell, S. C., Pennington, J., Rintamaa, M., Osborne, M., Parker, C., & Rudd, M. (2017). Supplemental literacy instruction in high school: What students say matters for reading engagement. *Reading & Writing Quarterly*, 33(1), 54–70.

doi *Cantrell, S. C., & Rintamaa, M. (2020). The nature of rural high school students' reading engagement. *Reading & Writing Quarterly*, 36(4), 297–319.

doi Catalano, T., Kiramba, L. K., & Viesca, K. (2020). Transformative interviewing and the experiences of multilingual learners not labeled "ELL" in U.S. schools. *Bilingual Research Journal*, 43(2), 178–195.

doi Compton-Lilly, C., Rogers, R., & Ellison, T. L. (2021). *Making sense of literacy scholarship: Approaches to synthesizing literacy research*. Routledge.

doi Deroo, M. R., & Watson, V. W. (2020). "Air I breathe": Songwriting as literacy practices of remembrance. *Journal of Literacy Research*, 52(2), 158–179.

doi Edmonds, M. S., Vaughn, S., Wexler, J., Reutebuch, C., Cable, A., Tackett, K. K., & Schnakenberg, J. W. (2009). A synthesis of reading interventions and effects on reading comprehension outcomes for older struggling readers. *Review of Educational Research*, 79(1), 262–300.

doi Finlayson, K., & Dixon, A. (2008). Qualitative meta-synthesis: A guide for the novice. *Nurse Researcher*, 15(2), 59–71.

doi Flores, N., Phuong, J., & Venegas, K. M. (2020). "Technically an EL": The production of raciolinguistic categories in a dual language school. *TESOL Quarterly*, 54(3), 629–651.

doi *Frankel, K. K. (2016). The intersection of reading and identity in high school literacy intervention classes. *Research in the Teaching of English*, 51(1), 37–59.

doi Frankel, K. K., Brooks, M. D., & Learned, J. E. (2021). A meta-synthesis of qualitative research on reading intervention classes in secondary schools. *Teachers College Record*, 123(8), 31–58.

doi García, O. (2009). Emergent bilinguals and TESOL: What's in a name? *TESOL Quarterly*, 43(2), 322–326.

doi *Gerber H. R., Abrams S. S., Onwuegbuzie A. J., & Benge C. L. (2014). From Mario to FIFA: What qualitative case study research suggests about games-based learning in a U.S. classroom. *Educational Media International*, 51(1), 16–34.

doi *Ginsberg, R. (2020). Dueling narratives of a reader labeled as struggling: Positioning, emotion, and power within four differing English course contexts. *Journal of Education for Students Placed at Risk*, 25(1), 1–27.

doi Glick, Y., & Walquí, A. (2020). Affordances in the development of student voice and agency: The case of bureaucratically labeled long-term English learners. In A. Kibler, G. Valdés, & A. Walquí (Eds.), *Reconceptualizing the role of critical dialogue in American classrooms* (pp. 23–51). Routledge.

*Goering, C. Z., & Baker, K. F. (2010). "Like the whole class has reading problems": A study of oral reading fluency activities in a high intervention setting. *American Secondary Education*, 39(1), 61–77.

doi *Greenleaf, C. L., Schoenbach, R., Cziko, C., & Mueller, F. L. (2001). Apprenticing adolescent readers to academic literacy. *Harvard Educational Review*, 71(1), 79–129.

*Harmon, J., Wood, K., Smith, K., Zakaria, N., Ramadan, K., & Sykes, M. (2016). Teaching and learning in high school reading classes: Perspectives of teachers and students. *Reading Psychology*, 37(7), 962–994.

Hernandez, S. J. (2017). Are they all language learners? Educational labeling and raciolinguistic identifying in a California middle school dual language program. *CATESOL Journal*, 29(1), 133–154.

Hoon, C. (2013). Meta-synthesis of qualitative case studies: An approach to theory building. *Organizational Research Methods*, 16(4), 522–556.

*Houchen, D. (2013). "Stakes is high": Culturally relevant practitioner inquiry with African American students struggling to pass secondary reading exit exams. *Urban Education*, 48(1), 92–115.

Kangas, S. E., & Cook, M. (2020). Academic tracking of English learners with disabilities in middle school. *American Educational Research Journal*, 57(6), 2415–2449.

Kibler, A. K., & Valdés, G. (2016). Conceptualizing language learners: Socioinstitutional mechanisms and their consequences. *The Modern Language Journal*, 100(S1), 96–116.

Kim, W. G. (2017). Long-term English language learners' educational experiences in the context of high-stakes accountability. *Teachers College Record*, 119(9), 1–32.

Kiramba, L. K., & Oloo, J. A. (2023). "It's OK. She doesn't even speak English": Narratives of language, culture, and identity negotiation by immigrant high school students. *Urban Education*, 58(3), 398–426.

Larson, J., Duret, E., Rees, J., & Anderson, J. (2021). Challenging the autonomous wall: Literacy work in an urban high school. *Journal of Literacy Research*, 53(2), 174–195.

*Learned, J. E. (2016). "The behavior kids": Examining the conflation of youth reading difficulty and behavior problem positioning among school institutional contexts. *American Educational Research Journal*, 53(5), 1271–1309.

Learned, J. E., Frankel, K. K., & Brooks, M. D. (2022). Disrupting secondary reading intervention: A review of qualitative research and a call to action. *Journal of Adolescent & Adult Literacy*, 65(6), 507–517.

Leung, C., & Valdés, G. (2019). Translanguaging and the transdisciplinary framework for language teaching and learning in a multilingual world. *The Modern Language Journal*, 103(2), 348–370.

Linares, R. E. (2021). Creating and navigating a transborder writing space: One multilingual adolescent's take-up of dialogue journaling in an English-medium classroom. *Reading Research Quarterly*, 56(4), 673–692.

Martínez, R. A. (2018). Beyond the English learner label: Recognizing the richness of bi/multilingual students' linguistic repertoires. *The Reading Teacher*, 71(5), 515–522.

Martínez, R. A., Martinez, D. C., & Morales, P. Z. (2022). Black lives matter versus Castañeda v. Pickard: A utopian vision of who counts as bilingual (and who matters in bilingual education). *Language Policy*, 21(3), 427–449.

*Masterson, J. E. (2020). Reading in "purgatory": Tactical literacies in a remedial reading class. *Reading Research Quarterly*, 57(1), 91–109.

May, S. (Ed.). (2014). *The multilingual turn: Implications for SLA, TESOL and bilingual education*. Routledge.

McMurtry, T. (2021). With liberty and Black linguistic justice for all: Pledging allegiance to anti-racist language pedagogy. *Journal of Adolescent & Adult Literacy*, 65(2), 175–178.

doi *Paterson, P.O., & Elliott, L.N. (2006). Struggling reader to struggling reader: High school students' responses to a cross-age tutoring program. *Journal of Adolescent & Adult Literacy*, 49(5), 378–389.

Sandelowski, M., & Barroso, J. (2007). *Handbook for synthesizing qualitative research*. Springer.

doi *Sarroub, L.K., & Pernicek, T. (2016). Books, boys, and boredom: A case of three high school boys and their encounters with literacy. *Reading & Writing Quarterly*, 32(1), 27–55.

doi Seltzer, K. (2020). "My English is its own rule": Voicing a translingual sensibility through poetry. *Journal of Language, Identity & Education*, 19(5), 297–311.

doi *Skerrett, A. (2012). "We hatched in this class": Repositioning of identity in and beyond a reading classroom. *The High School Journal*, 95(3), 62–75.

doi Street, B. (1998). New literacies in theory and practice: What are the implications for Language in Education. Linguistics and Education, 10(1), 1–24.

doi Umansky, I.M., & Dumont, H. (2021). English learner labeling: How English learner classification in kindergarten shapes teacher perceptions of student skills and the moderating role of bilingual instructional settings. *American Educational Research Journal*, 58(5), 993–1031.

Valdés, G. (2018). What's in a name: An argument for the use of accurate and specific language in both research and practice [Paper presentation]. 2018 *Annual Conference of the American Association of Applied Linguistics*, Chicago, IL.

doi Valdés, G. (2020). (Mis)educating the children of Mexican-origin people in the United States: The challenge of internal language borders. *Intercultural Education*, 31(5), 548–561.

doi Vasudevan, L., & Campano, G. (2009). The social production of adolescent risk and the promise of adolescent literacies. *Review of Research in Education*, 33(1), 310–353.

doi Wu, C.H., & Coady, M.R. (2010). 'The United States is America?': A cultural perspective on READ 180 materials. *Language, Culture and Curriculum*, 23(2), 153–165.

CHAPTER 3

An ethnetnography of (non)belonging
The transliterate practices of a Muslim refugee-background mother

Fares J. Karam & Amanda K. Kibler

University of Nevada, Reno | Oregon State University

This chapter aims at presenting ethnetnography as an innovative qualitative methodology for studying multilingual literacy practices in Applied Linguistics. An ethnetnography combines elements of a traditional ethnography with a netnography (focusing on participants' online interactions). To showcase how to conduct an ethnetnography, we draw upon a study that traces how a Muslim refugee-background participant negotiates (non)belonging within the resettlement context of the United States. We share how to collect, analyze, and present the data and reflect on the rewards and challenges of adopting ethnetnographic methods. Methodological implications are presented on how an ethnetnographic approach can provide for a more complete, equitable, and ethical examination of the literacies of refugee-background individuals on the move.

Keywords: ethnetnography, ethnography, netnography, transliteracies, resonance, ambivalence, refugee, multilingual

Introduction

This chapter presents ethnetnography as an innovative qualitative methodology for studying multilingual literacy practices in Applied Linguistics. An ethnetnography combines elements of a traditional ethnography with a netnography (focusing on participants' online interactions). To showcase how to conduct an ethnetnography, we draw upon a study that traces how a Muslim refugee-background (RB) participant negotiates (non)belonging within the resettlement context of the United States. We define and expand upon our conceptualization of ethnetnography later on in the chapter, but for now, we assert our belief in the need to *rethink data* in a world where resettlement is no longer restricted to isolated experiences

https://doi.org/10.1075/rmal.11.03kar

within the geographical confines of the host country. Technology and social media have opened doors for immigrant and RB individuals to connect with friends, family, and significant others (other immigrant groups or refugees, in some cases) across a variety of interwoven contexts (both in-person and online), drawing on rich multilingual repertoires and experimenting with different modalities (e.g., Karam, 2021). Indeed, to focus on one type of data or limit data collection sites without examining how data *speak to each other* across contexts could entail presenting an incomplete story of resettlement and render invisible the increasingly complex literacy practices with which RB individuals engage.

As an increasing number of people are forcibly displaced each year across the globe (UNHCR, 2021), RB individuals continue to face xenophobic and discriminatory attitudes that attempt to render them voiceless and without agency. The assets that they bring — including their rich linguistic repertoires and their diverse life experiences — are often ignored in educational contexts, and they are often subjected to state policies of exclusion. The most recent wave of such policies was during the Trump presidency, described by Rumbaut (University of Colorado Boulder Institute of Behavioral Science, 2020) as the Great Exclusion of 2017–2020 when, among other policies, a presidential executive decision banned travel from Muslim majority countries, including Syria, the home country of our focal participant in this study. In addition, RB individuals are often represented through media images taken without their consent that depict them in vulnerable times (e.g., images of refugees receiving aid or being rescued). Such depictions reinforce their loss of agency and strengthen feelings of non-belonging due to the propagation of narratives of victimhood and dependency on state resources.

Milani and Levon (2019) have contended that some refugees experience "the viciousness of belonging — an affective attachment to a *place* that can nevertheless never be one's true home" (p. 624, emphasis ours). In an increasingly digitized and interconnected world where literacies are constantly on the move (Stornaiuolo et al., 2017), *place* can be a physical location, an online context, or an interwoven space between the two. To parallel this complexity, innovative research methods are needed more than ever to examine the literacy development of people on the move — across spaces, times, languages, and modalities. With this movement comes what Lorimer Leonard (2013) referred to as the "paradox of mobility" (p. 17) — the assumption that with mobility comes simultaneous restrictions and hurdles that impede movement. For example, while mobile literacy practices may suggest additional flexibility and freedom of expression, one should still pay close(r) attention to power structures that impede this mobility and marginalize specific groups of people, their languages, and their literacy practices. As such, language and literacy scholars should be cognizant of "who and what moves, how, why, and under what conditions" (Stornaiuolo et al., 2017, p. 70).

Recent research has shown that digital literacy and engagement in online contexts and social media in particular can be effective for refugee-background multilingual learners of English (RMLEs) to voice their concerns and to resist stereotypical representations and restrictions on what literacies matter and how they should be utilized (Karam, 2018; Moriarty, 2019; Omerbašić, 2015). Thus, there is a need to better understand the interconnections between RMLEs' resettlement and literacy practices in both in-person and in online contexts, which is the purpose of this study. More specifically, our research questions ask: How does negotiating (non)belonging influence a Syrian refugee-background mother's literacy practices? What literacy practices "resonate" in such negotiations across in-person and online contexts via social media platforms? In this chapter, we draw upon findings pertaining to these research questions to share how we collected, analyzed, and presented the data from an ethnographic perspective. We also reflect on the rewards and challenges of engaging in ethnetnographic research and methods. We conclude by sharing methodological implications on how an ethnetnographic approach can provide a more complete, equitable, and ethical approach to examining the literacies of RB individuals on the move.

Overview of the study and its findings

In this section, we provide an overview of our study. More specifically, we describe the context of the study, explain our theoretical framing around literacies, situate the study in a relevant body of literature, and briefly present our findings — which we draw upon to discuss our research design (ethnetnography) in the following section and how we engaged in rethinking data for this study.

Context and focal participant

This chapter draws upon an ongoing longitudinal study that started in 2017. The study's setting is a mid-sized city in the western United States. The focal participant is Maria (all names are self-selected pseudonyms), a Muslim RB woman from Syria. Maria and her family (husband and three elementary school-aged children) were forcibly displaced to Turkey in 2013 in order to escape the civil war in Syria before moving to the United States in 2016. Data sources for this study included field notes from weekly visits, semi-structured and informal interviews with Maria, and artifacts from the family's apartment.

Maria had learned some English during high school (the highest level of formal schooling she completed) in her home country. In the United States, she studied hard to earn her pharmaceutical assistant certification and obtain a job in a local pharmacy. Our focus on Maria in particular is motivated by her extensive use of social media to stay in touch with family and friends in Syria and other countries and to navigate resettlement in her new country. For example, she is part of a social media group of transnational Syrian women who use the platform to problem-solve, ask questions, get information, and even engage in buying and selling objects and artifacts that are not easily found in the U.S. resettlement context. The first author visited Maria and her family at their home on a weekly basis.

Theoretical frame

To frame our research questions, we drew upon two theoretical lenses: transliteracies (with a focus on resonance as one of the tools to enact a transliteracies framework) and ambivalence. Transliteracy is "the ability to read, write and interact across a range of platforms, tools and media from signing and orality through handwriting, print, TV, radio and film, to digital social networks" (Thomas et al., 2007, para. 3, as cited in Stornaiuolo et al., 2017 p. 71). Stornaiuolo and colleagues (2017) built on that definition to develop a transliteracies framework that transcends individual ability to examine how literacies and mobility are intertwined across social and material relationships and diverse temporalities and spaces. A central tenet of this framework is a critical focus on the paradox of mobility — a recognition that with the free flow of things, people, and literacies, facilitated mainly by today's technological advancements and social media platforms, comes the need to examine power structures that limit such mobility in literacy practices. This is particularly important in the case of transnational RMLEs who have experienced forced displacement and who are trying to navigate resettlement in new (and often unwelcoming) environments. To operationalize a transliteracies framework, Stornaiuolo and colleagues (2017) proposed four tools for analytical inquiry, one of which is *resonance:*

> As a conceptual metaphor, resonance highlights how phenomena mirror, echo, parallel, and weave together across spaces, people, texts, and times [...]. In considering resonance, transliteracies inquiry attends to whose meanings and practices are amplified or muffled in which systems, and how and why some objects and forms find resonance and persist while others wane. [...] Equally important in using resonance as an inquiry tool is attention to what does not resonate over time.
>
> (p. 81)

While other conceptual tools are equally helpful, resonance is particularly insightful for this study as it allows us to not only examine which literacy practices of the focal participant resonate across different spatial and temporal contexts (in-person and online), but also which literacy practices are muffled, censored, or rendered invisible as Maria navigates the uncertainties and ambivalence that accompany resettlement in a new country.

Indeed, ambivalence is often experienced by RMLEs in resettlement contexts (e.g., Warriner, 2013). Tazreiter (2019) has explained ambivalence as a "feeling, attenuation, or attitude — as a response to life's risks and uncertainties" (p.5) that accompany migration from one's home country. Indeed, ambivalence can explain many of the uncertainties and contradictions that accompany the process of migration. For example, Warriner (2013) reported on how one RB woman from Bosnia experienced an ambivalence of place, expressing both positive feelings about life in the United States and fear that her new country of resettlement is too geographically far from her home country. In the first author's own research, Karam (2021) analyzed how Maria and her husband wrote a bilingual and multi-modal bedtime story for their children while negotiating their ambivalence about maintaining the original version of the story or modifying parts of it to fit within the socially accepted norms of their resettlement context. For example, Maria did not want to include details that suggested the story would scare the children into sleep because she believed it was unacceptable to do that in the U.S. context. In short, ambivalence is a common, yet understudied phenomenon in refugee studies, especially in online contexts and in relation to multilingual literacy practices.

Relevant literature

Important and recent scholarship has been produced on the academic and social needs and challenges that RB populations face within the U.S. context, including many recent projects such as a special issue edited by experts in the field (McBrien et al., 2017) and entire books and edited volumes on the resettlement experiences and the education of RB populations across the lifespan (e.g., Shapiro et al., 2018; Warriner, 2021). In the field of Teaching English to Speakers of other Languages (TESOL) in particular, there have been calls in *TESOL Quarterly* to spur TESOL professionals to act as advocates for RB students through gaining a better understanding the refugee experience and addressing issues of discrimination in the TESOL classroom (Duran, 2019) and in TESOL teacher education (Karam, Oikonomidoy, & Kibler, 2021). This plethora of recent publications is a testament to the importance of this topic and reflects an urgency to learn more about refugee experiences, especially with the recent increase in violent acts of forcible displacement across the globe. Indeed, "refugee resettlement has never been more urgent" (Warriner, 2021, p.1).

Within the U.S. context, education literature mainly focuses on challenges faced by RMLEs. For example, most students experience trauma prior to resettlement and an interruption in their formal schooling due to forced displacement

(McBrien, 2005). They are expected/pressured to learn English as an additional language in a very short period of time (Bartlett et al., 2017) despite the increasing xenophobic and discriminatory practices that they face upon arrival and as they resettle in a new environment (Duran, 2019; Portes & Rumbaut, 2001). Highlighting these various challenges that RMLEs face is very important, yet it is also important to acknowledge the heterogeneity of refugee populations and how they can face different levels of discrimination based on their religions, countries of origin, linguistic backgrounds, or social statuses, among other factors (Bartlett et al. 2017). Muslim RMLEs in particular face increasingly unwelcoming attitudes, especially after the September 11th attacks and the recent Great Exclusion of 2017–2020 (University of Colorado Boulder Institute of Behavioral Science, 2020) — hence the need for educators to adopt flexible and student-centered approaches to teaching (Bartlett et al., 2017) and incorporate RMLEs' experiences in their planning (De Costa, 2010).

Despite these challenges, the literature presents a few cases that document the sense of agency and resistance that RMLEs employ as they navigate the U.S. school system. For example, Shapiro and MacDonald (2017) documented how one RB participant used his oral and written narratives to resist deficit perspectives of refugees and reframe his experiences from an asset point of view. In our own research, we have focused on the construct of agency and how RB adolescents use multilingual and multimodal means to resist discriminatory positionings (e.g., Karam, Barone, & Kibler, 2021). Other studies have also asserted the important role of RMLEs' involvement in out-of-school multimodal literacy practices. For example, Omerbašić (2015) documented nine Thai female refugee adolescents' out-of-school multimodal literacy practices and how digital spaces enabled them to interact with peers with similar experiences and histories.

Indeed, "social media sites provide an accessible platform which can and are being used by groups of refugees and asylum seekers to counter mass invisibility and silence" (Moriarty, 2019, p. 155). However, there remains an imperative need for methodological and theoretical innovations that examine not only the affordances of mobile and digital literacies but also the limitations, constrictions, and power structures that undervalue RMLEs' literacies and multilingual repertoires. If we are to respond to such calls to learn more about RMLEs in order to become better advocates, and indeed better educators (Duran, 2019), then it becomes increasingly important to be cognizant of RMLEs' literacy practices and how they use language (in multilingual and multimodal means) to express their opinions and counter invisibility — with particular attention to the silencing mechanisms that can further marginalize their voices both in-person and online. Furthermore, if the struggle to belong or establish a new sense of self in an unwelcoming environment is one of the most daunting challenges that RB individuals may face

(McBrien, 2005), then there is a need to learn more about how this challenge is navigated across modalities.

Findings

To answer our research questions (*How does negotiating (non)belonging influence a Syrian refugee-background mother's literacy practices? What literacy practices "resonate" in such negotiations across in-person and in online contexts via social media platforms?*), we analyzed the data using an iterative and hybrid inductive-deductive thematic analysis-based strategy (Fereday & Muir-Cochrane, 2006). As a result, three prominent themes emerged, and these related to how Maria was trying to claim or negotiate (non)belonging as a citizen of the United States, (non)belonging as a local community member, and (non)belonging as a transnational Syrian woman and mother. In this chapter, we present samples of our findings related to the third theme: negotiating (non)belonging as a transnational Syrian mother. Our choice of that theme in particular was informed by the relevant data's potential to serve as an illustrative example of the methodology used and its affordances. In line with our research question, we focus on what literacy practices resonate (or not) as Maria claims the identity of a Syrian mother and a naturalized citizen of the United States.

بعد غياب 7 شهور اشتقتلا كتير والله الحوسة
بدونا ما بتسوا شي احلا هدية بتجيني

Translation: 'After 7 months of absence I miss her a lot I swear to God without her it is not worth it the best gift that I have received'
Thank you XXXX so much for all nice gift and thanks for my birthday gift

Figure 1. The Squeegee, Al Howsa, or الحوسة

In this sample from Maria's online posts on one of the social media platforms, she celebrates her acquisition of a squeegee (حوسة in Arabic, Figure 1). Back in Syria, floors were made out of marble, and a squeegee was essential to making sure that Maria had clean floors, something which she regarded as an essential responsibility of a wife and mother. She would clean the floors with soapy water and use the squeegee to direct and dry up the water with a mop mounted on the squeegee. Upon arrival to the United States, Maria did not know how to clean the hardwood floors and was trying to acquire a squeegee which she used in Syria to clean the tile flooring. One problem she faced was that she did not know what a حوسة was called in English and she could not find any squeegees in stores. To address this problem, Maria resorted to her online community of Syrian women in the United States. Upon sharing her problem with this online community, she was not only able to identify the English word, but one of her friends was able to get her a squeegee and deliver it on time as a birthday gift. As evident by her online post, Maria was ecstatic. Although she did not really need the squeegee (she could not wash her apartment floor with water), the squeegee was a part of the home that she left behind, and having the squeegee made her feel more complete. As she explained, it was the best gift she had ever received.

Maria described the important role of social media in helping her negotiate resettlement. "I wouldn't have survived without social media!", Maria shared in an interview. She explained how her online community helped her find a sense of belonging and comradery, knowing that many other Syrian women had faced some of the same problems and were there to help her. How Maria was able to both use her multimodal and multilingual repertoires and draw upon the help of her online network are examples of how digital literacies can provide affordances to RB individuals to negotiate resettlement and problem-solve efficiently. In this case, Maria's literacy practices "resonated" with her online community, who helped her find and acquire a squeegee! From a transliteracies perspective, the squeegee as an artifact allows us to examine "how literacies become threaded across the material world in dynamic and unpredictable ways" (Stornaiuolo et al., 2017, p. 75).

Although Maria's online post was a successful example of how the mobility of literacies (threading multilingual, multimodal, and artifactual literacies via a digital milieu across different spaces and actors) can provide affordances to RB individuals in resettlement contexts, we have to keep in mind the paradox of mobility and the inequitable dimensions that accompany such mobility in literacy practices online, as the following excerpt from an interview with Maria shows:

> One time I posted [online] a video of my daughter crying. She was not sobbing or anything, but she had what I believed to be cute tears. I posted it because I wanted to show her being cute. Right after I posted the video, I started receiving

> comments and questions asking if my daughter was OK. People were worried that our family was suffering or unhappy. Soon, I received a phone call from our resettlement agency, asking me to delete the video in order to avoid any negative reflections on their work. She (the agent) did not want people to think that they were not taking care of us and that the children were miserable here. I deleted the video, and I realized that I needed to be careful about what to post.

The above excerpt shows how increased mobility online is not without limitations. Maria had to delete her online post as the content did not resonate with the resettlement agency and their perceived role as successful mediators of resettlement. Maria explained that the image of a crying "refugee" child did not align with the resettlement agency's efforts to maintain a positive online presence that focused on what they were doing to help the recently resettled refugee community. Maria could not have refused the resettlement agent's request to delete the post, as her family was dependent on the aid and services provided through that agency. In addition, this example shows how the online and in-person contexts are intertwined and how this act of censorship of Maria's multimodal artifact of what she believed was a "cute" video was misconstrued. From a transliteracies perspective, this data emphasizes the need to attend "to whose meanings and practices are amplified or muffled in which systems, and how and why some objects and forms find resonance and persist while others wane" (Stornaiuolo et al., 2017, p.81). On a methodological level, we see how an ethnetnographic design can capture resonance (and dissonance) across online and in-person contexts, and how these contexts are intricately intertwined.

Methodological discussion: Rethinking data for more equitable research

This study adopts an innovative qualitative ethnetnographic design. While ethnographic case studies and ethnographies are well-established in research in Applied Linguistics and have been used to examine people's lived experiences and learning trajectories (e.g., De Costa, 2010; Wei, 2020), netnographies remain rare (Kessler et al., 2021) and netnographers continue to face ambiguities and challenges regarding ethical decision-making (Kessler et al., 2023). To date, there have been no studies combining ethnographic and netnographic approaches to examine the resonance of literacy practices across languages in the resettlement experiences of RB individuals and families; such is the purpose of this study. In this section, we provide example netnographies that have been recently conducted before we shift to a discussion of how we engaged in rethinking data for this ethnetnography to aspire for more equitable research with RMLEs such as Maria.

Netnographies in second language acquisition research

Kozinets (2019) described netnographies as "a form of qualitative research that seeks to understand the cultural experiences that encompass and are reflected within the traces, practices, networks and systems of social media" (p.14). Thus, a netnography draws upon ethnographic techniques and methods to examine the lived experiences of individuals or communities on social media platforms. Kessler et al. (2021) have contended that the research site and the types of data collected are the two main features that differentiate netnography from ethnography. While ethnographies examine physical locations, netnographies examine online contexts. As for data, ethnographies often involve fieldnotes, observations, interviews, and various artifacts from a physical location. Netnographies also rely on observations but focus more on participants' *online traces* resulting from interacting with others in online contexts and posting various types of data, including audio, video, and images (Kozinets, 2019).

While netnographers may solely rely on studying participants' online traces, adding ethnographic data to these online traces is not an uncommon practice. In relation to collecting this data, Kessler et al. (2021) have identified three different types of data operations: investigative, interactive, and immersive. Investigative data collection operations emphasize the online traces themselves by focusing on participants' normal online activities and what participants post on social media without researcher interference. This is different from interactive data collection operations where participants respond to specific prompts presented by the researcher. For example, the researcher posts an online question for participants to engage with or comments on the participants' posts and interacts with them as a member of the online environment. The third type of data collection operation is immersive in that the researcher maintains an immersion journal whereby they document various aspects of the study (e.g., observations of synchronous activities and other descriptive and methodological notes). This immersion journal is similar to fieldnotes written in traditional ethnographies.

To date, there have been few netnographies in SLA research, although there has been a recent increase in interest in this type of research (e.g., Dovchin, 2015; Isbell, 2018; Kessler, 2023; Kulavuz-Onal, 2013; Neuschafer, 2022). For space considerations, we provide summaries of two of the most recent netnographies (Kessler, 2023; Neuschafer, 2022) and use these to later compare and contrast with our own data collection and data analysis procedures.

Kessler (2023) combined quantitative methods with netnography to examine the written corrective feedback sought and provided in WordReference Forums, an asynchronous online community where discussion boards (forums) are dedicated to assisting users in learning languages. Prior to data collection, Kessler started by engaging in pre-study observations to learn more about the practices of the users in these forums and familiarize himself with the online context. From those initial observations, Kessler was able to identify some of the rules or processes that governed these forums. For example, second language (L2) users of English would post questions that are answered by speakers whose first language (L1) is English. Users could not request translations of chunks of text, and such requests were removed by the moderators. Although collecting data from public online forums does not require IRB approval, Kessler obtained IRB approval for his study and sought participants' online consent (five L2 speakers and five L1 English speakers). Kessler observed these participants' online activities over four months and collected questionnaire data and randomly selected forum postings from each focal participant during each observation, which took place once or twice per week for around an hour. Qualitative analysis of the data involved utilizing codes from the literature and engaging in a thematic analysis of the data — which led to identifying new types of written corrective feedback that did not exist in the literature prior to Kessler's study (e.g., supply requests where users asked the feedback provider to choose between two or more words that were considered appropriate to use in the text). Based on these new findings, Kessler proposed a new typology/classification system to better understand the intricacies of online feedback. Another contribution of that study was its unique examination of written corrective feedback in out-of-school contexts (e.g., in online language forums).

Neuschafer's (2022) study adopted a qualitative netnographic design to examine Duolingo discussion board posts pertaining to learners of Spanish and German. More specifically, Neuschafer assessed learners' needs as they progressed from one unit to another in Duolingo, a language learning app. Unlike Kessler, Neuschafer did not seek consent from participants and collected randomly sourced posts on publicly available discussion boards. Users of these discussion boards adopted usernames and avatars. As some users might have used their real names as usernames, Neuschafer refrained from reporting usernames in the study to help protect users' identities. "The criteria for the selection of users and their data from discussion boards included identifying information that was relevant, active, interactive, diverse, and provided rich details" (Neuschafer, 2022, p.4). One important limitation of this netnography, acknowledged by the author, was the fact that the data collected may not be representative of the typical Duolingo user, as many users of the app may not post their views and comments on these discussion boards. Regarding data analysis, Neuschafer adopted Kozinets's (2010) six steps of analyzing netnography data. These steps include coding, noting, abstracting, comparing, checking information, generalizing, and theorizing. Findings suggested that compared to German users, Duolingo Spanish users "had the benefit of being immersed in discussions that included many native-speaking Duolingo Spanish users, which increased the accuracy of answers and cultural immersion in the language" (Kozinet, 2010, p. 12). Importantly, Spanish speakers were more tolerant of the dynamic nature of language and more accepting of variations and seeming inconsistencies of the Spanish language used by learners.

Ethnetnographies and rethinking data for equitable research Apart from citing a need for additional netnographies in multilingual contexts, Kessler et al. (2021) have contended that future research should consider investigating "both the online and in-person aspects of language learning" which would afford a "fuller picture of both the community and its members along with characteristics related to how languages are learned in/across different spaces" (p. 20). Thus, an innovative *ethnetnographic* approach, combining both ethnographic and netnographic data sources, can yield a more comprehensive picture of multilingual language and literacy development in general, and in this particular case, of how RMLEs like Maria might draw upon their multilingual and multimodal repertoires to share their experiences of resettlement and belonging in a new environment.

Ethnetnography: Towards a definition

Drawing upon Kessler's call, and based on our own work, we define an *ethnetnography* as a form of qualitative research that combines both ethnographic and netnographic approaches to collect and analyze data with the purpose of examining the experiences of (transnational) individuals across multiple languages, spaces, temporalities, and modalities. An ethnetnographic research design invites constant reflection regarding conducting meaningful and ethical research as ethnetnographers traverse participants' lives on a deeper level — across physical and online contexts and across various timescales and languages, which would necessitate a rethinking of data. Needless to say, engaging with such research comes with both numerous rewards and challenges at the same time. In the following paragraphs, we describe our positionality as researchers in addition to our ethnetnographic design (data collection and analysis processes). We also reflect on the rewards and challenges encompassing ethnetnographic research and discuss ethical dimensions pertaining to ethnetnographies.

Researcher positionality, recruitment, and ethical considerations

With respect to our positionality, we have worked with immigrant and RB individuals and families both in the United States and in other contexts, such as Lebanon. We are both committed to contributing to an asset-based body of literature that challenges stereotypical representations of this marginalized group of multilingual learners. In our research we continuously strive to adopt innovative research designs and methodologies that amplify the voices of immigrant and RB children, youths, and adults.

Maria and her family were recruited for our study back in 2017 by the first author. Institutional Review Board (IRB) approval was acquired and Maria and her family signed informed consent and assent forms that were translated into Arabic by the first author, who also explained the purpose of the research to all participants in both English and Arabic. In our case, it was important for the first author to take the time to explain the research and consent and assent process to the family in their first language and answer their questions. Also important was our approach in positioning the family as a source of knowledge, explaining to them that one of our objectives was to learn *from* their experiences of language learning and resettlement. Indeed, in one of our previous research projects, the family visited the first author's TESOL methods classroom and shared their resettlement stories and teaching tips with students seeking TESOL certification on how to address the needs of RB families (Karam, Oikonomidoy, & Kibler, 2021). As such, the family members were perceived as sources and creators of knowledge who could inspire educators and the RB families they work with.

The reason we share these details is to illustrate how ethical research transcends typical IRB processes. Initially, the IRB did not request back-translations of the consent/assent documents. However, a recent IRB random audit highlighted the fact that back-translations were not available on file and recommended submitting these documents. Back-translations of consent and assent documents were submitted. The IRB compared these translations with the English language versions on file and reported that the documents were adequate, approving the back-translations. While IRB safe-guards — such as ensuring that back-translations — are provided to ensure the accuracy of the consent and assent forms — are important, conducting ethical and collaborative research with RB families often transcends such mechanisms. Due to their importance, we integrate ethical considerations and reflections in subsequent sections as we elaborate on our vision of conducting ethnetnographies. Such attention to ethical considerations is in line with recent research that brings additional attention to ethical issues in Applied Linguistics (e.g., Cinaglia et al., 2024) and research involving social media and online environments (Kessler et al., 2023; Marino et al., 2024).

Ethnetnographic data collection operations

Our data collection approach was in line with our perspective on prioritizing participants' knowledge. Reflecting an ethnetnographic design, our data sources for this study combined both ethnographic and netnographic data sources. Consequently, our data included not only ethnographic fieldnotes from the first author's weekly visits, semi-structured and informal interviews with Maria, and artifacts from Maria's living place; our data also included multilingual and multimodal *online traces* from Maria's social media accounts and her descriptions of them. Our ethnographic approach helped produce rich longitudinal data related to how Maria negotiated resettlement and belonging through her multilingual literacy practices.

Extended time in the field is a prominent feature of ethnographies which allows researchers to observe participants over a prolonged period of time and therefore enable a deeper understanding of routines, rituals, rules, roles and relationships that are at the center of complex human interactions (Saldaña & Omasta, 2021). In an increasingly connected and digitized world where transnational families and their literacies are constantly on the move, it is wise not to ignore the realm of social media where RB families and individuals communicate with friends and family across the globe and share their experiences of finding a new home in resettlement contexts.

As mentioned earlier, Kessler et al.'s (2021) recently proposed set of guidelines to conduct netnographies in multilingual contexts guided this study. More specifically, we adopted an "investigative data operations" (Kessler et al. 2021, p. 8) approach where the focus was on collecting the data without the researcher's interference or prompts. Such an approach positioned the researcher as an outsider and was a good fit for this study in particular as we wanted to highlight the participant's voice and lived experiences of resettlement and belonging rather than prescribing how to use her social media accounts or prompting her to do so by being a participant-observer. This outsider online positionality was contrasted with a more involved (insider) role of the first author within the family's life in the physical context. We contend that there is no right or wrong way to embrace or reject such a duality in the researchers' outsider/insider positionalities, but this dual vision can rather provide different lenses that enrich observations and allow deeper insight into what "resonates" across these contexts.

In addition to the longitudinal background knowledge (gained through ethnographic observations and interviews) that the first author had of how Maria negotiated resettlement and belonging, we were interested to learn more about what meanings and practices resonated (or not) between in-person and online literacy contexts. As such, the first author asked Maria to share how she used language to document or express her resettlement experiences on social media. To protect Maria's identity, we refrained from specifying which social media platform(s) she was active on. However, she was very excited to share how social media played a significant role in her resettlement experiences, emphasizing, "I would not have survived without social media." Maria also explained that after she acquired her pharmaceutical technician certificate and started to work at a pharmacy, she had less time to post on social media. She shared that she now mostly posts about "significant" events in her family's life. When asked for examples, Maria picked up her phone and started to share online traces of these significant events. These included such events as the family's first arrival at the airport into the United States, getting a driver's license, acquiring the pharmaceutical assistant certificate, and obtaining citizenship. Not all "significant" events were landmark events that had to do with resettlement, but they were significant events to the family at an emotional or spiritual level (e.g., celebrating one of her daughters wearing the hijab and celebrating her son's awards and academic achievements at school).

Regardless of the type of event, Maria shared what she believed were important events with the first author. As she shared, he asked Maria if he could take photos of these posts, and Maria approved. Toward the end, Maria even handed him her mobile device and invited him to go through her social media platforms and capture whatever he was interested in, explaining, "There is nothing private there that I would not want to share with you." Nevertheless, one's mobile phone is a very personal device that most people would not entrust to others. The first author was faced with the dilemma of either rejecting the offer to go through the phone or to search the phone for relevant data and posts that were not originally highlighted or shared by Maria. Applied linguists often face similar dilemmas (Cinaglia et al., 2024; De Costa, 2016) related to protecting participants' privacy, especially in online environments (Marion et al., 2024). To address this dilemma, he explained to Maria that there were only a few posts that he still wanted to take screen shots of — those that Maria discussed earlier but he did not have the chance to capture. Maria agreed and left her mobile phone in his custody while she prepared food and then invited him to stay and have lunch with the family. The first author took photos of the posts that he was interested in and handed the device back to Maria. Those photos were all of events that Maria had previously shared with him and did not include moments from events on the phone. This incident required "thinking on one's feet" in terms of decision making and how to honor Maria's *trust* and *perspective* — two important points we elaborate on below.

Maria trusted Fares with her phone. This sense of trust did not come in a short period of time, but was rather the result of prolonged engagement with the family and a research partnership that prioritized the family's needs over research objectives, especially during the first few months of resettlement. The priority was never to collect data; rather, in assisting the family with their immediate needs primarily, opportunities along the way to collect data arose. Such trust could not have been achieved with a pure netnographic approach that focused solely on extracting participants' online data. An ethnographic approach allows for trust to build over time with participants and can therefore facilitate data collection operations, whether in-person or online.

With such trust comes the responsibility of honoring participants' perspectives. As our research aimed at amplifying Maria's voice and presenting resettlement and negotiating belonging through her own experiences, we endeavored to highlight the events or experiences that she chose to share with us. We do acknowledge the inherent subjective role of the researcher in influencing how findings are presented, but we also wanted to honor Maria's trust and perspective by avoiding selectively extracting data from her phone. This approach goes beyond the investigative data operations (Kessler et al., 2021) where the researcher avoids influencing participants' behaviors online. In our case, we honored Maria's sense of agency in selecting what stories, events, and experiences she wanted to highlight and share about how she negotiated belonging in the resettlement context. Preserving participants' sense of agency, in our opinion, is essential. While this may not be a focus from a netnographic perspective where netnographers do not necessarily develop a personal relationship with participants, it is extremely important from an ethnographic perspective, especially with marginalized populations such as RMLEs who have been stripped of their agency through acts of violence or persecution that have forced them to flee their home country. In short, an ethnetnographic approach to investigative data operations adds another layer of consideration for participants' sense of agency that is usually not as prioritized through a pure netnographic approach.

Ethnetnographic data analysis

Similar to ethnographies, netnographies (or ethnetnographies in the case of this study) are flexible, and although researchers may approach data with certain theoretical lenses, researchers should engage with open inquiry and let the data guide their findings (Kessler et al., 2021). In line with this thinking, we analyzed the data using an iterative and hybrid inductive-deductive thematic analysis-based strategy (Fereday & Muir-Cochrane, 2006) where a priori codes were derived from the literature, in addition to codes evolving from the data itself in the form of emergent themes.

In coding and analyzing ethnetnographic data, some data sources may be more prevalent than others. Just as mixed methods designs sometimes lean more heavily on their quantitative or qualitative data sources, a similar process may be at play in ethnetnographic designs. In other words, ethnetnographers may draw more, less, or equally upon ethnographic data (e.g., field notes, interviews, and physical artifacts) or netnographic online traces (e.g., audio, video, images, or texts posted online). Thus, ethnographic or netnographic data may be a primary or secondary source of data, depending on the research and its objectives. For those reasons, we developed the distinctions below, which we hope can be helpful for researchers interested in utilizing ethnetnographic methods.

1. **ETHnetnography:** ethnographic data and methods have a primary role with a more prolonged time in the field focused on physical contexts; netnographic data and methods are complementary
2. **ethNETnography:** ethnographic data and methods have a secondary role; heavier reliance is on netnographic data and methods with prolonged engagement in and observations of online contexts
3. **ethnetnography:** a more balanced design that draws equally upon ethnographic and netnographic designs with prolonged observations and time in the field and in both physical and online contexts

In our study, ethnographic data collected over the span of around six years was our primary data source. Netnographic data of Maria's online activity played a complementary yet important role. As such, our study aligns with an ETHnetnography within the above categorizations. While we did not purposefully assign netnographic data a secondary function, it is important to acknowledge that we started this project as an ethnography, collecting all types of traditional ethnographic data. However, we soon realized how our participants' resettlement experiences were not limited to the in-person context. We knew from the literature that transnational families used technology to maintain contact with family and friends, but we also soon realized that this was not the sole purpose that social media platforms played in the family's lives.

References to social media started emerging from our extended time with the family. For example, they shared stories of how the two daughters were bullied online because of their hijab; they shared how social media was used to help the children learn Arabic; and they shared videos and pictures documenting their travels and events with the first author through one social media app. Soon, we came to the realization of the complex role of social media in the family's lives and how inseparable those platforms were from their daily lives and routines, especially in Maria's case. This realization influenced how we decided to frame the study and challenged us to identify new theoretical and methodological approaches that could honor the complexities of the family's and Maria's multilingual and multimodal literacy practices. As the first author had access to only one of the social media platforms that the family was active on, we decided to ask Maria to show us the social media posts that she believed were important to her and her family, regardless of the platform, timing, language, or modality. That came with both rewards and challenges that we discuss in the next section.

Rewards, challenges, and limitations

Engaging in ethnetnographic research comes with a unique set of rewards, challenges, and limitations. It is rewarding in the sense that an ethnetnographic approach can provide a more complete picture of how individuals engage in learning languages, meaning making, and different literacy practices. In the case of RMLEs, it can also provide a more comprehensive picture of their resettlement experiences. This carries an increased importance with transnational and transliterate individuals who are constantly on the move. Another reward is how combining ethnographic and netnographic approaches and methods can be an important source of triangulation that transcends temporalities, modalities, and spaces. However, it is important to note that netnographic data in our study was not merely an additional source of triangulation. In fact, netnographic data was essential to trace resonance across physical and online contexts in how Maria negotiated resettlement and belonging through multilingual literacy practices. In tracing resonance, we did not look for triangulating data, but we were more interested in tracing tensions, discrepancies and ambivalence.

Challenges in ethnetnographic research include how to navigate ethical dilemmas. With tracing participants' lives both in-person and online comes a deeper knowledge of their lives and intimate routines and rituals. This yields incredibly rich data but also creates a significant challenge for researchers on how to process and analyze this wealth of data while examining resonances, dissonances, and tensions. Pervading this process is the challenge of maintaining participants' identities and honoring their perspectives. To ensure anonymity, researchers need to take extra measures beyond using pseudonyms and adopting best practices relating to data maintenance. In an ethnetnography that combines data from online and in-person contexts, the risk of revealing participants' identities is double-fold. In our case, we chose not to reveal which social media platforms Maria was active on. We also took screen shots of the images and ran a search using the powerful Google lens on an Android phone to make sure that none of the results led to revealing the participants' identity. We also cropped aspects of the images that we used in this chapter to make it more difficult to trace the participant's online trail. In addition, we tried to take the time to explain these details to the participants. Having prolonged time with the family within the in-person context facilitated this aspect, and it was interesting to observe how Maria explained to her daughter during one of the interviews that "Fares will not use your real name in his research" to reassure her.

With respect to honoring the participants' perspectives and voices, member checking is critical in ethnetnographies, mainly due to the intimate and longitudinal nature of this type of research. In line with this belief, we shared our findings with Maria, who was in agreement with our analysis and how we presented the data. She emphasized how online contexts and social media can have both positive effects on one's life and how they can also be limiting — a theme that we explored in our chapter.

Ethnetnographies, although powerful, come with certain limitations. Participants, just like the rest of us, may have different ways of expressing their views or projecting their identities online through diverse literacy practices. As such, ethnetnographers should come with an open mind and allow for ambiguities, discrepancies, and ambivalence. Prolonged observations, both in-person and online, can account for such differences and yield exciting, if not sometimes contradictory, explanations. In addition, decision making on what data to include or exclude can also be a limitation. In our case, we only included netnographic data that was highlighted by Maria. While this amplifies Maria's perspective, it can also limit a more comprehensive understanding of how Maria uses social media. In all cases, researchers should provide a rationale for their decisions on which data to include or exclude in their analyses.

Implications for qualitative research on multilingual literacy development

This study offers multiple insights into qualitative research of multilingual literacy development across modalities, particularly as researchers are challenged to rethink data in an increasingly digital and multimodal world. Ethnographic perspectives center on the lived experiences of participants, and such a viewpoint allows us to see that online worlds are neither distant nor distinct from face-to-face communication and meaning making. For refugees, immigrants, and other displaced populations in particular, online modalities play a key role in offering a sense of belonging in their resettlement experiences, and as Maria's case demonstrated, these experiences cross both languages and modalities. We contend that ethnetnographic approaches offer a uniquely comprehensive picture of multilingual literacy development that would be difficult to capture otherwise. They also complement particular theoretical approaches to multilingual literacy (such as transliteracies) and the refugee or immigrant experience (such as belonging and ambivalence), all of which exist across contested ideological and sociopolitical spaces.

For those researchers interested in employing such a methodological approach, we urge them to avoid superficial uses of ethnetnography and instead to deeply consider the methodological considerations outlined in this chapter. Such an approach influences all aspects of the study, from research questions to theoretical perspectives and positionality, and from data collection and analysis to findings and implications. Ethnetnography also requires particular attention not only to time, trust, and relationship-building with participants — cornerstones of ethnography — but also to clear ethical guidelines that are needed to navigate the complex and dynamic world of technology and online communication. Methodological choices should be carefully made and clearly presented in ethnetnographic reports, such that the body of evidence and theory behind this methodological innovation can grow in meaningful and coherent ways.

Future studies adopting ethnetnographic designs also have to grapple with many unanswered questions. For example, how and when do you decide to engage in an ethnetnography? In our study, we started with ethnography and pivoted to an ETHnetnography. We are curious if researchers can do the opposite and how that would look (e.g., to start with a netnography and add an ethnographic layer). Better still, what does adopting an ethnetnographic approach with an equal focus on eth- and net-nographic approaches look like? What procedures are involved in recruitment, consent, and data collection and analysis in this approach? How will that help us further rethink data in qualitative research on multilingual literacy development? And how might researchers conduct a larger scope ethnetnography with a group rather than a single case study participant? We are only beginning to scratch the surface of adopting innovative research designs and methods that can accompany a fast-paced world where people and their languages/literacies are on the move.

We extend an invitation to fellow researchers to continue to (re)imagine what a combined ethnographic/netnographic research design may look like and to continue to explore the possibilities of innovative qualitative designs to better understand the literacy development of multilingual individuals and families from immigrant and refugee backgrounds.

References

Bartlett, L., Mendenhall, M., & Ghaffar-Kucher, A. (2017). Culture in acculturation: Refugee youth's schooling experiences in international schools in New York City. *International Journal of Intercultural Relations*, 60, 109–119.

Cinaglia, C., Rabie-Ahmed, A., & De Costa, P. I. (2024). Introduction: Ethical issues in applied linguistics scholarship. In P. I. De Costa, A. Rabie-Ahmed, & C. Cinaglia (Eds.), *Ethical issues in applied linguistics scholarship* (pp. 1–7). John Benjamins.

De Costa, P. I. (2010). From refugee to transformer: A Bourdieusian take on a Hmong learner's trajectory. *TESOL Quarterly*, 44(3), 517–541.

De Costa, P. I. (Ed.). (2016). *Ethics in applied linguistics research: Language researcher narratives*. Routledge.

Dovchin, S. (2015). Language, multiple authenticities and social media: The online language practices of university students in Mongolia. *Journal of Sociolinguistics*, 19(4), 437–459.

Duran, C. S. (2019). On issues of discrimination and xenophobia: What can TESOL practitioners do to support and advocate for refugee students? *TESOL Quarterly*, 53(3), 818–827.

Fereday, J., & Muir-Cochrane, E. (2006). Demonstrating rigor using thematic analysis: A hybrid approach of coding. *International Journal of Qualitative Methods*, 5(1), 80–92.

Isbell, D. R. (2018). Online informal language learning: Insights from a Korean learning community. *Language Learning & Technology*, 22(3), 82–102.

Karam, F. J. (2018). Language and identity construction: The case of a refugee digital bricoleur. *Journal of Adolescent & Adult Literacy*, 61(5), 511–521.

Karam, F. J. (2021). Writing the story of Sabadullah: Transnational literacies of two refugee-background parents. In D. Warriner (Ed.), *Refugee education across the lifespan* (pp. 231–250). Springer.

Karam, F. J., Barone, D., & Kibler, A. K. (2021). Resisting and negotiating literacy tasks: Agentive practices of refugee-background students. *Research in the Teaching of English*, 55(4), 369–392.

Karam, F. J., Oikonomidoy, E., & Kibler, A. K. (2021). Artifactual literacies and TESOL: Narratives of a Syrian refugee-background family. *TESOL Quarterly*, 55(2), 510–535.

Kessler, M. (2023). Written corrective feedback in an online community: A typology of English language learners' requests and interlocutors' responses. *Computers and Composition*, 67.

Kessler, M., Marino, F., & Liska, D. (2023). Netnographic research ethics in applied linguistics: A systematic review of data collection and reporting practices. *Research Methods in Applied Linguistics*, 2(3), Article 100082.

Kessler, M., De Costa, P. I., Isbell, D., & Gajasinghe, K. (2021). Conducting a netnography in second language acquisition research. *Language Learning*, 71(4), 1122–1148.

Kozinets, R. V. (2010). *Netnography: Doing ethnographic research online*. Sage.

Kozinets, R. V. (2019). *Netnography: The essential guide to qualitative social media research*. Sage.

Kulavuz-Onal, D. (2013). *English language teachers' learning to teach with technology through participation in an online community of practice: A netnography of webheads in action* (Unpublished doctoral dissertation). University of South Florida.

Lorimer Leonard, R. (2013). Traveling literacies: Multilingual writing on the move. *Research in the Teaching of English*, 48, 13–39.

Marino, F., Liska, D., & Kessler, M. (2024). Ethical considerations for research involving computer-assisted language learning, social media, and online environments. In P. I. De Costa, A. Rabie-Ahmed, & C. Cinaglia (Eds.), *Ethical issues in applied linguistics scholarship* (pp. 73–87). John Benjamins.

McBrien, J. L. (2005). Educational needs and barriers for refugee students in the United States: A review of the literature. *Review of Educational Research*, 75(3), 329–364.

McBrien, J., Dooley, K., & Birman, D. (2017). Cultural and academic adjustment of refugee youth: Introduction to the special issue. *International Journal of Intercultural Relations*, 60, 104–108.

Milani, T.M., & Levon, E. (2019). Israel as homotopia: Language, space, and vicious belonging. *Language in Society*, 48(4), 607–628.

Moriarty, M. (2019). Regimes of voice and visibility in the refugeescape: A semiotic landscape approach. *Linguistic Landscape*, 5(2), 142–159.

Neuschafer, T. (2022). A netnographic analysis of how Duolingo supports German and Spanish learning needs. *Digital Culture & Education*, 14(3), 1–15.

Omerbašić, D. (2015). Literacy as a translocal practice: Digital multimodal literacy practices among girls resettled as refugees. *Journal of Adolescent & Adult Literacy*, 58(6), 472–481.

Portes, A., & Rumbaut, R.G. (2001). *Legacies: The story of the immigrant second generation*. University of California Press.

Saldaña, J., & Omasta, M. (2021). *Qualitative research: Analyzing life* (2nd ed.). Sage.

Shapiro, S., & MacDonald, M.T. (2017). From deficit to asset: Locating discursive resistance in a refugee-background student's narrative. *Language, Identity & Education*, 16(2), 80–93.

Shapiro, S., Farrelly, R., & Curry, M.J. (Eds.). (2018). *Educating refugee-background students: Critical issues and dynamic contexts*. Multilingual Matters.

Stornaiuolo, A., Smith, A., & Phillips, N.C. (2017). Developing a transliteracies framework for a connected world. *Journal of Literacy Research*, 49(1), 68–91.

Tazreiter, C. (2019). Temporary migrants as an uneasy presence in immigrant societies: Reflections on ambivalence in Australia. *International Journal of Comparative Sociology*, 60(1–2), 91–109.

Thomas, S., Joseph, C., Laccetti, J., Mason, B., Mills, S., Perril, S., & Pullinger, K. (2007). Transliteracy: Crossing divides. *First Monday*, 12(12).

UNHCR. (2021, June 18). *Figures at a glance*. UNHCR. www.unhcr.org/en-us/figures-at-a-glance.html

University of Colorado Boulder, Institute of Behavioral Science. (2020, October 9). The Wall: American Nativism, Immigration Policy, and the Great Exclusion of 2017–2020; Ruben G. Rumbaut. [Video]. YouTube. https://www.youtube.com/watch?app=desktop&v=OcZL _lxSe-o&feature=youtu.be

Warriner, D. (2013). "It's better life here than there": Elasticity and ambivalence in narratives of personal experience. *International Multilingual Research Journal*, 7, 15–32.

Warriner, D.S. (2021). *Refugee education across the lifespan*. Springer.

Wei, L. (2020). Ethnography. In J. McKinley & H. Rose (Eds.), *The Routledge handbook of research methods in applied linguistics* (pp. 154–164). Routledge.

CHAPTER 4

Communicating selves

Immigrant, emergent multilingual students' voices and agency through their multimodal artworks

Hsiao-Chin Kuo & Sanela Sprečić
Northeastern Illinois University | Western Michigan University

This chapter features integrating multimodal data sources (e.g., visual-arts and associated conversations) and critical multimodal analysis as an innovative methodological approach. Through multimodal literacies, we investigated how two immigrant, emergent multilingual students communicated their dialogical self with their multimodal artworks. This study is then used as a basis for the methodological discussion about multimodal data sources to give immigrant students agency to articulate their developing identities as a part of their complex, transnational lived experiences, which would have been missed by the researchers if only monomodal, verbal data sources were utilized. Implications are drawn around researchers' professional learning of multimodal research design and future research directions to create more equitable engagement for emergent multilingual participants.

Keywords: emergent multilinguals, multimodal literacies, visual arts, equity, identity

Introduction

> ...because [of] my grandma. She used to live in the village, so I really think about her, because she was sick when she was in the village, and that's why I decided to draw about it.　　　　　(Lora, emergent multilingual student from Congo)

What happens when emergent multilingual students are provided with opportunities to express themselves beyond the traditional monomodal (i.e., only verbal) way of communication? The above interview excerpt highlights how through creating visual artworks, such as drawings and sketches, an immigrant, emergent

https://doi.org/10.1075/rmal.11.04kuo

multilingual student, Lora, communicated her developing self and brought forward rich meanings about her transnational, lived experiences through the drawing of her grandmother's house during an interview process.

Through multimodal literacies, this chapter features how visual-arts data, along with associated conversations and critical multimodal analysis, serves as an innovative methodological approach. Such approach is particularly important for research with immigrant, emergent multilingual students as these students articulate their developing identities, which play a significant part of their complex, transnational, lived experiences and would have been missed by the researchers if only monomodal, verbal data sources were utilized. Drawing from a primary research project situated in a self-contained ESL newcomer-program in a Midwestern, urban middle school, we start this chapter by presenting a qualitative case study (Yin, 2009) that investigated how two focal immigrant, emergent multilingual students created multimodal artworks to express their developing selves (i.e., one's self-perception about lived experiences and different roles in the world). The presented study is theoretically framed by the notion of dialogical self (Hermans, 2001, 2022; Hermans et al., 1992) and conceptualized through multimodal literacies (Jewitt & Kress, 2003; Kress, 2010; Serafini, 2015). We present an overview of this theoretical framework along with relevant literature, research context, the demographic information about the two focal students, data collection and analysis, and findings in the first part of the chapter.

In the second part of the chapter, drawing upon the presented study, we discuss aspects of methodological decisions and the research process. Particularly, with multimodal data sources that include visual-art data and the opportunity for participants to explain their artworks, we challenge the norms about research data that are predominantly collected and analyzed via monomodal and verbal meaning-making. Thereafter, we clarify the affordances and opportunities of integrating visual arts, along with the participants' interpretation of their artworks, and of utilizing critical multimodal analysis, especially for research with emergent multilingual participants. In particular, we discuss how an integration of visual arts and verbal communication embodies knowledge that would have been missed by the researchers if only monomodal, verbal data sources were utilized. Furthermore, employing critical multimodal analysis scrutinizes the dominant deficit viewpoint of immigrant, multilingual students and expands our understanding of these students' literacy development and complex, transnational, lived experiences. Finally, we discuss ethical considerations of integrating visual arts around issues of anonymity and ownership. The present study and the methodological discussion shed light on qualitative research on multilingual literacy development with four implications for researchers: (1) to consider multimodal data sources in their research design, especially for more equitable access and possibilities for multilingual participants, (2) to treat multimodal data meaningfully and through a critical lens, (3) to address professional learning for researchers to develop their multimodal literacy knowledge, and (4) to further investigate the use of multimodal analysis and multimodal research disseminations.

Overview of the study

Theoretical framework

The study presented in this chapter is theoretically framed through two perspectives: dialogical self and multimodal literacies. The first perspective, dialogical self, suggests that the self conceives a dynamic, multifaceted, and dialogical whole of "I-positions" (i.e., self-positionings externally and internally toward others and oneself; Hermans, 2001, 2022; Hermans et al., 1992). According to Hermans (2001), the dialogical self merges characteristics of continuity that connect various self-positionings, as well as discontinuities that disagree with one another among the opposing voices within oneself while bounded and positioned in different times and spaces. These characteristics of a dialogical self are especially distinctive in lived experiences of immigrant communities. For example, Bhatia and Ram (2004) investigated how a second-generation Indian-American woman, Sayantini DasGupta, positioned herself in a typical White, Midwestern, American suburban neighborhood and constructed a sense of self in a constant and intensive dialogical negotiation among multiple, coexistent, yet contested voices: (1) one that racialized her as a Brown and ugly girl based on the White beauty standard; (2) one that perceived her as exotic and mysterious through the West's fascinated views about the East; and (3) one from her own community that expected her to remain pure and loyal to her culture by avoiding marriage outside her ethnic group. The case of DasGupta's dialogical self, negotiated among the assorted I-positions in connection with her American peers and within her diasporic communities, interrogates the traditional perception that views immigrant identities as reflecting a one-way, linear assimilation process from one's country of origin to the new host country. Bhatia and Ram (2004)'s example unpacks the complexity of immigrant identities that reflect the aforementioned characteristics of a dialogical self, formed in a process "that involves an ongoing, contested negotiation of voices from here and there, past and present, homeland and host land, self and other" (p. 237).

The second perspective of the theoretical framework, multimodal literacies, establishes the foundation for how literacy is conceptualized in this study. Multimodal literacies refer to the process in which "meanings are made, distributed, received, interpreted and remade in interpretation through many representational and communicative modes" (Jewitt & Kress, 2003, p. 1. See also Serafini, 2015). In this context, the term "modes" refers to units of semiotic resources, such as images and speech, that are socially and culturally shaped overtime to communicate meanings (Kress, 2010). In the present study, we ground our use of multimodal literacies in the following characteristics. First, we acknowledge the participants' social agency in their active and strategic use of semiotic resources to communicate their emerging selves, represented in their artworks and sketches (Höglund, 2022; Jewitt & Kress, 2003). Second, we emphasize the plurality and the multimodal nature of the term "literacies" to highlight its intertwined and multifaceted features (Sanders & Albers, 2010). Furthermore, we emphasize the notion that all modes are "partial in relation to the whole of the meaning" and "equally significant for meaning and communication" (Jewitt & Kress, 2003, p. 3). In the data sources of the presented study, the visual mode (i.e., the participants' artworks and sketches) and the verbal mode (i.e., their spoken interpretation of their visual artworks) complement each other and both play critical roles to depict a fuller picture of the students' developing identities and their lived experiences. More specifically, we view the visual mode as a primary semiotic resource which interacts with the participants' interpretation of their multimodal artworks while both inform their emerging selves (Pauwels, 2015).

Similar to the focus of the presented study in this chapter, some studies on multimodal literacies and emergent multilinguals focus on students' use of these literacies to communicate their transnational and transcultural identities, as well as their immigrant experiences. For example, scholars of multimodal literacies, such as Omerbašić (2015), Karam et al. (2021), and Paulick et al. (2022), advocate using physical and digital artifacts, including pictures and social media posts, that are observed in immigrant families' everyday activities and practices to understand immigrant students' transnational experiences and identities. More specifically related to visual artworks, in Ghiso and Low (2013)'s research on immigrant students' multimodal artworks of their transnational experiences, an eight-year-old girl of Indian heritage created a six-panel comic that portrayed the tragic loss of her uncle and their family trip to India. Similarly, the literacy scholars of multimodal practices Campano and Low (2011) discussed an eight-year-old Latina child's comic story about a journey of a snowman moving to a new land, which reflected the child's lived experiences as it metaphorically demonstrated "migration, transformation, and rebirth in a new place" (p. 383). As indicated in Ghiso and Low (2013) and Campano and Low (2011), students' complex lived experiences and emotions were documented in their multimodal literacy artworks and would have been missed by the researchers if only written data sources were collected because of the unique affordances and limitations of these different communication modes, which are further discussed in the second part of this chapter.

Furthermore, the findings in both studies disrupt the ideological view about immigrant experiences as a one-way process to "assimilation and meritocracy" (Parini, 2012, as cited in Ghiso & Low, 2013, p. 33). Nonetheless, in these studies, the participants' comics were interpreted mainly through the researchers' speculations with limited to no student explanation to guide the researchers' understanding of their multimodal works.

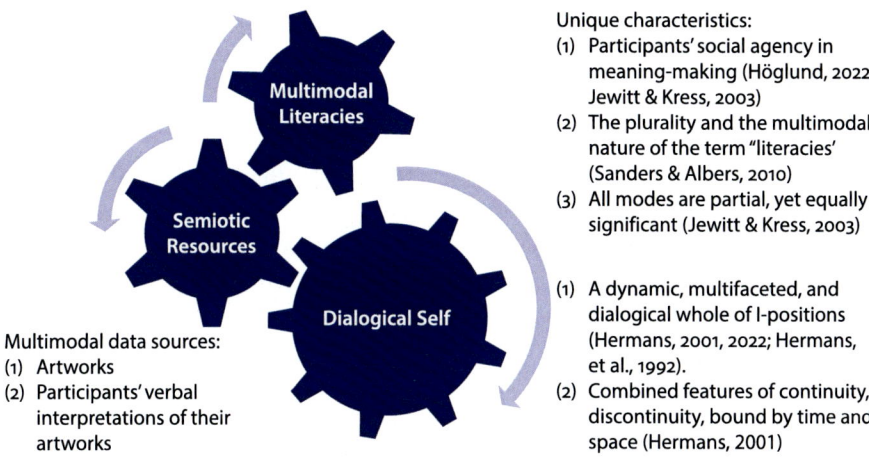

Unique characteristics:
(1) Participants' social agency in meaning-making (Höglund, 2022, Jewitt & Kress, 2003)
(2) The plurality and the multimodal nature of the term "literacies" (Sanders & Albers, 2010)
(3) All modes are partial, yet equally significant (Jewitt & Kress, 2003)

(1) A dynamic, multifaceted, and dialogical whole of I-positions (Hermans, 2001, 2022; Hermans, et al., 1992).
(2) Combined features of continuity, discontinuity, bound by time and space (Hermans, 2001)

Multimodal data sources:
(1) Artworks
(2) Participants' verbal interpretations of their artworks

Figure 1. Theoretical framework

In summary, as illustrated by the metaphor of interlocking gears in Figure 1, the interaction between the above two theoretical perspectives, dialogical self and multimodal literacies, along with their associated key features, plays a significant role in this study. The unique characteristics of multimodal literacies drive the two main multimodal data sources, artworks and participants' verbal interpretations, as semiotic resources that mediate participants' communication of their emerging selves. Underpinned by the above theoretical framework and to address the gaps in literature, the presented study is guided by the question: How did the focal, immigrant, emergent multilingual students communicate a sense of self through multimodal artworks, along with their verbal interpretation of their artworks? In the following sections, we discuss the research context and methodology, as well as a brief overview of the findings that respond to this research question.

Research context and participants

The study presented in this chapter focuses on two immigrant, emergent multilingual students, drawing from a primary research project that was situated in a self-contained ESL newcomer program in a Midwestern middle school in an urban setting. The student population in the school represented 85 different countries, with over 60 languages spoken. The objective of the ESL newcomer program was to provide sheltered content instruction for students classified as English language learners (ELLs) while at the same time they developed English language and literacy proficiency. The program contained two classes, designed for students at either Level One (Entering) or Level Two (Beginning), based on WIDA's *Performance Definitions for the Levels of English Language Proficiency in Grades K-12* (WIDA Consortium, 2012). Once the students reached the desired English language proficiency level, Level 3 (Developing) and above based on WIDA's Performance Definitions, they would move to mainstream classes in their district with English language development support.

The two focal participants, Fernanda and Lora (both pseudonyms) were students from the Level Two (Beginning) class of the ESL newcomer program. Both students were recruited in this study by Author 2, who was the instructor in the program and had contextual knowledge about students and their artworks, while Author 1 was a university faculty member in the same region. As Fernanda noted in the interview, she moved to the United States with her mother from Tegucigalpa, the capital of Honduras, because Fernanda's mother wanted to pursue a better education for Fernanda. When Fernanda missed her brother and sister who were in Honduras, she would tell herself that she had to separate from them in order to give them a better life in the future. Fernanda and her mother spoke mostly Spanish at home. According to Fernanda, as her mother started learning English at an adult ESL program, Fernanda would sometimes speak English to her mother because she wanted to help her mother learn English so that people would not look down on them. The other focal participant, Lora, moved with her mother from Brazzaville, the capital of the Republic of the Congo, also purportedly for the purpose of pursuing a better education. Lora described life being poor and the lack of a good education back in Congo. After moving to the United States, Lora missed her friends and relatives, such as her aunts and cousins. At home, Lora and her mother spoke several languages, primarily French, and sometimes Lingala and Munukutuba, two other national languages commonly used in Congo.

Data collection and analysis

Data were collected through multiple sources to strengthen the research trustworthiness (Stahl & King, 2020). The primary data were the artworks created by the two focal participants in the ESL newcomer class. Other data were collected through two rounds of semi-structured, individual interviews, conducted in English with the two students, and additional sketches and drawings that the students created during the interview process. Both the first and the follow-up interviews with Fernanda were conducted by Author 1 and Author 2. With Lora, the first interview was conducted by Author 1 and the follow-up interview was conducted by both authors. In the first interview, students were asked to explain their artworks, including their thinking and design process of creating the in-class artworks, their interpretation of these artworks, and the connection of these artworks to their sense of selves. For example, Author 1 asked Fernanda the following questions to start the conversation about Fernanda's artwork: "Can you tell us anything, either a story or things, that you wanted to express through this? What do you want to tell us?"

Fernanda and Lora were also asked in the interviews to draw something that represented who they are. The following is an example of these questions. The beginning of the conversation below touches on Fernanda's preference of communication modes between verbal and visual. Then Author 1 guided the conversation by asking if Fernanda would like to make another artwork during the interview to express herself in a more personal way.

Author 2: Do you think you can tell people about yourself by doing some [art] project?
Fernanda: Yes. Yes, I can tell them who I am and dream by making some draw[ings], what I like, you know.
Author 1: So, um, do you prefer to draw to tell people [about you]? Or do you prefer to just talk to people?
Fernanda: (…) I mean, to draw what I like.
Author 1: (…) we [met] for the first time, right? And then, so I saw this [in-class artwork] to know something about your country. But if I give you another chance to draw or just make another, another artwork to tell me about you.
Fernanda: OK, about me?
Author 1: Yeah.
Fernanda: OK.
Author 1: Do you want to do that?
Fernanda: Yes.
Author 1: OK. And you can do it any way you want.

After drawing during the first interview, students were then asked to explain their sketches created in the interview. Afterwards, a follow-up, second interview was conducted with both students to clarify questions and to further investigate issues identified from the first interview.

Data analysis included the following procedure. The semi-structured interviews were audio recorded and transcribed. For students' accounts in the interviews, a thematic analysis (Braun & Clarke, 2021) was conducted to search for emerging "themes and patterns" (Glesne, 2021, p.184), which were then utilized to triangulate with the results from analyzing students' artworks and sketches. The analysis of students' artworks and sketches was conducted primarily by Author 1 and involved two discursive stages. The initial analysis of students' artworks and sketches was guided by the following questions, adapted from Albers (2007, p. 154):

- What is the student trying to convey?
- What immediately comes to my mind?
- What visual features are used?
- What impressed me?

Preliminary themes, such as expressions of feelings and emotions, and visual features, such as shapes and colors, were identified in the initial analysis. At the second stage, critical multimodal analysis was employed to closely examine the students' artworks and sketches with a focus on identifying thematic components (Riessman, 2008) and unpacking the multimodal layouts such as visual compositions (Kress & Van Leeuwen, 2021). Further explanation and examples of critical multimodal analysis are presented in the Methodological Discussion section of the chapter.

In the sections below, we present the artworks and sketches created by the two focal students, Fernanda and Lora, along with a discussion of how their developing selves emerged from the above analysis. For the purposes of maintaining confidentiality about the two focal participants and respecting their ownership of the artworks, instead of displaying the actual artworks, their works are presented through thick description (Geertz, 2017) and in a form of schematic illustrations, created by Author 1 to highlight the visual structure and composition of students' artworks. Excerpts from the interviews are not corrected grammatically in order to authentically demonstrate the participants' accounts. Square brackets "[ ]" are used in the excerpts to clarify meanings while parentheses "(...)" are used to indicate an omitted portion of the original account.

Artworks and sketches

The artworks created by the two focal students were collected from a class project, titled *Wonders of Our Native Countries*, which was the final part of the students' book report for *Wonders of the World* by Joshua Davis, a part of the *System 44* series published by Scholastic in 2009. The goal of this assignment was for each student to identify a wonder that the student considered significant in their native countries and create a project for an annual family event, which students' parents and family were invited to attend. The class project was presented in a poster of paper collage that included three kinds of multimodal arts: a drawing of the wonder, an outline map of the student's native country along with a description about the wonder written inside the map, and a small paper flag representing the student's native country. Through online research, Fernanda's art project was about Copán Ruinas, an important World Heritage site representing the Mayan civilization in Honduras (UNESCO World Heritage Convention, n.d.). On the top of her poster, she drew a temple of the Copán archaeological site, for which she got the inspiration from a website. In the middle of her poster is her description about Copán Ruinas, titled "COPAN THE LAST CITY," written inside the shape of a Honduras outline map. On the bottom, Fernanda drew the Honduran flag, which contains three horizontal, blue-white-blue stripes, with five blue stars in the white strip.

Lora's art poster was about the Basilica of St. Anne of Congo, a monumental religious architecture located at Brazzaville that represented "Congolese history and the resilience of its people" (Borchard, 2021, par.1). For the Basilica of St. Anne of Congo, Lora drew the interior scene of the building, focusing on the frontal view facing the church altar. In the middle of her poster, right next to the church drawing, is the shape of a Congo outline map. Inside the map, she wrote a description titled "Basilica of St. Anne." On the left side of Lora's art poster is a flag of Congo that included three horizontal, green-yellow-red stripes.

In the interviews, Fernanda and Lora also drew sketches to express more about who they are, as prompted by Author 1. The schematic illustration in Figure 2 highlights Fernanda's artwork. Her sketch of a comic strip includes a large horizontal panel, occupying the whole upper section of the sketch paper, and three smaller panels on the bottom section of the paper. On the left-hand side of the upper panel, she drew two human figures with big smiles, representing her and her best friend, who was in Tucson, Honduras. The right-hand side of the upper panel includes a bright, shiny, yellow sun and two green mango trees. In the bottom-left panel, Fernanda drew two more human figures, both representing herself: the one on the left under the caption "before" shows a sad expression, while in the one on the right under the caption "after", she wears a smiling face. Above these two human figures were five beamed notes that symbolized music. For these two distinctive self-portraits in this bottom-left panel, Fernanda explained in the interview: "Sometimes I get sad or I get bored. So when I listen to music, I feel more better (...) music, for me, it's like something big. So when you listen music, I feel free."

In the bottom middle and right panels, each includes two human figures, representing herself and her friend. In the interview, Fernanda indicated that the middle panel tells a story in Honduras in which her friend was crying while Fernanda, with a smiling expression, tried to comfort her friend. For this middle panel, Fernanda explained, "(...) when I see people sad, I don't like when people sad, so I try to make them feel better." The bottom-right panel tells a story in the context of the United States in which Fernanda and her friend were both smiling.

Left-hand side of the upper panel:		Right-hand side of the upper panel:
A portrait of Fernanda and her best friend in Honduras, both wearing big smiles, standing on a street in Honduras.		A bright, shiny, yellow sun in the sky and two green mango trees on the street.
(Gutter)		
Bottom-left panel: Five music notes on the top Before | After 	Bottom-middle panel: Fernanda comforting a crying friend	Bottom-right panel: Both Fernanda and her friend are smiling

Figure 2. Schematic illustration of Fernanda's comic strip

As Fernanda further clarified in the follow-up interview, this bottom-right panel expresses her wish to be with her Honduran friend again.

During her interview, Lora drew a picture of a village in Congo, as illustrated in Figure 3, in which she positioned her grandmother's house in the center of the sketch paper. She drew a large self-portrait, wearing an orange dress and standing on the left-hand side next to her grandmother's house. On the top-left corner, above her self-portrait, she drew a bright, shiny, yellow sun. On the other side next to the house is a large, green tree. Under the tree are four human figures in a much smaller size, as well as four red flowers. In front of the house is a large grass field. In the interview, Lora explained that in the drawing, she was playing with the neighbors' kids while the adults were working and cooking inside the house.

Left-hand side:	Middle:	Right-hand side:
Lora's self-portrait with frontal view facing the viewers, standing under a big, yellow sun.	Lora's grandmother's house, with a triangle purple roof, a red wall, a green window, and a blue door.	A large green treen, tree, four small human figures representing neighbors' children, and four small, red flowers.

Figure 3. Schematic illustration of Lora's drawing of Grandmother's house in the village

The multimodal analysis of the above artworks and sketches is discussed in the second part of the chapter, Methodological Discussion, which particularly focuses on how visual arts are adopted for the methodological decisions and the research process. In what follows, we discuss briefly the findings about students' developing selves through their visual artworks.

Brief overview of the research findings

The analysis of students' artworks and sketches shows that their developing selves are dialogical, including both a cultural self and a personal self. In Fernanda's case, her in-class art project and the sketch of the comic strip feature the discontinuities of I-positions in her dialogical self. Her artwork about Copán Ruinas highlights her cultural self that represents her Honduran heritage, while her comic strip demonstrates an individual, personalized self. Different from the cultural self, instantiated by her artwork about Copán Ruinas, Fernanda's comic strip illustrates how she positioned herself differently in times and spaces in her transnational experiences between Honduras and the United States.

On the other hand, Lora's artwork on the Basilica of St. Anne of Congo captures a continuity of her cultural self as an immigrant from Congo and her personal self as a Christian. In the interview, Lora told a story about her choice of the church building in her artwork:

> (...) that's very popular in my country, that people always go there and go pray. And it helped a lot of people, they don't have food, they don't have clothes, like you can sleep there. Yeah, it's very, it's a helpful church. That's why I decided to write about it.

Lora further explained the connection of the church building to her identity as a Christian and the importance of praying: "I would connect this by telling others that praying, it's like a good thing, because everywhere you go, God is watching you and everything you do. He's always watching you, even if you think He's not." More details about Fernanda's and Lora's artworks and sketches and the connections to their transnational lived experiences are addressed in the methodological discussion below.

Methodological discussion

In this section, we aim to focus on the methodological implications of rethinking data sources, including important issues about integrating multimodal data sources, employing critical multimodal analysis to deepen our analysis on the multimodal data, and foregrounding ethical considerations particularly for integrating visual data.

Rethinking research data sources: Issues about equity and integrating multimodal data

Historically, the norms about what counts as rigorous research design, data, and knowledge have been predominantly shaped by monomodal, verbal, or numerical meaning-making, while other modalities, such as art-based practices, have often been viewed as supplementary and secondary by educational researchers and policy-makers (Leavy, 2020). For example, as a common data-collection approach among qualitative researchers in social sciences and education, research interviews are often conducted primarily through verbal communication (Crabtree & Miller, 2022). However, not every research participant is equally capable of articulating themselves when verbal communication, a monomodal mode of meaning-making, is the only data source (Creswell & Creswell, 2023).

For emergent multilingual participants, issues about equity arise when the access and opportunities for them to articulate themselves in interviews is predominantly structured in a monomodal, verbal communication in a language — English in this case — in which they are just emerging. Furthermore, when the interview conversation involves abstract concepts, such as the concept of motivation in the question of "What's your motivation to....," it can be challenging for those who are less familiar with this concept in a formal setting to verbalize their thoughts. For emergent multilingual participants, challenges can occur when they misunderstand the interview questions or the participants may feel intimidated with probing questions, possibly due to their developing multilingual proficiency (Marshall & While, 1994) or concerns about prejudice against their identities (Steele & Aronson, 1995).

The study presented in this chapter illustrates these challenges. Lora seemed to be less communicative in the interviews than Fernanda. Several times in the conversations, Lora would respond "I don't know" or "yeah" without much attempt to elaborate her thoughts. The following excerpt is taken from the first interview with Lora after Author 1 and Lora discussed Lora's in-class artwork about the church building in Congo.

Author 1: (...) If I give you a chance to draw and then tell us who you are. Like something that represent[s] you here, like now, what would you draw?
Lora: If I had a chance to draw something
Author 1: Or make an artwork?
Lora: that represents, represent me?
Author 1: Yeah. Like tell us who you are or even your country. Do you want [to]?
Lora: I wanna draw like houses, that's in my country, because that represent where I'm from.

Author 1: Right. Do you want to draw something about you personally or about your country? Let's say, I mean, this is the first time I [met] you, right?

Lora: Um Hmm

Author 1: And you are creating something to tell me who you are. What would you draw?

Lora: I will probably draw our personalities? I don't know.

In this section of the interview, Author 1 asked Lora to draw something to tell others about her, and Lora's initial response was to draw houses in her country. Later Author 1 asked if Lora wanted to draw something about her personally or about her country. Lora's next response became uncertain: "I will probably draw our personalities? I don't know." In this case, Lora's minimum responses and hesitations could be a result of many factors, one of which could be not understanding the questions. Nevertheless, the subsequent drawing she made of her grandmother's house assisted Lora in elaborating about herself later in the conversation:

> Because like, my family, my, my, basically my grandma, she's in the village. But my mom had to put her in the city, because she got really sick. And my mom had to buy a house and stuff in my city so she can live and have a good life. And in my country, also in villages, they're killing people so much, that she had to move.

This suggests that Lora's drawing of grandmother's house in the village also led our conversation toward her view about living in Congo and in the United States, which addresses feelings of nostalgia and is further discussed under the section of Critical Multimodal Analysis. The visual expression of Lora's inner world, instantiated in her grandmother's village, is significant because it illustrates "the deeper area within the child that can be defined as the truth within (whether or not that 'truth' has any basis in reality) or, simply, what the child feels and believes" (Igoa, 1995, p. 46).

More importantly, the above example in Lora's case accentuates that feelings and emotions may not be equally articulated through monomodal, verbal communication alone. As pointed out by Jewitt and Kress (2003) above, all modes of communication are partial and constrained in some way. There are distinguishing differences regarding the affordances and limitations in verbal versus visual communication: while verbal communication (e.g., writing and speech) is often linear and sequential, visual communication is usually spatial and multidimensional (Gerber et al., 2012; Kress, 2000). Therefore, although verbal communication is prevalent in data collection and analysis, using it alone does not always fully capture abstract meanings or nuances of emotions. Particularly, emotions that immigrants and refugees have often experienced are complex and intense, and may be neglected in monomodal, verbal expression. For example, Igoa (1995) described a 10-year immigrant girl, Rosario, from the Philippines, who was seen as quiet by her teachers and peers and was labeled "non-English proficient" (p.54). Her feelings of loneliness and disconnection from peers was not understood until her drawing of a sad, lonely bear in her class art project.

To address the issue of equity in the research process, researchers need to consider multiple ways of meaning-making and communication. In the present study, visual arts are not only used for pedagogical purposes as in the class art project, *Wonders of Our Native Countries*, but are also employed in the research process. Furthermore, the issue of equity is addressed by integrating multimodal data sources, which involved participant-generated drawings and sketches (e.g., Fernanda's comic strip and Lora's drawing of her grandmother's house in the village), along with participants' verbal interpretations about the themes and visual design of their visual artworks (Pauwels, 2015). As pointed out by the above discussion and examples, integrating multimodal data in qualitative research can increase researchers' ability to capture abstract and difficult-to-articulate knowledge that would have been hidden in verbal communication alone, as well as to bring forward multiple perspectives that propel researchers to view things in new ways and gain a better, more holistic understanding of the research participants and their experiences (Leavy, 2020; Weber, 2008).

Critical multimodal analysis

In addition to including multimodal research data, it is important to analyze that data multimodally through a critical lens. As a part of the innovative methodological approach used in this study, particularly for deconstructing stereotypes about immigrant, emergent multilingual students' lived experiences and their developing identities, critical multimodal analysis was employed. Its use in this study contains two components: (1) a critical lens from Lewison et al. (2002)'s Critical Literacy, which positioned our attitudes while analyzing the participants' artworks; and (2) analytical actions that were guided by Kress and Van Leeuwen (2021)'s work of visual design. In this section, our discussion is structured by the three aspects of Lewison et al. (2002)'s Critical Literacy model: "(a) disrupting the commonplace, (b) interrogating multiple viewpoints, (c) focusing on sociopolitical issues" (p.382). Along with a discussion, we introduce visual analysis strategies through Kress and Van Leeuwen (2021)'s work as supported by examples from Fernanda's and Lora's artworks and sketches.

For the first aspect, "disrupting the commonplace" (Lewison et al., 2002, p.382), we aim to problematize the prevalent positioning of immigrant students through a deficit view that oversimplifies their lived experiences. For example, in Fernanda's interview, her account about the poor living conditions and her family's need to pursue better opportunities and education depicts the common stigmatized discourse about lives in Latin American countries. Yet, our analysis of Fernanda's comic strip (Figure 2) revealed stories of being courageous and resilient. Particularly, the three sequential panels in the lower section (Figure 4) mirror the left-versus-right, landscape orientation in Kress and Van Leeuwen (2021)'s visual composition model,[1] which communicates a movement of continuous message from given information on the left to new information on the right, similar to reading English from left to right (Kress & Van Leeuwen, 2021). The bottom-left panel of Fernanda's comic strip serves as a "point of departure" (Kress & Van Leeuwen, 2021, p.187) that describes how Fernanda used music to lighten her mood from sadness to happiness. Next, the bottom-middle panel, in which Fernanda comforted a friend who was feeling sad in Honduras, continues the message. After that, the bottom-right panel concludes the message that in the context of the United States, Fernanda and her friend were both smiling. It also conveys Fernanda's feeling of wanting to be with her friend again. The continuity of the whole message flows across the three bottom panels of Fernanda's comic expression and communicates a sense of courage and resilience to the viewers. When we revisited her comic strip in our second interview, Fernanda explained that she wanted to be positive and present herself with courage: "I guess, I will be like, be myself. Like, I'm like, be myself. Don't be scared."

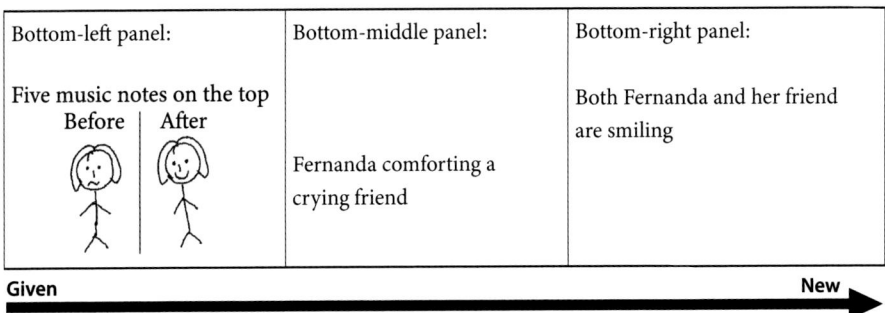

Figure 4. Given and new visual composition in Fernanda's comic story

---

1. While utilizing this left-to-right visual analysis to unpack Fernanda's artworks and sketches seemed appropriate because of her Spanish language background with a left-to-right, Latin alphabet writing system, researchers employing this left-to-right orientation of visual analysis need to consider their participants' cultural and linguistic roots, especially for research participants whose preferred languages are not written from left to right (Bergen & Chan Lau, 2012; Coulmas, 2003).

For the second aspect of the critical literacy lens, "interrogating multiple viewpoints" (Lewison et al., 2002, p.382), we examined multiple voices in particular relation to what is presented and what is hidden through the multimodal data. For example, similar to Fernanda, in the interview Lora also explained the poor conditions back in Congo that led to her mother and her both moving to the United States to pursue a better life and education. Lora's account mirrors the dominant discourse about immigrant experiences, as previously discussed: one linear direction from poor conditions in the past/back home to "assimilation and meritocracy" in the new society (Parini, 2012, as cited in Ghiso & Low, 2013, p.33). Nevertheless, Lora's drawing of her grandmother's house in the village (Figure 3) demonstrates feelings of nostalgia, which are difficult to articulate in verbal communication and could have remained unspoken if visual data were not collected. Lora's drawing portrays her lived experiences in Congo as she drew herself on the left-hand side of the house and the neighbors' kids on the right-hand side of the house. In the interview, Author 1 asked Lora about her visual design of this drawing:

Author 1: So is there a reason why you are on this side of the house, and their [the neighbors'] kids are on the other side of the house?
Lora: Basically because, like, basically in my country, houses are so close together, so you, like you can go ahead and find your neighbors. Think, they don't, they won't do anything, because there is a tree here, so our kids are playing. That's why I decided to be here and all the people like that.
Author 1: Oh, but it's not really your separating from them?
Lora: Mm Hmm.
Author 1: You are actually playing together.
Lora: Mm Hmm.

As Lora indicated in the above interview excerpts, because the houses in Congo were built closely next to one another, Lora and the neighbors' children were not distanced apart as illustrated in the drawing. Instead, Lora created a close-up shot that focused on her grandmother's house and everyone playing together outside the house. Lora further explained that she missed people back home in Congo because people were friendly. She explained how life in the United States is different and people may not be as friendly: "And if like in here, if you go to someone else's house, like if you don't ask them, you can go to the police, they can call the police on you." In our second interview when we revisited her sketch about her grandma's village, she elaborated that people in Congo are more open and welcoming, as they can visit friends and neighbors without asking in advance. Lora's drawing about her grandma's village describes the nuanced differences between her lived experiences in her home country and in the United States. Furthermore, her drawing brings out a sense of nostalgia, a subtle feeling of affection and long-ing for what was familiar and pleasant during her time in Congo.

Third, we drew upon Lewison et al. (2002)'s "focusing on sociopolitical issues" (p. 382) to scrutinize the sociopolitical system that affects emergent multilingual students' lived experiences. Our critical multimodal analysis of both Fernanda's and Lora's artworks and sketches demonstrate their exquisite multimodal literacy communication and skills, which are often undervalued in the mainstream, social semiotic system that privileges the English monomodal mode through practices such as English academic writing. In the case of Fernanda's in-class artwork about Copán Ruinas, she explained that her artwork of the temple at the Copán archae-ological site was inspired by an online photo (you may click on the following link to view the online photo: https://www.sheknows.com/living/articles/1023687 /frequent-flier-visiting-copan-ruinas-in-honduras/). In the photo, the viewers are positioned at eye level with the temple, which creates a sense of equal relationship between the object (i.e., the temple) and the viewers (Kress & Van Leeuwen, 2021). In Fernanda's artwork, she changed viewers' perspective to a higher angle facing down to the temple. This higher angle presented in Fernanda's drawing gives view-ers power (Kress & Van Leeuwen, 2021), by positioning the viewers from a top-down, bird's eye perspective. In our interview, Fernanda interpreted her drawing of the architecture and explained that she intentionally designed such a visual struc-ture with rich details of the architecture, such as the stairs, in order for the viewers to feel as if they were physically on the site climbing up the stairs, which leads to the top of the temple.

In Lora's case, the visual design of her drawing about her grandmother's vil-lage addresses one aspect of "the interactive meanings of images" (Kress & Van Leeuwen, 2021, p. 123) — social distances between the images and its viewers. Figure 5 demonstrates the schematic illustration of two components in Lora's drawing (which is presented in full in Figure 3). On the left-hand side of her drawing, Lora created a close shot of her self-portrait, which conveys a sense of intimacy between the character (Lora) and the viewers of the drawing. On the contrary, the long shot of the other four human figures to the right of her grandmother's house, in much smaller size, creates an impersonal feeling (Kress & Van Leeuwen, 2021, p. 124) between the four small human figures and the viewers. Lora explained that she made her self-portrait much bigger than the others because she was the one drawing the picture. Furthermore, the visual design of the characters' gazes is illustrated in Lora's self-portrait: her eyes were gazing at the viewers, which makes Lora's self-portrait an "image of a demand....demand[ing] that the viewer enter into some kind of imaginary rela-tions" (Kress & Van Leeuwen, 2021, p. 117) with Lora as she introduced her grand-mother's house and village.

Figure 5. Schematic illustration of Lora's self-portrait (left) and small human figures (right) (taken from Figure 3)

Similar to Igoa (1995)'s case presented above about Rosario, who was labeled with a deficit term, both Fernanda and Lora were looked down upon due to their lack of English language proficiency. When Fernanda left Honduras for the United States, she described a difficult initial transition to the first school she attended before moving to the newcomer program:

> It was kind of hard because, like, I was learning English, and the teachers there were not nicely. They just gave me the work and they say, 'If you not understand, it's your problem.' So I, I get stressful because I don't understand nothing. I'm just like, I can't understand. But I know I am good at school, but like I get mad at myself because I don't understand nothing.

Lora also described how she was made fun of by her peers at a previous school: "(...) And that was a problem because when I speak, when I spoke, people was always laughing at me because I didn't know how to speak." On the contrary, our critical multimodal analysis of both Fernanda's and Lora's visual designs of their artworks and sketches highlight their strategic uses of multimodal literacy skills, such as their abilities to communicate meaning visually. Their strategic uses not only show their active voices and agencies in the design process, but they also disrupt the stigma shaped by the deficit, monomodal focus on lacking English language proficiency.

The above discussion and examples highlight the importance of employing both the critical and the multimodal aspects of critical multimodal analysis. This analytical framework opens our eyes to view the complexity of immigrant, multilingual students' uprooting emotions and the nuances of their transnational, lived experiences, which would have been missed in the world that focuses on monomodal, verbal literacy practices and communications.

Ethical considerations: Anonymity and ownership

While we emphasize the significance of integrating visual art and other multimodal data sources as an innovative approach in qualitative literacy research design, particularly for providing more equitable access for emergent multilingual participants in interviews, we call attention to ethical considerations in two aspects. The first consideration regards the issue of anonymity. Particularly with photos taken by researchers for observations or made by the research participants, possibilities of breaking the research participants' anonymity occur when these photos are included in the dissemination of research findings (Mitchell, 2011; Pauwel, 2015). Pauwel (2015) has suggested one of the solutions is to postprocess the images, which could include blurring parts of the image. Another aspect is the issue of ownership, particularly for participant-created visuals such as drawings and artworks. For researchers, gaining access to analyze the visual data is different from getting participants' permission to use the visual data, especially for exhibition on a website, a presentation at a conference, or publication in a book or a journal article (Mitchell, 2011). To address these ownership issues, Mitchell (2011) has suggested that additional consent forms can be used to explain how the visual data may be published and to receive research participants' permission to do so.

In the present study, with the approval by the Human Subjects Institutional Review Board at the partnering university, we collected the bilingual parent/ guardian consent signed by the parents and the bilingual child assent signed by the multilingual students: an English-Spanish version in Fernanda's case and an English-French version in Lora's case. However, the information about transferring ownership of students' artworks and sketches for publication was not explicitly stated in the consent process. Therefore, to address the above two issues (i.e., maintaining a level of confidentiality and respecting the participants' ownership of their artworks), we employed two approaches to present our visual data in this chapter. One was to provide thick description (Geertz, 2017) through which we verbally depicted students' artworks, as demonstrated in the above section, Artworks and Sketches. We also created schematic illustrations to highlight the visual structure and composition of the students' actual artworks. To facilitate the translation process from visual to verbal for the present study, we applied Gerber et al. (2012)'s suggestion of using "a dialectic that employs a dynamic interaction between thematic analysis and artistic response to the data that emerge from art-based research" (p. 46). For example, through the thematic analysis on the interview data with Fernanda and via the multimodal analysis on her comic strip, we identified important thematic components. One, about Fernanda and her friends, was portrayed in her comic strip. Through the visual analysis on the bottom panels that delineate the continuity of the theme across the panels, especially the bottom middle and right panels (see Figure 4), her emphasis on friendship and her courage and resilience is revealed. At the same time, we reviewed her accounts in the interviews and further contextualized this component from both data sets. This process helps create the narratives in thick description about her artworks and produce the schematic illustration that highlight the visual layout of her works.

Nevertheless, in our reflexive decision-making, we encountered the dilemma of somehow compromising the meaning representation and complexity in translation (Gerber et al., 2012; Leavy, 2020), particularly due to the distinguishing affordances and limitations in visual and verbal representations, as previously discussed. For example, in Fernanda's and Lora's sketches produced during the interview process, they both included a bright, yellow sun that brought out pleasant ambience based on our visual analysis. However, this visual feature highlighted by its color is somewhat lost in the translation. This dilemma foregrounds a limitation of our study and points our attention to future research procedures to consider additional steps to clearly address the ownership issue in the consent process. More importantly, the process of post-processing visual data and the strategy employed to handle the translation across semiotic modes (i.e., visual to verbal) discussed in this section provide methodological implications that researchers can consider in dealing with multimodal visual data.

Implications

Through multimodal literacies, the study presented in this chapter sheds light on integrating visual-arts data, along with associated conversations, and critical multimodal analysis, as an innovative methodological approach to gain a holistic understanding about emergent multilingual students' developing identities, complex transnational lived experiences, and uprooting feelings and emotions that would be difficult to express by monomodal communication alone. The methodological discussion calls our attention to rethinking research data sources, issues about equitable access for emergent multilingual participants, the opportunities and affordances of integrating visual arts and applying critical multimodal analysis, and ethical considerations that address participants' anonymity and ownership of their creative artworks. In light of the above discussions, we draw implications for qualitative research on multilingual literacy development in the following aspects.

First, it is imperative for qualitative researchers to consider adopting visual arts or other multimodal literacies in their research design. In recent years, more and more studies on multimodality have been conducted, including those that address multimodal pedagogies and educational policies (e.g., Grapin & Llosa, 2020), ESL teachers' beliefs about multimodal practices (e.g., Choi & Yi, 2016), and multimodal assessment for emergent multilinguals (Grapin & Llosa, 2022). A theme that emerged across these studies is the urgency to provide emergent multilingual students with more equitable access to learning. With many academic-related tasks growing increasingly multimodal, we argue that greater consideration should be given to multimodal approaches in research methodology, such as the inclusion of online multimodal artifacts in Karam and Kibler and children's multimodal works in a play-based setting in Kim et al. (this volume), especially for research on emergent multilingual students, in order to both respond to this growing attention to multimodality in classrooms and to address issues of equity in the research process.

Second, we urge researchers to handle multimodal data as primary, instead of secondary or decorative, and to treat multimodal data meaningfully through a critical lens. As suggested by Serafini (2015), to truly understand visual images and multimodal texts, the analysis needs to go beyond the image's literal meanings and potential meanings constructed by the viewers and further consider sociocultural and sociopolitical context to critically examine stereotypical and ideological aspects. As demonstrated in the above section, the critical multimodal analysis proposed in this chapter provides a specific framework to guide researchers' actions through visual analysis (e.g., Kress & Van Leeuwen, 2021) and to equip researchers with a critical lens in three aspects (Lewison et al., 2002).

Furthermore, we urge qualitative researchers to increase their multimodal literacy knowledge, as well as to engage in professional learning of its application in research design and implementation. We also contend that such knowledge and training about multimodal literacies should be incorporated into graduate research inquiry and methodology courses and include insights about the critical role of multimodal literacies in research design, an understanding of different multimodal research methods, such as arts-based research practice (Leavy, 2020), and the learning of skills and strategies to analyze multimodal data. For researchers working with emergent multilingual participants of immigrant or refugee backgrounds, it is particularly important to understand how to utilize multimodal data, such as participant-generated artworks, to mediate meanings and obtain a more comprehensive picture about their complex transnational lived experiences.

Finally, we suggest directions for future research on integrating visual arts or other types of multimodal literacies in research design, especially when working with emergent multilingual participants and connections to their multilingual literacy practices. One direction is to investigate approaches to analyze visual data generated by multilingual participants of different language backgrounds. As previously discussed, the left-to-right orientation of visual analysis (Kress & Van Leeuwen, 2021) as seen in Fernanda's case can be problematic for participants whose preferred languages are not in a left-to-right writing direction. Since language mediates thinking and cognition (Vygotsky, 1978), it would be helpful to advance visual analysis approaches for participants from diverse language writing systems, such as those that are oriented right-to-left or use non-Latin-alphabet systems. Another research direction is to create opportunities for multimodal research dissemination in professional conferences and academic journals, especially given the notion as mentioned in Jewitt and Kress (2003) that all modes are partial and equally significant to a whole message. Particularly for sharing research findings that involve arts-based research practice, we need to explore ways that go beyond the traditional, monomodal focused approach and thus better communicate meanings that otherwise cannot be fully expressed, such as feelings and emotions. An example of such innovation was seen at the Annual Meeting of the American Educational Research Association (AERA) in 2023, where Dr. Carolina Bergonzoni's academic presentation was a form of dancing performance in which she used her body movements to mediate meanings of her family history (Bergonzoni, 2023). Moreover, as academic publication is still predominantly managed in a monomodal, printed-based format, when publishing findings of arts-based research, it is necessary to further inquire into issues of translation across modalities, such as the examples (e.g., color expression) discussed in the Ethical Consideration section of this chapter.

Through multimodal literacies, in this chapter, we aimed our attention on the integration of visual arts with verbal conversations in the interviews, as well as on critical multimodal analysis as an innovative methodological approach. At the heart of our discussion is the focus on the voice and agency of emergent multilingual students by viewing them as designers of their multimodal artworks. That is, through these students' exquisite multimodal literacy communication and skills, they purposefully utilize various representational resources and modes in particular structure and composition to communicate selves and to "implement the purposes of the designers" (Kress, 2000, p.340). Such a perspective contests the prevalent deficit view that perceives emergent multilingual students as passive, failing, and lacking in abilities. The present study and discussion in this chapter expands the horizons with more equitable access and opportunities for emergent multilingual participants, especially immigrants, refugees, and other groups from historically marginalized communities, to be included in the co-construction of research possibilities.

References

Albers, P. (2007). *Finding the artist within*. International Reading Association.

Bergen, B. K., & Chan Lau, T. T. (2012). Writing direction affects how people map space onto time. *Frontiers in Psychology*, 3, Article 109.

Bergonzoni, C. (2023, April 13–16). *Family (hi)story in my dancing body* (Conference presentation abstract). 2023 AERA Annual Meeting, Chicago, IL, United States. https://tinyurl.com/2hlkly6x

Bhatia, S., & Ram A. (2004). Culture, hybridity and the dialogical self: Cases from the South Asian-American Diaspora. *Mind, Culture, and Activity*, 11(3), 224–240.

Borchard, G. (2021). *Basilique Saint-Anne-du-Congo, Brazzaville*. African state architecture – An academic research project funded by European Research Council (ERC). Retrieved on 15 November 2024 from https://www.africanstatearchitecture.co.uk/post/basilique-saint-anne-du-congo-brazzaville

Braun, V., & Clarke, V. (2021). *Thematic analysis: A practical guide*. Sage.

Campano, G., & Low, D. (2011). Multimodality and immigrant children. *Contemporary Issues in Early Childhood*, 12(4), 381–384.

Choi, J., & Yi, Y. (2016). Teachers' integration of multimodality into classroom practices for English language learners. *TESOL Journal*, 7(2), 304–327.

Coulmas, F. (2003). *Writing systems: An introduction to their linguistic analysis*. Cambridge University Press.

Crabtree, B. F., & Miller, W. L. (2022). *Doing qualitative research* (3rd ed.). Sage.

Creswell, J. W., & Creswell, J. D. (2023). *Research design: Qualitative, quantitative, and mixed methods approaches* (6th ed.). Sage.

Geertz, C. (2017). *The interpretation of cultures: Selected essays* (3rd ed.). Basic Books.

Gerber, N., Templeton, E., Chilton, G., Liebman, M. C., Manders, E., & Shim, M. (2012). Art-based research as a pedagogical approach to studying intersubjectivity in the creative arts therapies. *Journal of Applied Arts and Health*, 3(1), 39–48.

Ghiso, M. P., & Low, D. E. (2013), Students using multimodal literacies to surface micronarratives of United States immigration. *Literacy*, 47(1), 26–34.

Glesne, C. (2021). *Becoming qualitative researchers: An introduction* (5th ed.). Pearson Education.

Grapin, S. E., & Llosa, L. (2020). Toward an integrative framework for understanding multimodal L2 writing in the content areas. *Journal of Second Language Writing*, 47,

Grapin, S. E., & Llosa, L. (2022). Multimodal tasks to assess English learners and their peers in science. *Educational Assessment*, 27(1), 46–70.

Hermans, H. J. M. (2001). The dialogical self: Toward a theory of personal and cultural positioning. *Culture & Psychology*, 7(3), 243–281.

Hermans, H. J. M. (2022). Dialogical self theory. In V. P. Glăveanu (Ed.), *The Palgrave encyclopedia of the possible*. Palgrave Macmillan.

Hermans, H. J. M., Kempen, H. J. G., & Van Loon, R. J. P. (1992). The dialogical self: Beyond individualism and rationalism. *American Psychologist*, 47, 23–33.

Höglund, H. (2022). The heartbeat of poetry: Student videomaking in response to poetry. *Written Communication*, 39(2), 276–302.

Igoa, C. (1995). *The inner world of the immigrant child*. St. Martin's Press.

Jewitt, C., & Kress, G. R. (Eds.). (2003). *Multimodal Literacy*. Lang.

Karam, F. J., Oikonomidoy, E., & Kibler, A. K. (2021). Artifactual literacies and TESOL: Narratives of a Syrian refugee-background family. *TESOL Quarterly*, 55(2), 510–535.

Kress, G. R. (2000). Multimodality: Challenges to thinking about language. *TESOL Quarterly*, 34(2), 337–340.

Kress, G. R. (2010). *Multimodality: A social semiotic approach to contemporary communication*. Routledge.

Kress, G., & Van Leeuwen, T. (2021). *Reading images: The grammar of visual design* (3rd ed.). Routledge.

Leavy, P. (2020). *Method meets art: Arts-based research practice* (3rd ed.). Guilford Publications.

Lewison, M., Flint, A. S., & Van Sluys, K. (2002). Taking on critical literacy: The journey of newcomers and novices. *Language Arts*, 79(5), 382–392.

Marshall, S. L. & While, A. E. (1994). Interviewing respondents who have English as a second language: challenges encountered and suggestions for other researchers. *Journal of Advanced Nursing*, 19, 566–571.

Mitchell, C. (2011). *Doing visual research*. Sage.

Omerbašić, D. (2015). Literacy as a translocal practice: Digital multimodal literacy practices among girls resettled as refugees. *Journal of Adolescent & Adult Literacy*, 58(6), 472–481.

Parini, J. (2012). The American mythos. *Daedalus*, 141(1), 52–60.

Paulick, J. H., Karam, F. J., & Kibler, A. K. (2022). Everyday objects and home visits: A window into the cultural models of families of culturally and linguistically marginalized students. *Language Arts*, 99(6), 390–401.

Pauwels, L. (2015). *Reframing visual social science: Towards a more visual sociology and anthropology*. Cambridge University Press.

Riessman, C. K. (2008). *Narrative methods for the human sciences*. Sage.

Sanders, J., & Albers, P. (2010). Multimodal literacies: An introduction. In P. Albers, & J. Sanders (Eds.), *Literacies, the arts & multimodalities* (pp. 1–43). National Council of Teachers of English.

Serafini, F. (2015). Multimodal literacy: From theories to practices. *Language Arts*, 92(6), 412–423.

Stahl, N. A., & King, J. R. (2020). Expanding approaches for research: Understanding and using trustworthiness in qualitative research. *Journal of Developmental Education*, 44(1), 26–29.

Steele, C. M., & Aronson, J. (1995). Stereotype threat and the intellectual test performance of African Americans. *Journal of Personality and Social Psychology*, 69(5), 797–811.

UNESCO World Heritage Convention. (n.d.). *Maya Site of Copan*. https://whc.unesco.org/en/list/129

Vygotsky, L. S. (1978). *Mind in society: The development of higher psychological processes*. Harvard University Press.

Weber, S. (2008). Visual images in research. In J. G. Knowles & A. L. Cole (Eds.), *Handbook of arts in qualitative research* (pp. 41–53). Sage.

WIDA Consortium. (2012). *The English Language Learner Can Do Booklet.* Retrieved on 15 November 2024 from https://wida.wisc.edu/sites/default/files/resource/CanDo-Booklet-Gr-9-12.pdf

Yin, R.K. (2009). *Case study research: Design and methods* (Vol. 5). Sage.

CHAPTER 5

Commentary: The instability of 'data' in a postdigital era
Key challenges for qualitative multilingual researchers

Amy Stornaiuolo
University of Pennsylvania

This commentary on Part 1 of *Innovative Qualitative Methodologies in Multilingual Literacy Development Research: Amplifying Voices from Immigrant, Transnational, and Refugee Communities* focuses upon some of the ways in which qualitative literacy researchers have begun to rethink data. Complex ethical and conceptual challenges that arise in multilingual literacy research in a postdigital era are contextualized in the work of the three chapters in Part 1 before directions for future research are offered.

Keywords: qualitative, literacy, multilingual, methodology, data

Introduction

In a *postdigital* era in which digital technologies are inextricably intertwined with the material world (Jandrić et al., 2018), multilingual literacy researchers face challenges not only in conducting qualitative research but also in conceptualizing people's meaning-making practices across languages, cultures, and systems characterized by instability and precarity (Stornaiuolo et al., 2017). With digital technologies so deeply entangled with everyday social practices and broader systems, the boundaries between the virtual and material are blurred and the 'digital' might be less visible to literacies researchers (Bhatt, 2023). Scholars in education and beyond have been theorizing the postdigital like other 'post' phenomena (e.g., postmodern, posthuman) — meaning not that we are *beyond* the digital or that digital technologies are *other* to everyday life but that we must critically appraise and hold the digital to account as it becomes increasingly intertwined with how we act in the world (Knox, 2019). For multilingual literacies researchers who want to engage in equitable and ethical research, the postdigital requires a criti-

https://doi.org/10.1075/rmal.11.05sto

cal reimagining of *data* in research, especially as digital platforms hide the complex datafication processes that condition people's literacy practices and are tied to commercial enterprises (e.g., Pangrazio et al., 2022).

The authors with contributions in this section of the book — "Rethinking *Data* in Qualitative Research on Multilingual Literacy" — all explicitly tackle the complex ethical and conceptual challenges that arise in multilingual literacy research in a postdigital era. While chapters by Brooks (Chapter 2), Karam and Kibler (Chapter 3) , and Kuo and Sprečić (Chapter 4) each offer different innovative methodological approaches to multilingual literacy research, collectively they highlight three challenges helpful for researchers to consider in designing equitable research. First, all three chapters emphasize the ethical and practical challenges of identifying and capturing data in a complex multimodal and multimedia landscape. Second, these authors argue for the importance of expanding *what counts* as data to include people's lived experiences and emotions in a fuller and more holistic manner. Finally, all chapters raise the question of representation and, specifically, how researchers might position themselves in relation to participants to make their experiences, histories, and meaning making practices visible to others. These three challenges are core issues facing multilingual literacy researchers in a postdigital age and require new methodological approaches that reimagine *data* from a critical perspective.

The challenge of data on the move: Methods for moving with

At the core of each of these chapters is the central tension about how researchers cope with people and things on the move, as they engage with new methodologies to take into account the material and virtual entanglement of physical and digital spaces and unbounded field sites (Burrell, 2009). This question of how people move across languages and spaces is particularly fraught for those who have been displaced from their homes by war, economic precarity, climate change, or other systemic injustices — and requires multilingual literacy researchers to think carefully about their own positionality as they 'move with' people and practices in dynamic and unpredictable ways. The authors in this section all propose different methods for researchers to *move with*: move with participants (Karam and Kibler, Chapter 3), move across data (Kuo and Sprečić, Chapter 4), and move across existing scholarship (Brooks).

Karam and Kibler (Chapter 3) offer the most direct discussion of this challenge of rethinking data on the move, proposing an *ethnetnographic* approach that combines ethnography and netnography to help researchers better understand how participants move across multilingual and multimodal repertoires. In a study

with one Muslim refugee-background woman named Maria who navigated resettlement and belonging after experiencing civil war in Syria and displacement to
Turkey and the US, Karam and Kibler discussed how Karam 'moved with' Maria
across online/offline contexts to trace how she remained connected with loved
ones and navigated the US context, especially through social media. They focus
on what resonated with Maria across spatial and temporal contexts, and particularly the tensions that emerged as social media facilitated some opportunities
(e.g., learning from other Syrian women the English word for a household item;
posting a video of her daughter crying to connect with others) and at the same
time opened her up to surveillance and censorship (e.g., she heard concerns about
the video's optics on the resettlement agency). Karam and Kibler suggest that ethnetnography provided them a more comprehensive view of Maria's resettlement
experiences as a transnational and transliterate individual, an approach that offers
researchers different ways of moving with participants to see those tensions and
triangulating data across temporalities, modalities, and spaces.

Kuo and Sprečić (Chapter 5) offer an approach that invites researchers to
move across data in new ways, particularly by collecting and analyzing multimodal and arts-based data that facilitate multilingual individuals in making
meaning with researchers as agentive designers and communicators. They argue
that the researchers' positionality and interpretive approach needs to be informed
by a critical lens, which helps to center the perspectives of multilingual students
that are not always recognized when viewed through primarily linguistic data.
They examine the artworks created by two immigrant students, Fernanda and
Lora, who were enrolled in a beginner class of a self-contained ESL newcomer
program in a midwestern middle school. Through thick description of the arts-
based data, Kuo and Sprečić examine the participants' multimodal and multilingual repertoires and argue that researchers should learn how to 'move across'
such data in their collection and analysis efforts to expand equitable access for
participants.

Brooks (Chapter 2) proposes that a helpful tool for researchers is the qualitative metasynthesis, an approach to analyzing and interpreting findings across a
broad body of research. Brooks argues that qualitative metasynthesis foregrounds
the interpretive work of the researchers as they 'move with' the scholarship to
make sense of it for multilingual policy and practice. She offers two critical
questions that can help researchers highlight multilingual participants' voices by
focusing on both bureaucratic language classifications and participants' multilingual orientations. Such a critical orientation can illuminate gaps and elisions
in the research base and help researchers avoid overgeneralizing about students
identified as English learners (ELs), whose experiences and voices may not be
centered or nuanced in much research. In all three chapters, the question of how

multilingual literacy researchers move in a complex, dynamic, and unstable landscape is a central tension that has high stakes for how equitable literacy research can more fully capture the ways people are drawing on wide repertoires in systems that do not value or recognize their voice, agency, or capacity as communicators and meaning makers.

The challenge of what counts as data: Methods to expand data

One of the central challenges for researchers in a complex multimodal landscape is in making decisions about how to decide *what counts* as data. Traditionally, data with and about people's language practices have been conditioned and structured by normative understandings about language and competency, and all three chapters focus on expanding beyond limited understandings of people's multilingual practices. One way the authors think about this expansion is to center participants' experiences, identities, and voices in the research. Brooks (this volume), for example, explores young people's experiences with being classified with reading intervention and EL labels. Brooks (Chapter 2) found that many studies reviewed for her metasynthesis did highlight students' multilingual practices and experiences. However, Brooks could not draw broader conclusions about the students' experiences in relation to their identities because so many of the studies did not report students' language backgrounds and institutional labels in any consistent or explicit way. She argues that given the ways that those labels shaped young people's experiences and trajectories, "[t]his type of explicit discussion of bureaucratic labels is important because it allows research to illustrate how the institutional labeling that impacts their daily lives. It highlights who is educated within these stigmatized spaces" (p. 35). In her chapter, Brooks argues for critically rethinking data from a more expansive perspective that includes both institutional labels and how young people navigate and make sense of those classifying practices.

All three chapters argue that including multimodal data is one expansive way to center participants' voices and experiences in multilingual research. Given the ways people make meaning across language and other modes, the authors argue that researchers need to move beyond collecting language data alone if they want to capture the complexity and fullness of people's understandings. For Karam and Kibler (Chapter 3), that multimodal data included multilingual online artifacts (images, videos, etc.) that were read alongside ethnographic fieldnotes and interviews to understand participants' "rich linguistic repertoires and their diverse life experiences [that] are often ignored in educational contexts and [...] subjected to state policies of exclusion." For Karam and Kibler, such expansion of multimodal and multilingual data entails researchers "examining how data *speak to each other* across contexts" (emphasis original) in both data collection and analysis in order to understand and make visible a more complex story of the literacy practices of refugee-background individuals. Their approach to ethnetnography involves engaging in deep ethnographic inquiry into the lived experiences of multilingual participants, including online modalities that serve an important connective function in linking immigrants, refugees, and displaced populations, in particular, to other people and places as they navigate belonging in and across new cultural, geographic, and linguistic contexts.

While qualitative multilingual education researchers have long been making the case for expanding what counts in research to include multimodal data, the chapters focus heightened attention to the felt, embodied, and affective dimensions of people's meaning making practices – to include a richer and more complete portrait not just of people's experiences, identities, and ways of being/moving/making sense of the world but also their feelings and emotions. For example, Kuo and Sprečić (this volume), highlight that their participants drew on the expressive capacities of art to communicate their experiences as transnational youth in ways that could not be communicated through verbal communication alone. They suggest that multimodal data should be seen as a primary data source, not a supplement or ornamental addition, for multilingual researchers committed to expanding equitable access for participants to share their emotions and feelings. They draw on critical approaches to multimodal analysis (e.g., Serafini, 2015) to center deeper analysis that takes into account the sociocultural and sociopolitical factors shaping young people's emotions and experiences. All three chapters consider these sociocultural and sociopolitical factors as they collect expanded forms of data that center people's experiences, including Maria's feelings of ambivalence in Karam and Kibler (Chapter 3) and young people's experiences with reading intervention classes in Brooks (Chapter 2).

The challenge of representation: Methods for making visible

The third challenge these chapters all highlight is a challenge of representation: How should researchers navigate the ethical and relational terrain involved with representing other people's experiences, feelings, and stories across multiple languages and cultures? When working with individuals and communities who have experienced histories of oppression, trauma, or displacement, such issues of representation are heightened. So too are the dilemmas navigated by multilingual literacy researchers working across diverse languages, cultures, and identities themselves, even if they think of themselves as 'insiders' (Jackson, 2004).

As Karam and Kibler (Chapter 3) make clear, building relationships over time built on shared histories and trust is a key way of navigating the ethics of representation. Fares was in constant, reciprocal conversation with Maria about which online artifacts he could collect and report on, dialogue facilitated by the trusting relationship he had developed over time through a family and research partnership in which he prioritized the family's resettlement needs and wellbeing over the research. Such an ethical, humanizing, and person-centered approach to research guided Karam and Kibler's decision-making about what to represent (and how), an issue more fraught with online data that can compromise anonymity. In ethnetnography, they argue, it is important to operate from such a position, thinking creatively and adaptively to center participants' agency in making decisions about how and under what circumstances to share data. Rethinking data, from this perspective, means also reconsidering how researchers collaborate and build relationships with participants to co-construct and negotiate what data are appropriate to collect and share.

Brooks (Chapter 2) thinks about the importance of representation in researchers' data collection and reporting of findings, and particularly calls attention to the role of the researcher in shaping that interpretive process. In examining how linguistic bureaucratic labels like EL are not neutral but embedded in broader "ideologies about language, language learning, youths themselves, their abilities, and their communities" (p. 36), Brooks calls attention to the ideologies that underpin the systems and structures shaping people's lives and experiences as multilingual individuals. She argues that all literacy researchers need to focus on the literacy practices of multilingual students, paying close attention to how participants and their linguistic backgrounds are described and not shying away from explicitly reporting and discussing their institutional labels in multiple sections of the research report. While she reports that some authors may refrain from reifying these ideological categories in their reporting, "the failure to explicitly name the official English language acquisition status of students is not beneficial for equity-focused research." (p. 36). In other words, if equity-oriented literacy researchers want to recognize and honor the multilingual and multimodal repertoires of participants, they need to expansively report on participants' experiences and identities alongside institutional labels and classifications that certainly shape those identities and experiences.

Kuo and Sprečić (Chapter 4) literally propose that researchers make participants' thinking, identities, and experiences visible through the incorporation of arts-based methods, specifically using graphic representations to 'show' a fuller picture. They offer ways to do so without compromising participant privacy in re-representing young people's drawings through their own. Through thick description and schematic illustrations, the authors re-present the young people's artwork to preserve anonymity and respect the participants' ownership of their creative work. While Kuo and Sprečić recognize what is lost in researchers' interpretive representation of youth artworks, they weigh those losses with their ethical duty to take care in how they present participants' multilingual and multimodal work.

Moving forward: Centering ethics and equity in working with data

All three of these challenges outlined above are vitally important for multilingual literacy researchers to grapple with: moving with people and data in new ways while expanding what counts as data and making critical decisions about how to represent participants in humanizing and ethical ways. What connects these chapters is a deep and profound concern with ethical and equitable approaches to addressing these three challenges. Given that these challenges will only grow more complex as people navigate an increasingly precarious multimodal and multilingual world, researchers must be alert to new ways to address them.

One future direction that researchers may want to consider as they engage in ethnetnography, metasynthesis, and multimodal research is how normative systems and structures condition and are conditioned by platforms. From digital platforms that help people learn languages (e.g., Duolingo), interface with government agencies for visas (e.g., USEmbassy.gov), regulate language testing in schools (e.g., WIDA's ACCESS for ELLs), or connect with loved ones across time and space (e.g., Zoom, WhatsApp), it is clear that digital platforms are integrally connected to how transnational and multilingual participants navigate everyday activities across languages, cultures, and places. Critical scholarship on platform studies in education (e.g., Nichols & Garcia, 2022) can offer important insights for multilingual literacy researchers, particularly as digital platforms seem like neutral connectors that mask how they mediate processes of datafication (Pangrazio et al., 2022). As researchers move beyond a focus on individuals, other dimensions like the business models, governance structures, and ownership dimensions of digital platforms can become salient to analyses (van Dijck et al., 2018). Brooks (Chapter 2) suggests an excellent methodological approach to bring forward these dimensions in her critical orientation to metasynthesis, which offers researchers "an invitation to discuss the other bureaucratic and socially significant categories that shape the lives of young people in schools" (p. 41). As algorithms continue to shape people's practices in profound and inequitable ways (e.g., Benjamin, 2019; Buolamwini, 2023), multilingual literacy researchers will need to develop new methods of accounting for the ways these shape people's multilingual and multimodal communication practices.

A second direction for multilingual literacy researchers to take up more fully is what it means to engage in multilingual research in a postdigital era — specifically as we move away from distinctions between online and offline and think more about people's sociomaterial practices across space and time (Wang & Canagarajah, 2024). Specifically, how can researchers take on the critical perspectives needed to engage ethically with data in hybrid contexts? What are the limits of what researchers can and should know or ask? What about when researchers learn or collect more than what participants intended? Or when the repercussions might not be easily anticipated? When might they refuse, or open space for refusal by participants? Kuo and Sprečić (Chapter 4) and Karam and Kibler (Chapter 3) all pose such questions as they propose methodological approaches that encourage researchers to take up ethical and critical positions. There are no easy answers as the instability of data in such a postdigital world means that researchers are constantly having to adapt to shifting ethical terrain (see Franzke et al., 2020). That is why having guidance about how these authors are rethinking *data* alongside participants is such an important contribution to the field of multilingual literacy research.

References

Benjamin, R. (2019). *Race after technology: Abolitionist tools for the new Jim Code.* John Wiley & Sons.

Bhatt, I. (2023). Postdigital literacies. In P. Jandrić (Ed.), *Encyclopedia of postdigital science and education* (pp. 1–5). Springer Nature Switzerland.

Buolamwini, J. (2023). *Unmasking AI: My mission to protect what is human in a world of machines.* Random House.

Burrell, J. (2009). The field site as a network: A strategy for locating ethnographic research. *Field Methods,* 21(2), 181–199.

Franzke, A.S, Bechmann, A., Zimmer, M., Ess, C. & the Association of Internet Researchers. (2020). Internet research: Ethical guidelines 3.0. Retrieved on 15 November 2024 from https://aoir.org/reports/ethics3.pdf

Jackson, J.L. (2004). An ethnographic *Film*flam: Giving gifts, doing research, and videotaping the native subject/object. *American Anthropologist,* 106(1), 32–42.

Jandrić, P., Knox, J., Besley, T., Ryberg, T., Suoranta, J., & Hayes, S. (2018). Postdigital science and education. *Educational Philosophy and Theory,* 50(10), 893–899.

Knox, J. (2019). What does the 'postdigital' mean for education? Three critical perspectives on the digital, with implications for educational research and practice. *Postdigital Science and Education,* 1(2), 357–370.

Nichols, T.P., & Garcia, A. (2022). Platform studies in education. *Harvard Educational Review,* 92(2), 209–230.

Pangrazio, L., Stornaiuolo, A., Nichols, T. P., Garcia, A., & Philip, T. M. (2022). Datafication meets platformization: Materializing data processes in teaching and learning. *Harvard Educational Review*, 92(2), 257–283.

Serafini, F. (2015). Multimodal literacy: From theories to practices. *Language Arts*, 92(6), 412–423. http://www.jstor.org/stable/24577533.

Stornaiuolo, A., Smith, A., & Phillips, N. C. (2017). Developing a transliteracies framework for a connected world. *Journal of Literacy Research*, 49(1), 68–91.

Van Dijck, J. Poell, T., & de Waal, M. (2018). *The platform society: Public values in a connective world*. Oxford University Press.

Wang, C., & Canagarajah, S. (2024). Postdigital ethnography in applied linguistics: Beyond the online and offline in language learning. *Research Methods in Applied Linguistics*, 3(2), 100111.

PART 2

Challenges and affordances of qualitative methodological approaches
Rethinking "theory" in qualitative research on multilingual literacy

CHAPTER 6

Korean American children's voices in translanguaging Play-Based Family Literacy (PBFL) through the *suda* (수다) approach

Jinhee Kim, Su-Jeong Wee & Sohyun Meacham
Kennesaw State University | California State University Los Angeles | University of Northern Iowa

In this chapter we propose *suda* (수다) [*suda* is a type of conversation similar to small talk, but it entails a significant length of time with several emergent stories in Korean culture] as a tool for rethinking theory and methodological innovation in qualitative research, emphasizing culturally responsive and sustaining perspectives through examining Korean American children's translanguaging Play-Based Family Literacy (PBFL) at home during the COVID-19 pandemic. This chapter focuses on how our rethinking of *suda* to include the voices of multilingual children as well as researchers themselves can be an innovative qualitative research tool that facilitates the examination of PBFL practices, which encourage natural literacy practices within play contexts, diverging from traditional school-like literacy activities. Introducing how *suda* is utilized as data collection and analysis, this study also presents implications of rethinking *suda* for culturally responsive and sustaining research that can amplify the voices of multilingual children and researchers in the context of translanguaging PBFL practices. Our findings also highlight the importance of PBFL practices for early childhood development and literacy research.

Keywords: culturally responsive and sustaining methodology, Korean American children, multilingual literacy, play, Play-Based Family Literacy (PBFL), *suda* (수다) approach, translanguaging practices

https://doi.org/10.1075/rmal.11.06kim
© 2025 John Benjamins Publishing Company

Introduction

Play has been considered an essential context for children's learning since Plato's time (Hirsh-Pasek & Golinkoff, 2008; Panksepp, 2007). When children explore, manipulate tools and materials, construct, and have joyous emotions during play, they can further develop their interests in seeking knowledge about what they handle. However, scholars have observed the disappearance of play not only in schools but also in childhood homes (e.g., Han, 2021; Nicolopoulou, 2010) because of such obstacles as unsafe play environments, hurried lifestyles, over-scheduling, heavy use of screen-based entertainment media, and academically oriented skill training (Miller & Almon, 2009). Since the 1990s, several scholars have started paying more attention to the relationship and interface between play and literacy (e.g., Christie, 1991; Christie & Roskos, 2015; Roskos & Christie, 2000, 2001) and thus play-literacy research has burgeoned. At the same time, along with globalization, researchers are increasingly considering the play of children from diverse backgrounds and finding that emergent bilingual children's translanguaging practices are often observed when they play (e.g., Bengochea & Gort, 2022; Halmari & Smith, 1994; Kyratzis, 2010). For example, Bengochea and Gort (2022) found that preschool-aged Spanish-English emergent bilingual children used translanguaging practices to justify their play ideas and communicate with their peers.

Our study employs a Play-Based Family Literacy (PBFL) framework, which diverges from narrow school-like views of literacy. It allows us to describe the rich literacy processes of researchers' children, which exhibited in-depth intercultural knowledge and translingual competence. We introduce the term PBFL to describe our comprehensive approach to understanding the play-literacy activities in this study, and in doing so, our study can offer a unique contribution to the fields of literacy and early childhood education. Family literacy approaches based on the home-school partnership approach, which promotes more school-like literacy activities in families, have prevailed in the literature. In particular, the concept of family literacy based on play has been implied in previous literature. For example, Anderson et al.'s (2010) review of naturalistic studies of literacy embedded in families across various sociocultural contexts described many play-literacy contexts, such as dramatic play (e.g., play school) and board game play. The term PBFL stems from the frameworks of family literacy (Anderson et al., 2013; Gonzalez et al., 2023; Taylor, 1983) and play-literacy (Christie, 1991; Christie & Roskos, 2015; Han, 2021) because the frameworks facilitate play-based literacy with family learning at home.

Our PBFL framework includes authentic play contexts that promote naturalistic application and use of literacy practices rather than didactic practices. We as early childhood educators seek to promote children's play-literacy, particularly with families who have young children. To support children's literacy development through play, establishing authentic play is prerequisite. While research on adult-children interaction in play has confirmed that adults' guidance or facilitation can support the children's literacy processes, child-led play remains critical (Meacham et al., 2013). When a high degree of freedom is ensured, children's spontaneous participation is an important characteristic of PBFL. Informed by multimodal (Jewitt & Cress, 2003) and sociocultural perspectives (Heath, 1983), our view of literacy in PBFL goes beyond "simple views of reading" (Gough & Tunmer, 1986; Juel, 1988) which only look at text decoding and linguistic comprehension as reading skills and overlook many sociocultural factors in literacy practices. Like Heath (1983), we see literacy as a social practice. Family, as a social context for literacy practices, is a context for children's literacy learning.

The PBFL framework incorporates elements of family literacy. However, it distinguishes itself from traditional family literacy, which employs didactic literacy teaching approaches rooted in simplistic views of reading. In particular, the PBFL framework is suitable for the unique context of multilingual families because in play contexts, compared to didactic contexts, children can more freely explore their language resources. Emergent multilingual children have linguistic repertoires spanning multiple languages "from which they select features *strategically* to communicate effectively" (García & Wei, 2014, p. 22, italics in original), a phenomenon described as translanguaging practices. In play contexts, compared to didactic contexts, children have more opportunities to use and develop their translingual competence, which allows them to "negotiate meaning when varied, and often divergent, semiotic resources come into contact with one another" (Kang & Pacheco, 2020, p. 428). PBFL includes many types of playful literacy processes that take place within families and allow a high degree of freedom and creativity: storytelling, emergent book club/book talk, arts and crafts, songmaking, and extended use of online technology tools for entertainment, creation, and communication. Within the PBFL framework, children can develop their own authentic voices and ways to use literacy for many aspects of their lives.

While conversations about emergent multilingual practices in play are growing, there remains a scarcity of research on play among Asian American children, especially concerning translanguaging play and literacy at home. When play intersects with translanguaging family literacy, emergent bilingual children from Asian American families can derive numerous benefits. According to Budiman and Ruiz (2021), Asians constitute the nation's fastest-growing racial/ethnic group and are projected to become the largest immigrant group by 2060. Notably, about 34% of Asians in the U.S. solely speak English at home, while the remaining 66% speak a language other than English. Therefore, it is crucial to focus more on understanding Asian American children's play-literacy experiences at home. At the same time, there is a noticeable lack of diverse methodological approaches to examine the diverse play and literacy activities of multilingual children at home. Understanding these children's play-literacy experiences necessitates consideration of their family cultures. There is a clear need for a culturally sustaining methodology to delve into these aspects (See Chapter 7 for a similar argument applied to children's out-of-school learning). Therefore, we propose *suda*, which is rooted in Korean culture, as a tool for rethinking theory and a methodological innovation in qualitative research, emphasizing culturally responsive and sustaining perspectives through examining Korean American children's translanguaging play-based family literacy (PBFL).

Overview of the study

In this section, we briefly discuss a study in which we employed *suda* to explore how our children's translanguaging literacy was intertwined specifically with their play at home in the authors' families across different U.S. regions during the COVID-19 pandemic. We address the innovative and culturally sustaining aspects of *suda* as theoretical framework and methodology, which ethically enables the examination of multilingual children's voices in PBFL practices at home. Scholars have raised questions about the deficit perspectives on the family literacies of children from diverse backgrounds (e.g., Gonzalez et al., 2023; Xu & Hee, 2023), calling for cultural sensitivity, a celebration of diversity, and empowerment of parents while emphasizing a rhetoric of strength. Moving beyond the post-deficit perspective, we believed we should go forward with strength-based approaches by considering the diverse literacy practices within different families at home.

While *suda* traditionally refers to oral conversations among adult women in Korean culture, we rethought this theory in two ways. First, we applied the concept of *suda* to explore children's PBFL across diverse modalities in this study. In doing so, we expanded the use of *suda* within the worlds of multilingual children, moving beyond limited, gendered adult conversations to better understand and appreciate children's voices. In this sense, *suda* helped to broaden our perspectives of children's literacy beyond mere reading and writing. It also enabled us to pay more attention to the play-literacy practices emerging from children's everyday lives within natural settings, particularly at home. Second, we undertook *suda* ourselves as a culturally sustaining qualitative research tool encompassing both theoretical framework as well as methodology. In the following section we explain more about what *suda* is and how the approach was used by researchers to analyze children's nuanced voices in PBFL while analyzing how children and families engaged in *suda* within translanguaging PBFL at home. We then describe our positionality and the data collection and analysis we undertook before presenting a short summary of the findings, which are explored in more detail later in the chapter.

What is *suda* (수다)?

Suda is a term used in Korean culture to describe engaging in intensive, leisurely conversations. *Suda* is not commonly employed for casual chats with individuals from different cultures, underscoring its cultural specificity. In simplified English, *suda* is commonly rendered as "chatting intensively." Although the adjective "talkative" is frequently employed to convey the adjective form of *suda* (suda-seu-rup-da) into English, talkativeness does not precisely capture the essence of *suda*, which encompasses the emotions of the conversants. Unlike small talk or casual chatter in English, *suda* conversations involve deep discussions, although they feel leisurely to the conversants (Oh, 2005). *Suda* embodies deep dialogue, ontological (ways of being) and epistemological (ways of knowing) exploration, and cultural significance, where participants in these conversations openly express their uncertainties with vulnerability and embark on a journey to find certainties. Characterized by its open-ended and fluid nature, *suda* allows us to discover fresh perspectives on our lived experiences, serving as an onto-epistemological lens (ways of being and knowing) for us to gain new insights. While *suda* conversations typically do not have predetermined agendas or specific objectives, they can help us clarify issues or problems and find answers to our questions. Similarly, *suda* does not adhere to strict rules or hierarchies among participants, such as a predetermined sequence or a designated leader, thus creating a safe environment (Kim et al., 2021, 2024; Meacham et al., 2022; Wee et al., 2023). Because of this characteristic, when *suda* is employed within learning-teaching contexts, children can find it playful (Han et al., 2023; Wee et al., 2023). *Suda* has been a gendered term used mainly to describe the everyday conversations of Korean women (Oh, 2005). Compared to men's conversations, which were deemed important for matters concerning national politics or business in society, *suda* was often regarded as encompassing trivial and insignificant topics typically associated with women. While men in Korea have knowingly or unknowingly participated in *suda*, the patriarchal society tended to prevent them from recognizing and acknowledging it. Korean feminist sociologist Sookhee Oh (2005) has reinterpreted *suda* as socio-cultural functions embracing Korean culture rather than as a gendered binary conversation, which tends to be limited to women in Korean cultural communities, challenging this traditional gendered perception of *suda*.

In this study, we broaden the application of *suda* to multilingual children, extending beyond gendered adult conversations. We view *suda* as defying traditional gender roles, welcoming all family members, including fathers, into profound conversations without set objectives. As female researchers who came from Korean cultural communities and are familiar with *suda*, we were privileged to capture children's *suda* through PBFL at home, and then to analyze that data through our own *suda* conversations. The development of the *suda* as a framework and methodology stemmed from our efforts to describe and explain our research practice. We have sought to reclaim its educational significance and its criticality in qualitative research (e.g., Kim et al., 2021, 2024; Meacham et al., 2022; Wee et al., 2023).

Due to the open-ended nature of *suda*, which allows for the exploration of personal and profound topics, it has proven to be a suitable framework for us to gain new insights about our lived experiences. Our approach to rethinking the theory of *suda* — by expanding it to the literacy practices of our multilingual children and ourselves as researchers — serves as our theoretical framework, research methodology, and analytical tool. *Suda*, initially used as a data collection method in our earlier co-autoethnographic study, has evolved into a central conceptual framework (see Kim et al., 2021, 2024; Meacham et al., 2022; Wee et al., 2023).

Who we are

As transnational mothers and immigrant teacher educators from South Korea, we share similarities such as being multilingual and working in higher education after graduate studies. However, our home literacy practices vary significantly due to differences in family composition, primary language spoken at home, and sociocultural contexts. These variations have directly shaped our children's literacy practices at home. During the study, our children, ranging from pre-K to 4th grade, were all U.S.-born and used varying degrees of translanguaging between Korean and English at home. The kids showed different levels of proficiency in Korean. Each family had distinct language dynamics — each husband of two authors, who came from Korea at a young age, used both Korean and English equally, while the other author's non-Korean husband primarily spoke English with some Spanish. Additionally, factors like the number and genders of siblings, community diversity, and involvement in the Korean community, including access to heritage language programs, influenced our children's home language practices. Our diverse positionalities as transnational mothers and immigrant teacher educators, coupled with the specificities of our family dynamics, language use patterns, and community engagement, contributed to a rich and multifaceted exploration of home literacy practices. This positionality provides a unique lens through which to examine the complexities of language development and literacy practices in our multilingual children's worlds. *Suda*, particularly when used as emotionally engaging action, facilitates an ethical exploration of children's worlds because it naturally creates comfortable and safe environments for participants to share their voices and listen to others. *Suda* also fosters a profound understanding of their literacy practices because it encourages researchers to approach these practices in a participatory and dialogic manner. This suda process represents our cultural practice, which felt entirely natural to us.

Data collection and analysis

The data were initially obtained through a collaborative self-study among the researchers, adopting the approaches of self-study scholars (e.g., Clift et al., 2005) while intertwining our intersectional roles of a teacher educator and a parent researcher. While our institutions have different IRB policies for self-study (the IRB process were waived for two researchers at their institutions, while one researcher's self-study obtained the IRB approval), we asked our children if observations and the collection of artifacts during their play could be included in the study, and we informed them that they could withdraw their consent at any time during the research period. We also continuously monitored our children's willingness to participate in the study. This study utilized a two-layered data collection process through *suda*: (1) *suda* among the researchers, and (2) *suda* with children (preK-4th grade) during the research period (2020–2021) in subsequently analyzing the data. The data consisted of (1) field notes during our observations of children's PBFL, (2) photos and audio-video recordings of children's PBFL activities (e.g., creating and singing their original hip-hop songs and role-playing), (3) a collection of the children's artifacts (e.g., drawings, paintings, and writing samples), and (4) recordings of online conferences (*suda* sessions) among us. Initially, we collected our children's literacy practices integrated with play (PBFL). *Suda* allowed us to immerse ourselves in children's worlds naturally and deeply invited us to understand their PBFL at home. During these interactions, we avoided imposing anything on the children and instead engaged in open conversations, sharing our experiences and actively listening to them. The *suda* dialogues between family members included us as researchers and children; they were recorded through various methods such as note-taking, picture-taking, and audio-and video-recording (mostly through our cell phones) to capture the children's translanguaging PBFL experiences at home.

Second, *suda* served as our analysis tool, engaging us in multiple sessions over a year to analyze the collected data. The *suda* approach is ongoing, collaborative, participatory, and recursive. We conducted both individual and collective analyses during these *suda* sessions. *Suda* enabled us to conduct collective interpretations regarding our children's literacy practices, extending our reflections to include the perspectives and insights of multiple researchers. Initially, we individually reviewed the data from each family, exploring emerging themes and cases through open coding guided by the theoretical frameworks supporting translanguaging PBFL practices. Each of us generated multiple open codes, such as translanguaging, types of play, book club, bookmaking, and family literacy. These open codes were then compared and contrasted with other data sources. In our individual analysis, we reviewed field notes and samples of children's work, such as drawings, stories, and poems, to identify specific themes.

Later on, we shared our experiences and thoughts collaboratively, with mutual engagement among the researchers, which combined with each researcher's interpretations of the data from the process of the collaborative analysis process. In order to achieve consensus, we discussed central themes and codes derived from individual analysis. Our analysis through *suda* was more dialogical than traditional qualitative data analysis, as it creates a safe space for engaging in the sharing and discussion of the inseparable data from researchers' lived experiences, which researchers can even feel vulnerable (see Kim et al., 2021, 2024; Meacham et al., 2022; Wee et al., 2023).

During our analysis process, we engaged in sharing and discussing our respective reflective journals. We actively raised questions and addressed uncertainties that arose during our individual analyses, fostering a collective exploration and understanding of the data. We began by recording our views separately, then provided comments and feedback on each other's interpretations. We transcribed our recorded *suda* sessions among researchers and collaboratively reanalyzed them. The process produced a more comprehensive and nuanced understanding of PBFL at home. (See Chapter 8 for another example of a collaborative and dialogic approach to data analysis employed by qualitative researchers exploring families' literacy practices.)

Key findings

By employing *suda*, we found that children actively engaged in various multimodal forms of translanguaging PBFL at home (e.g., storymaking/storytelling, book club/book talk, role-play/creative drama, drawing/writing, and paper/digital reading). Through these activities, which involved both Korean and English, children explored social issues such as racism and unequal treatment, raising pertinent questions. PBFL helped children better understand social issues in their environments, which schools may not address with adequate sensitivity. Below, we address how rethinking theory with *suda* helped us arrive at these findings.

Suda: Methodological discussion

This chapter contributes to rethinking theory by highlighting *suda* as an innovative, culturally responsive and sustaining approach to the study of literacy, which we undertook by: (1) expanding the theory of *suda* itself beyond gendered adult conversations to the multilingual interactions of children and their families, as well as to researchers themselves; and (2) using this same theory as a tool to bridge theory and methodology, undertaking concrete analytical steps that a theoretical commitment to *suda* implied. In the four sections below, we demonstrate the opportunities that rethinking theory with *suda* provided us in this study. Example (1) demonstrates the ways in which *suda* allowed us to arrive at a collective analysis among researchers. Examples (2)–(4) show new aspects of children's literacy practices that our expanded notion of *suda* uncovered: we saw that these practices defied clear boundaries between literacy and play (Example (2)), represented complex translingual interactions among family members (Example (3)), and played an important role in shaping children's narrative abilities (Example (4)).

Example 1: *Rethinking theory to arrive at a collective analysis*

As we mentioned earlier, *suda* refers to culturally specific everyday conversations, commonly among women (Kim et al. 2021, 2024; Meacham et al., 2022; Oh, 2005; Wee et al., 2023). Reflecting patriarchal norms within the culture, *suda* has tended to be underestimated as a trivial conversation among women. Without any agenda or specific aim to achieve, *suda* can be a naturalistic tool for researchers to access participants' accounts and be engaged in listening to their voices. *Suda* can create a critical space for researchers to collect and analyze data respecting and valuing participants' accounts in nuanced ways (Kim et al., 2021, 2024). Without any hierarchy or assigned roles among participants, *suda* can also serve as an effective vehicle for seeking meanings in conversations between adults and children (Wee et al., 2023). As *suda* begins without specific goals, conversants have much freedom to move from one topic to another. The following transcript exemplifies our collaborative analysis through *suda* among researchers. The example transcript for the collaborative analysis shows the nature of *suda*, focusing on the episode of Claire and Lily making bookmarks after the online book club (see the finding section for the episode of Claire and Lily):

Jinhee: … 그래서 Claire가 'racism으로부터 protect 할 거라고 우리 family를.' 그렇게 얘기를 해서. Pandemic 때 사람들이 너무 Asian people 미워한다고. 그랬더니 Lily 가 '나도 알아' 하면서 이제 계속 얘기가 이어갔어요. 근데 자기들끼리 이렇게 주고받고 하는 그런 얘기들을 저는 그냥 계속 관찰 했었거든요. 근데 이게 수다랑 놀이가 함께 가고, 자기들끼리 계속 수다를, 수다의 그 특성 중에 하나가 갑자기 어떤 주제가 정해진 게 아니

라 자연스럽게 그냥 natural 한 상황에서 계속 나오고 그런 거잖아요 [So Claire said, 'I wish I can protect our family from racism.' That's how the conversation started. During the pandemic, people started hating Asian people too much. Lily chimed in, saying, 'Oh, yes, I know.' And the conversation continued from there. I just kept observing these exchanges they had among themselves. It was a mix of chatting and playing, where they kept conversing among themselves. One characteristic of their conversation was that it was not about pre-decided topics; it naturally flowed from the situations they were in].

Soh: 그러니까 이게 이런 주제가 갑툭튀잖아. 완전히 갑자기 툭 튀어나 갑툭튀라고 얘기한다며. 이게 이런 말이 이렇게 그냥 수월수월 나올 수 있다. 얘네 둘이 되게 얘기를 서로 즐기는 거야. 서로 그냥 앉아서. 그리고 이런 게 노는 거잖아. 그러면서 그냥 계속 수다 떠는 게 노는 거잖아. 그 사이에 이렇게 이런 주제가 갑자기 툭 튀어나올 수 있다는 게 되게 신기하네 [This is about how suddenly, out of the blue, this topic pops up, totally out of nowhere, and they call it a sudden pop-up. They seem to really enjoy talking with each other, just sitting around and fooling around like this. While doing that, they just keep chatting, enjoying themselves. It's quite amazing how suddenly a topic like this can just pop up between them].

Su-Jeong: 맞아 자매들끼리 대화가 되게 심도가 있는데 racism에 관해서 얘기하고. 근데 애들이 막 이거를 되게 어려워하지 않고, 이거에 관련해서 막 bookmark를 만들어서 놀이로 또 연결 짓고 [Right, the conversations between the sisters are quite profound, they talk about racism. But the kids don't find it too difficult; they make bookmarks related to it and then play, making connections with it].

Soh: 그러니까 나도 어릴 때 생각해 보면 동생이랑 같은 방을 썼는데, 아침에 일어나면 동생이랑 그냥 미주알 고주알. 이름이 오백원이라는 강아지가 있었데. 강아지가 뒷산에 올라갔는데, 다른 강아지 500원 강아지가 5천원 강아지를 이런 식으로. 계속 우리 둘이 주거니 받거니 하면서, 그냥 수다 떨면서 얘기를 만든 거. 이게 되게 되게 재미있었던 기억이 아직도. 진짜 몇 십 년 전 얘기야 막 1학년 이럴 때. 그러니까 그런 거가 여기서 느껴지네. Lily랑 Claire 사이에 [So, when I look back to my childhood, my sister and I used to share the same room. In the mornings, we'd wake up and pretend there was a dog named '500 Won' in the backyard. This imaginary dog would interact with other imaginary dogs, like the '5,000 Won' dog, and we would create stories and *suda* while playing with them. It was such a fun memory that I still cherish. It feels like it was decades ago, back when I was in first grade, experiencing those kinds of things. That is the vibe I get between Lily and Claire].

Jinhee: 그리고 놀이 자체도, 그게 내가 이걸 해야지 하고 하는 게 아니라, 특정 목적이 없이 그냥 시작하는 거잖아요. 결국에는 수다도 어떻게 보면은 특정한 목적이 없이 계속 뭔가가 이어져 나가는 거고. 그래서 우리 오숙희 선생님이랑 얘기했을 때 '비언어적인 수다'. 놀이가 어쩌면 비언어적인 수단일 수도 있다라는 생각이 지금 드네요. 그러면서 그 놀이 안에 literacy가 들어가고, 그게 계속 연결되는 거가 지금 생각이 나서. 여기는 비언어적인 수다하고, 만들기도 하고 다른 거를 drawing하면서, 자기 언어를 생각을 표현

하고 또 Claire하고 Lily하고 또 대화를 언어적으로, 또 수다를 하면서 그것도 발전시키고, 같이 동시에 일어난 그 oral language의 형태의 수다가 일어나지만, 또 아이들이 이렇게 뭘 만들고 play하면서 같이 literacy가 들어가는. 또 다른 형태의 수다가 동시에 이렇게 아이들이 안에서 일어나는 [And play itself is not about setting out to do something; it is initiated without a specific goal in mind. Eventually, *suda*, in a way, continues without a specific purpose, and that is connected about 'non-verbal *suda*' when we talked to Sookhee Oh [Korean feminist sociologist]. It suddenly struck me that play could potentially be a form of non-verbal *suda*. Amidst this, literacy gets involved in play, continuously intertwining. Here, non-verbal *suda* is established, things are created, drawings are made, expressing one's language, while Claire and Lily engaged in conversations, enhancing both literacy and *suda*. Simultaneously, *suda* as a form of oral language occurs, but children, while creating and playing, engage in another form of *suda* where literacy is simultaneously involved].

Su-Jeong: 수다랑 놀이가 상호 보완적으로 이루어지니까 더 생각이 깊어지고 play를 더 깊게 만들고 oral conversation을 하면서 다른 형태의 non-oral communication 도 같이 이루어지네 [Since *suda* and play complement each other, thoughts become deeper, enhancing play and engaging in oral conversations, while also facilitating other forms of non-verbal communication].

As depicted in the preceding transcript excerpt, our *suda* sessions facilitated the merging of individual analyses into a collective analysis, integrating diverse interpretations and profound insights from each other. We freely exchanged interpretations and questions without a fixed sequence. *Suda*-ing itself was like a culturally responsive communication in that it created opportunities for us to explore our in-depth perspectives (Kim et al., 2024) on our children's translanguaging PBFL while collectively reflecting on our cultural aspects and positionalities.

Similarly, children can do *suda* with their family members to openly share their thoughts, experiences, and feelings during their literacy activities. Children can engage in *suda* by telling their own stories without worrying about being moderated, corrected, or evaluated. Viewed through the lens of *suda*, children's conversation is not dismissed as trivial or insignificant. Through *suda* with their family members at home, children can construct their own understandings and expand their thinking more than in institutionalized settings. In particular, children's conversations in translanguaging are embraced without any judgments, fostering greater acceptance and understanding. Methodologically, *suda* in literacy research is innovative in that it can create more space for emergent bilingual children to share their voices through PBFL, and it can help analyze children's voices in nuanced ways while providing deep insight into children's translanguaging accounts.

Epistemologically, *suda* allowed our interactional positionalities as Korean American transnational mothers, teacher educators, and researchers to come alive through embodying our own cultural approaches to doing and knowing, rather than feeling marginalized by Western knowledge hegemony. Kim et al. (2024) also claimed that *suda* created a culturally sensitive space for seeking our own voices and attempting to dismantle hegemonic knowledge as other feminist epistemologies have sought to do (e.g., Dillard, 2002; Pérez & Saavedra, 2017; Rhee, 2021). In *suda*, we often used translanguaging — shifting between Korean and English without prioritizing one. Every language in *suda* carries equal value and importance. *Suda* provided us with space and time where we were engaged in non-hierarchical, dialogic, fluid, therapeutic, and emotional conversations and reflected, analyzed, and clarified our lived experiences that were oftentimes scattered and unrecognized (Han et al., 2023; Kim et al., 2021, 2024; Meacham et al., 2022; Wee et al., 2023). As our culturally sustaining onto-epistemology, *suda* opposes the binary lens through which we perceive knowledge as civilized versus savage or valid versus invalid.

Suda is not a clear-cut space but rather a continuously developing and changing process as ideas are (re)routed and connected with each other in new ways/perspectives. That is, "suda produces the endless 'intermezzo' in Deleuze and Guattari's (2004) concept" (Meacham et al., 2022, p. 630). Intermezzo is a rhizomatic space of in-betweenness, which has "a perpendicular direction, a transversal movement" rather than an average (Deleuze & Guattari, 2004, p. 25). *Suda* has been instrumental in helping us recognize that play and literacy are not separate in children's lives, cherish various types of children's literacy, and broaden traditional literacy research to various types of literacy emergent from children's everyday lives in natural settings, particularly children's play at home. For example, when our children played, they often started drawing fragmented and simplified objects, but as their play progressed, their drawings frequently turned into more complex literacy practices. Sometimes they showed and explained their pictures to their families, and their drawings became more elaborate over time. Furthermore, *suda* was also deeply associated with PBFL in that our children were *suda*-ing in PBFL at home with their family members. The fluidity and flexibility of *suda* are strongly connected with PBFL, as children's play emerges spontaneously, and literacy is often represented through play. In this study, our children freely expressed and shared their translanguaging literacy through PBFL with their siblings and other family members at home. All the children's play was naturally initiated by them, and their play was connected to literacies, which provided opportunities for their families to participate in PBFL. *Suda*-ing among family members, including us, played a critical role in capturing children's PBFL at home. *Suda* helped us to rethink our data regarding a wide range of multimodal translanguaging PBFL activities at home.

Example 2: *Suda approach for children's play and literacy in an online book club*

Engaging in *suda* with children enabled us as adult researchers to closely listen to children's perspectives and voices through the intersections of play and literacy. We discovered that the distinction between children's literacy activities and play lacks a clear boundary, offering insights beyond what their written literacy portrays. For example, while Claire and Jaimee (4th graders) were doing their book club online, their siblings often joined them, played with them, and produced literacy practices.[2] During the pandemic, Jinhee's daughter Claire had a book club with Soh's daughter Jaimee via Zoom. The book club started when the two girls felt bored and wanted to interact with the world because they could not meet their friends during the first wave of the COVID-19 pandemic. While Jinhee and Soh worked on other research projects, they had several meetings online. The girls sometimes saw the meetings and passed behind the two authors' screens, curious about what we were discussing. Around that time, Claire wanted to have a book club with other kids and shared her idea with Soh's daughter Jaimee, so the book club started with only two girls. Although they had never met in-person before the book club, they planned what to do without any adults' help. They sometimes read aloud to each other or silently read certain pages, shared their thoughts, wrote related books, or made artifacts such as bookmarks. While they actively participated in the book club, they showed their toys and other stuff in their rooms through their tablets. In addition, while they read *Wishtree* (Applegate, 2017), they decided to make bookmarks to write their own wishes and hang them on house plants. In the book, people wrote their wishes and hung them from the tree's branches. The two girls got the idea to make bookmarks from the book and agreed to make them while they were in the Zoom meeting together. Although the book club members were only two girls, the meetings were sometimes expanded to include their siblings. For example, Lily (2nd grader), Claire's younger sister, heard Claire and Jaimee reading together from the book and wanted to join in. Lily read some parts of a page of the book too. After finishing the Zoom meeting for the online book club, Claire showed a bookmark (see Figure 1) to her younger sister Lily. Lily also wanted to make one and made it together with Claire. As the children started to make more bookmarks with various materials, they engaged in translanguaging PBFL. For example, Lily asked Claire, "언니 (sister), can you give me 가위 (scissors)? How can I make this hole?" Claire asked Lily, "뭐라고 쓸 거야 (What do you want to write) for wishes?"

---

2. All children's names are pseudonyms in this chapter.

Figure 1. Claire's bookmarks created during the book club

One of Claire's wishes ("protect me and my family") was related to her concerns and fears emerging from accelerated anti-racism during the first wave of the COVID-19 pandemic. When Lily asked about Claire's wishes, Claire elaborated on her wishes further.

Lily: Claire, what do you want to protect from?

Claire: I want to protect my family from racism. During this pandemic, people hate people of color, especially Asians.

Lily: Oh, yes. I know.

Through dialogic and non-hierarchical *suda* among the siblings as conversants, Claire expressed her concerns that emerged from the intersectionality of the spreading COVID-19 virus and anti-Asian racism. Listening to children's *suda* can aid adult researchers in understanding their play connected with literacy activities and the social issues relevant to their lives.

Example 3: *Drawing and translanguaging literacy in family conversations*

Exploring the intersection of drawing and translanguaging literacy within family conversations (*suda*) provides valuable insights into how children express themselves and navigate language use at home. When Aiden (2nd grader) voluntarily drew something about COVID-19 for the first time, it was nothing but a small red virus in the middle of the paper. Then, he added what he had discussed with his mom, Su-Jeong, and his father about what we should do during the pandemic, such as wearing a mask, washing hands, staying at home, and not going to crowded public places, to his drawing. Centering on a red coronavirus in the middle, he added a mask, hands with soap and water, a house where children were inside, and a big X on a crowd of people. When Su-Jeong asked him about what he drew, he explained the names of the items in his drawing. A few days later, Aiden worked together with his twin brother Dave to create a short comic book titled *Rock, Paper, Scissors* in which a rock wins over paper and scissors. The boys drew the illustrations and added texts in speech bubbles or in an empty space on the paper. When his dad saw their comic book, he commented in Korean, '가위, 바위, 보에서 바위가 이기는 거야? (Does Rock always win among rock, scissors, and paper?)' It became a cue for connecting between rock, scissors, and paper and the similar version of Korean play called "scissors, rock, and cloth wrapper." After that, the boys attempted to write 가위, 바위, 보 in Korean on the cover page (see Figure 2).

Figure 2. Storybook pages from Rock, paper, scissors

Then, Dave wrote *Rock vs. Covid 19*, which is a sequel to *Rock, Paper, Scissors*. In *Rock vs. Covid 19*, this time the champion Rock from the original story faces the coronavirus. Then Rock is transformed into actor Dwayne Johnson, known by his ring name, The Rock! The comic book does not show who wins exactly, but it depicts an ongoing fight between the two characters. Dave and Aiden invited their youngest brother Bryan (preschooler) to color their storybooks. Later on, the boys scanned their pages and created a pdf file of the book. The three brothers engaged in ongoing and non-hierarchical conversations while creating a creative and imaginary story. Initially, their intention was not to create a book or reach a definitive conclusion for the story. *Suda* facilitated the boys in presenting more elaborate and expanded ideas, leading to a structured development of the story. Neither *suda* nor collaborative book-making was suggested by any adult; it naturally emerged among the boys. During their continuous *suda*, they shared laughter and welcomed and reflected upon different ideas and opinions through collaboration and sequential work. On the cover page, they wrote the title both in Korean and English (see Figure 3). The children's drawings and *suda* during their play were intertwined with literacy and their father's comment on rock, paper, and scissors in Korean, and the similar game in Korea led them to use these translingual words in their story-making process.

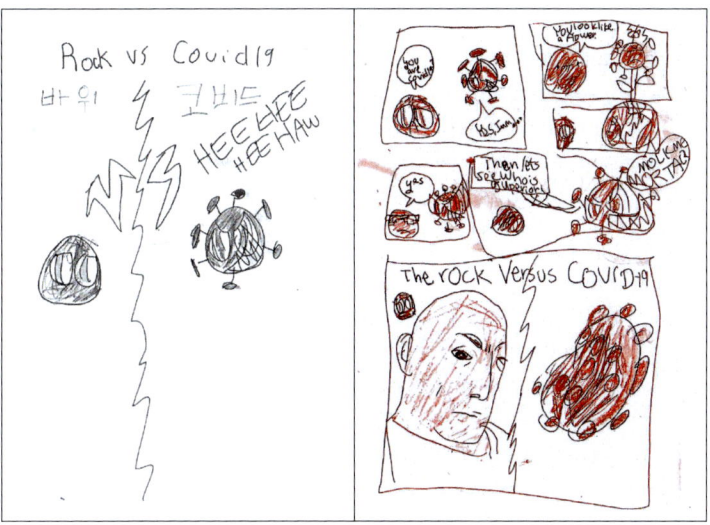

Figure 3. A sequel storybook titled Rock vs. Covid 19

Example 4: *Children's playful translanguaging interactions in making a story*

Playful translanguaging interactions through *suda* played a pivotal role in shaping the children's narrative abilities. In the creative process of making stories, we found the nuances of translanguaging, where language boundaries blur, and the children skillfully incorporated diverse linguistic elements into their narratives. The children expressed themselves through storytelling, showcasing the inherent fluidity and flexibility in their language practices.

In the example below, there was not a clear boundary between play and literacy. One day, Shaun (2nd grader), a Korean African American who is Soh's son, decided to create a picture book after a PBFL moment involving *suda* described below. His story exhibited his everyday life focusing on how he played with his pajama pants, his cat, and his sister at home. His story naturally portrayed his mother's Korean language use around him, and his authentic hip-hop songs were influenced by his dad's cultural heritage. He used lyrics from his original hip-hop song (e.g., "What we do for fun?") and he came up with an idea to transform his pajama pants into special clothes for his hip-hop performance. As he regularly does for Hip Hop literacy practice, he wrote his lyrics as follows:

I pulled my pajama pants up. Now they are covering my bae-kkop
(배꼽: belly button in Korean).
They reach my chest. Unbelievable!
Omma (Mom) says 'ajossi baji.' (old man's pants)
Appa (Dad) says 'hey silly pants.'
We laugh and laugh out loud.
Omma says, '배꼽이 빠져라 웃었네.' (English translation: I laugh
so hard so my belly button popped out!)
I say, 'my belly button reaches to the sky.'

...

I look at these jukebox pajama pants. I know I can have fun with
these.
I need special clothes for my Hip Hop performance.
I put my arms in the pajama pants.
I roll my arms to the back. Cool! Now it is a swag bomber jacket!
'What we do for fun?'
'What we do for fun?'
'I play with my pajama pants.'
I am flashing my two dimples!

This moment felt to Sho like a typical *suda* moment in which she would engage
with other Korean people because her family members chatted extensively and
humorously with one another about a topic while being emotionally engaged. For
her, such moments typically involve lively interactions with fellow Koreans, mir-
roring the animated and humorous conversations within her family that use English as the primary language for the African American husband and Asian African
American biracial children. The familiarity and depth of discourse on a particular topic resonated with the essence of what she considers a typical and culturally
rich "*suda*" moment. In this *suda* moment, Soh and her family members infused
some Korean words such as "bae-kkop" (belly button) and "ajossi baji" (old man's
pants) to enhance the humor. This *suda* interaction and the picture book writing
that emerged from it make a representative PBFL moment.

Implications for qualitative research on multilingual literacy development

Rethinking theory with *suda* provided a space for data analysis and triangulations
between the children who participated in PBFL and the adult researchers. When
we chose *suda*-ing as the term to emphasize the process of *suda* with our children,
we could read the children's voices more closely and understand them more
clearly. At the same time, during the collective analytic process, we were also

able to deeply analyze the voices children presented in PBFL. Our study confirms that *suda* is a critical and natural tool to understand and appreciate children's voices in PBFL, which may get less attention in school contexts. Paralleling the dialogic and fluid characteristics of *suda*, PBFL also provides a space for more child-directed literacy practices, in which children's natural literacy can emerge from play rather than any adult-led intervention. Rethinking theory with *suda* also allows researchers to observe and analyze children's translanguaging literacy through a culturally responsive and sustaining approach to data analysis.

This study provides several implications for literacy researchers and future research agendas. First, more attention should be given to the relationships between children's play and literacy within translanguaging practices in children's homes, despite some existing literature on translanguaging practices in children's homes (e.g., Song, 2016). This study provides valuable insight into the critical role PBFL practices can play for researchers who closely examine children's play in diverse home environments. By valuing each child's home culture, researchers can examine how diverse children's family literacy is intertwined with play and how schools can support those children better.

Second, this study demonstrated that rethinking *suda* as theory, which allowed us to utilize it as a culturally specific literacy framework as well as a methodology, can be a critical tool for listening to our Asian American children's voices, which have been neglected in the literature on play-literacy and family literacy. While *suda* is rooted in Korean culture, its lens highlighting openness and multiplicities of topics to be addressed among conversants can extend to other research areas and other cultures. The topics in *suda* are open rather than fixed, respecting the conversants as individuals rather than fitting them into predefined roles of listeners, speakers, or authorities on specific topics. The core characteristics of *suda* can be applied by researchers to listen to young children's voices, particularly multilingual children with an asset-based lens, as well as in other research contexts with various cultural settings. *Suda* is one way of challenging more traditional focus group dynamic where the interviewer holds authority and participants serve merely as informants. Instead, it aims to foster a dialogic environment where all participants share equal authority (Kim et al., 2024). *Suda* opens up the possibilities for researchers to truly listen to participants' voices, fostering collaborative research devoid of hierarchical relationships. Similar to pláticas as Chicana/Latina culturally responsive methodology grounded from small talk among Chicana/Latina communities (Delgado Bernal et al., 2023; Fierros & Delgado Bernal, 2016), *suda* contributes to building a respectful space to share voices of cultural communities. As shown in the findings, PBFL gave our children more freedom to express their voices related to social issues in multimodal literacy formats, and through *suda*, we could listen carefully to their nuanced voices related to their PBFL. *Suda* does not always demand insider positionality but rather fosters a space to intimately engage with insider perspectives, avoiding hierarchical relationships between a researcher and the researched. It allows researchers to see participants beyond their roles as subjects of study, promoting a more holistic understanding.

Third, as other scholars documented the importance and characteristics of social-emotional dimensions for culturally racially marginalized children (e.g., Albritton et al., 2024; Hayashi et al., 2022), this study suggests that literacy research should not overlook those children's social emotional dimensions. We propose that the concept of *suda* can be extended to encompass social and emotional dimensions. Collaborative for Academic Social and Emotional Learning [CASEL] (n.d) delineates five competencies crucial for social and emotional learning, namely self-awareness, self-management, social awareness, relationship skills, and responsible decision-making. The therapeutic attributes of *suda* (Oh, 2005; Meacham et al., 2022) are particularly pertinent to the processes involved in fostering children's self and social awareness, aligning with CASEL's framework. In the context of *suda*, children are presented with opportunities to recognize their emotions and cultivate empathy, creating a playful and secure learning environment where they can engage in open conversations with their peers. We suggest that families from multilingual contexts should encourage their children to develop PBFL rather than acquiring merely literacy per se, paying attention to their children's social emotional dimensions, which are deeply connected to their language development. Scholars have documented that learners' affect and emotion influence learners' cognitive development (Hawkins, 2017; Hohenberger, 2011). Considering the role of affect and emotion in language development, *suda* can be a critical tool for acknowledging children's feeling and emotion and boost their (multilingual) language development. When researchers consider emotions emerging from the process of participants' language development through culturally sustaining approaches, they can uncover more authentic voices of children to better understand children's language development. We suggest that *suda*, as a culturally sustaining approach, can be an imperative tool for researchers, particularly those studying in multilingual contexts because *suda* can foster equitable research contexts, shifting from traditional researcher's authority over the researched.

Traditional research on culturally and racially marginalized children's literacy tends to be conducted by outside adult researchers who spend time in the research contexts. Unlike outside researchers, we as mothers had been observing our children's translanguaging practices through PBFL for a long time. Compared to outsider researchers who have limited access to research contexts, we were in a privileged position to observe our children's PBFL and hear their voices more closely at home. We do not argue that research on the literacy of multilingual children from diverse backgrounds should only be conducted by parent researchers. Rather, we claim that *suda*, combined with our privileged research positions, allowed us to consider ethical issues in accessing children's worlds to better understand their literacy practices. For other outside researchers, this study can provide insights into culturally sustaining research methods for multilingual children from diverse backgrounds by sharing children's nuanced voices. *Suda* is also "an action-oriented noun" that "invites participants to be emotionally engaged in depth" (Meacham et al., 2022, p. 627) so that we as co-researchers could closely listen to children's voices and analyze the data deeply. For example, Claire's wishes ("Protect me and my family") on the bookmark and the sequel storybook by Su-Jeong's children reflected their fears and concerns about anti-Asian racism during the pandemic and the coronavirus. By understanding children's emotions reflected in children's literacy practices at home, we were situated to listen carefully to children's voices, which are often overlooked in the current literature. Rather than deriving data from the relationship between objectified child participants and researchers, this culturally sustaining approach creates an emotionally shared space to listen to children's voices entangled with PBFL. *Suda* can be utilized to outsiders beyond Korean cultural communities, as participants listen to each other and each other's emotion would be cared without holding judgment. This can help researchers to deliver children's accounts better while collecting children's voices. To better understand multilingual children's PBFL, we suggest that researchers need to reflect on their own positionalities and find/create an emotionally supportive space for hearing children's voices with more sincere and caring ears.

Having opportunities to reframe and rethink existing research approaches is critical for researchers to consider culturally sustaining research approaches toward minoritized children. As shown in this chapter, culturally sustaining research approaches can help researchers to hear nuanced voices presented in multilingual children's literacy practices in natural settings, respecting those children's affect and emotions. We hope this study can catalyze further discussions of (emergent) multilingual children's literacy research and culturally sustaining research for those children.

References

Albritton, K., Stuckey, A., Klatka, K., & Cruz, K. (2024). Systematic review of culturally adapted SEL interventions for racially and ethnically minoritized preschool children. *Journal of School Psychology*, 106, 101344.

Anderson, A., Anderson, J., & Teichert, L. (2013). Through a rear-view mirror: Families look back at a family literacy program. *School Community Journal*, 23(2), 33–54.

Anderson, J., Anderson, A., Friedrich, N., & Kim, J. E. (2010). Taking stock of family literacy: Some contemporary perspectives. *Journal of Early Childhood Literacy*, 10(1), 33–53.

Applegate, K. (2017). *Wishtree*. Feiwel & Friends.

Bengochea, A., & Gort, M. (2022). Translanguaging for varying discourse functions in sociodramatic play: An exploratory multiple case study of young emergent bilinguals. *International Journal of Bilingual Education and Bilingualism*, 25(5), 1697–1712.

Budiman, A., & Ruiz, N. (2021, April 29). *Key facts about Asian Americans, a diverse and growing population*. Pew Research Center. Retrieved on 15 November 2024 from https://www.pewresearch.org/fact-tank/2021/04/29/key-facts-about-asian-americans/

Christie, J. F. (Ed.). (1991). *Play and early literacy development*. State University of New York Press.

Christie, J. F., & Roskos, K. (2015). Play as a medium for literacy development. In D. P. Fromberg & D. Bergen (Eds.), *Play from birth to twelve: Contexts, perspectives, and meanings* (3rd ed., pp. 191–196). Routledge.

Clift, R. T., Brady, P., Mora, R., Choi, S., & Stegemoller, J. (2005). From self-study to collaborative self-study to collaborative self-study of collaboration: The evolution of a research team. In C. Kosnik, C. Beck, A. R. Freese, & A. P. Samaras (Eds.), *Making a difference in teacher education through self-study: Studies of personal, professional and program renewal* (pp. 85–100). Springer.

Collaborative for Academic Social and Emotional Learning [CASEL] (n.d.). *What is the CASEL framework?* CASEL. Retrieved on 15 November 2024 from https://casel.org/fundamentals-of-sel/what-is-the-casel-framework/

Deleuze, G., & Guattari, F. (2004). *A thousand plateaus: Capitalism and schizophrenia*. Continuum.

Delgado Bernal, D., Flores, A. I., Gaxiola Serrano, T. J., & Morales, S. (2023). An introduction: Chicana/Latina feminista pláticas in educational research. *International Journal of Qualitative Studies in Education*, 36(9), 1627–1630.

Dillard, C. B. (2002). Walking ourselves back home: The education of teachers with/in the world. *Journal of Teacher Education*, 53(5), 383–392.

Fierros, C., & Delgado Bernal, D. (2016). Vamos a platicar: The contours of pláticas as methodology. *Chicana/Latina Studies*, 15(2), 98–121.

García, O., & Wei, L. (2014). *Translanguaging: Language, bilingualism, and education*. Palgrave.

Gonzalez, J. E., Liew, J., Aguilar, S. D., Sainz, A. D., Sanchez, R., & Bumgardner, R. (2023). Family literacy practices and the home learning environment of Asian and Latino Americans: Path to literacy and social-emotional learning. In J. E. Gonzalez, J. Liew, G. A. Curtis, & Y. Zou (Eds.), *Family literacy practices in Asian and Latinx families: Educational and cultural considerations* (pp. 94–126). Springer.

Gough, P., & Tunmer, W. (1986). Decoding, reading, and reading disability. *Remedial and Special Education*, 7(1), 6–10.

Halmari, H., & W. Smith. (1994). Code-switching and register shift: Evidence from Finnish-English child bilingual conversation. *Journal of Pragmatics*, 21(4), 427–445.

Han, M. (2021). History of play and literacy research: contribution of Dr. James F. Christie. In M. Han, & J. Johnson (Eds.), *Play and literacy: Play & culture studies* (pp. 3–14), Hamilton Books.

Han, S., Kim, J, Meacham, S., & Wee, S. (2023). *Supporting Korean American children in early childhood education: Perspectives from mother-educators.* Teachers College Press.

Hawkins, J.A. (2017). *Feelings and emotion-based learning: A new theory.* Springer.

Hayashi, A., Liew, J., Aguilar, S.D., Nyanamba, J.M., & Zhao, Y. (2022). Embodied and social-emotional learning (SEL) in early childhood: Situating culturally relevant SEL in Asian, African, and North American contexts. *Early Education and Development*, 33(5), 746–763.

Heath, S.B. (1983). *Ways with words: Language, life and work in communities and classrooms.* Cambridge University Press.

Hirsh-Pasek, K., & Golinkoff, R. (2008). Why play = learning. In A. Petitclerc (Ed.), *Encyclopedia on early childhood development.* Retrieved on 15 November 2024 from http://www.child-encyclopedia.com/play/according-experts/why-play-learning

Hohenberger, A. (2011). The role of affect and emotion in language development. In D. Gökçay, & G. Yildirm (Eds.). *Affective computing and interaction: Psychological, cognitive and neuroscientific perspectives* (pp. 208–243). IGI Global.

Jewitt, C., & Kress, G. (Eds.). (2003). *Multimodal literacy.* Peter Lang.

Juel, C. (1988). Learning to read and write: A longitudinal study of 54 children from first through fourth grades. *Journal of Educational Psychology*, 80(4), 437–447.

Kang, H., & Pacheco, M.B. (2020). Translingual competence and study abroad: Shifts in sojourners' approaches to second language learning. *Language and Education*, 34(5), 425–439.

Kim, J., Han, S., Wee, S., & Meacham, S. (2024). Children's names and naming practices: Wrestling with racism in Asian American families. *Diaspora, Indigenous, and Minority Education.* 18(3), 182–194.

Kim, J., Wee, S., & Meacham, S. (2021). What is missing in our teacher education practices: A collaborative self-study of teacher educators with children during the COVID-19 pandemic. *Studying Teacher Education*, 17(1), 22–37.

Kyratzis, A. (2010). Latina girls' peer play interactions in a bilingual Spanish-English U.S. preschool: Heteroglossia, frame shifting, and language ideology. *Pragmatics*, 20(4), 557–586.

Meacham, S., Kim, J., Wee, S., Kim, K. (2022). ReZooming our academic home using the suda approach. *Qualitative Inquiry*, 28(6), 895–909.

Meacham, S., Vukelich, C., Han, M., & Buell, M. (2013). Preschool teachers' language use during dramatic play. *European Early Childhood Education Research Journal*, 22(5), 250–267.

Miller, E., & Almon, J. (2009). *Crisis in the kindergarten: Why children need to play in school.* Alliance for Childhood.

Nicolopoulou, A. (2010). The alarming disappearance of play from early childhood education. *Human Development*, 53(1), 1–4.

Oh, S. (2005). *Yes, let's Suda: Social psychological analysis of Suda* [그래, 수다로 풀자]. Woongjin.

Panksepp, J. (2007). Can PLAY diminish ADHD and facilitate the construction of the social brain? *Journal of the Canadian Academy of Child and Adolescent Psychiatry*, 16(2), 57–66.

Pérez, M.S., & Saavedra, C.M. (2017). A call for onto-epistemological diversity in early childhood education and care: Centering global south conceptualizations of childhood/s. *Review of Research in Education*, 41(1), 1–29.

Rhee, J. (2021). *Decolonial feminist research: Haunting, rememory and mothers*. Routledge.

Roskos, K.A., & Christie, J.F. (2000). *Play and literacy in early childhood: Research from multiple perspectives*. Lawrence Erlbaum Associates.

Roskos, K.A., & Christie, J.F. (2001). Examining the play — literacy interface: A critical review and future directions. *Journal of Early Childhood Literacy*, 1(1), 59–89.

Song, K. (2016). "Okay, I will say in Korean and then in American": Translanguaging practices in bilingual homes. *Journal of Early Childhood Literacy*, 16(1), 84–106.

Taylor, D. (1983). *Family Literacy: Young children learning to read and write*. Heinemann.

Wee, S., Meacham, S., & Kim, J. (2023). Being (Asian) American children: Children's exploration of racial/cultural identity and racism. *Race Ethnicity and Education*, 1–24.

Xu, Y., & Hee, P.J. (2023). Early literacy development in Asian and indigenous children of Hawai'i: A theoretical framework on multiple aspects of home literacy environments. In J.E. Gonzalez, J. Liew, G.A. Curtis, & Y. Zou (Eds.), *Family literacy practices in Asian and Latinx families: Educational and cultural considerations* (pp. 282–333). Springer.

CHAPTER 7

Bridging language and STEM

Using an Anzalduan framework to center Latinx
Elementary and Middle School students'
understanding of robotics

Rachel G. Salas & Lizeth I. Lizárraga Dueñas
The University of Nevada, Reno | The University of Texas at Austin

This chapter illustrates how combining an Anzalduan framework with
critical ethnography and social semiotics provides a unique approach
centering Latinx students' STEM knowledge, language, and literacy use as
legitimate ways of *conocimiento* and communicating. Using longitudinal
data, authors examine how Latinx middle-grade students use their linguistic
repertoires through multimodal representations to bridge their understanding of a real-world STEM FIRST LEGO League (FLL) challenge and their
community, conceptualized through Anzaldúa's (Moraga & Anzaldúa, 1983)
work on *mestizaje* and imagery of the *mestiza* body as a bridge. The chapter
further documents how to rethink Anzalduan theory through overlaying
Deleuze and Guattari's (1980/1987) characteristics of a *minor literature* as an
additional lens to deterritorialize language and promote equitable research
centering Latinx ways of languaging, knowing, and being.

Keywords: Anzalduan Theory, robotics, STEM, multilingual learners,
thinking with theory

Introduction

> Language is a mode of action, an ongoing implementation of relations of power,
> and all linguistic elements — phonemic, morphemic, syntactic and semantic —
> are involved in the generation of power relations via discursive practices.
>
> (Bogue, 2011, p. 133)

This chapter illustrates how combining an Anzalduan framework with multiple
methodological lenses, such as critical ethnography and social semiotics, provides
a unique approach centering the STEM knowledge, language, and literacy use

https://doi.org/10.1075/rmal.11.07sal

of Latinx students as legitimate ways of *conocimiento* (knowledge) and communicating. We draw on Deleuze and Guattari's characteristics of a *minor literature* (see Bogue, 2011) to underscore the power of an Anzalduan framework of linguistic resistance and empowerment. The focus of the study is an ongoing longitudinal project of an Out-of-School-Time (OST) FIRST (For Inspiration and Recognition in Science and Technology) LEGO League (FLL) program that explored multimodal language and literacy skill development through robotics/ STEM instruction for economically marginalized, multilingual, Latinx elementary and middle school students.

We position our research within Gloria Anzaldúa's (e.g., Moraga & Anzaldúa, 1983) work on *mestizaje* and imagery of the *mestiza* body as a bridge. Specifically, her symbolic use of constructing and traversing bridges, her concept of *Nepantla* – *tierra entre medio* – a liminal space for acts of resistance, and her claim that language identity is imperative to survival undergird the methodological process of this chapter. As Latinx ethnographic researchers, we identify as *mestizas* who understand that our *mestizaje* is part of our lens, bringing "a story of fusion, augmentation, code-switching, and translation" (Beltran, 2004, p. 606) to our work. Other researchers such as Garza et al. (2023) and McWhirter and Cinamon (2021) have used Anzaldua's theories on *Nepantla*, borderlands, and identity to examine underrepresentation in STEM; these studies focused on participants in higher education or older adults in the workforce. Our study focuses on Latinx elementary students in fourth and fifth grade and middle school students in sixth through eighth grade in an OST setting. Furthermore, we position ourselves as researchers and active participants and learners in the robotics/ STEM environment.

Latinx students continue to be underrepresented in STEM programs/majors and thus prevented/excluded from earning science and engineering degrees in higher education. Multiple factors persistently impact K-12 STEM education and student performance for Latinx and other racially and linguistically minoritized student populations (Burke et al., 2022). The Center for Advancement of Informal Science Education (CAISE, 2018) report shows that Latinx, Black, Indigenous, and other minoritized groups of children lack opportunities to explore STEM curriculum or activities, including consistent instruction to ignite possible early interest in STEM careers (Change the Equation, 2017; Djonko-Moore et al., 2017).

McGee and Robinson (2020) have argued that high-poverty schools with predominantly racially minoritized multilingual student populations continue to fall short in providing foundational STEM instruction. Often, these schools have technological assets funded by state or federal grants but not enough educators to deliver high-level computer science course instruction that advance problem-solving and critical and computational thinking skills (Ung et al., 2022).

Research suggests that OST or informal STEM instruction can support high-poverty schools that lack resources with increased STEM engagement (Ciechanowski et al., 2015).

Our study contributes to the OST STEM body of research by also investigating informal STEM instructional settings for Latinx students. We examined the ways by which multilingual Latinx elementary and middle school students used language and literacies to bridge their understanding of real-world STEM topics that impact them, their community, and the Latinx population. We also researched how an OST robotics/STEM program supports the literacy and language practices of the students. This chapter highlights how different theories and methodological tools worked together to inform our thinking and analysis of data generated through an Anzalduan framework. We use Deleuze and Guattari's three characteristics of a *minor literature* (Bogue, 2011) overlayed on Anzaldúa's framing to expand our discussion of thinking with theory for more equitable research. We end with a discussion on rethinking theory to produce more equitable research to center the participants' voices, ideas, and language in qualitative literacy research.

Overview of the study and its findings

> A bridge is not just about one set of people crossing to the other side; it's also about those on the other side crossing to this side.　　(Anzaldúa, 2002, p. 4)

Traditional and critical ethnography in education

The qualitative method of ethnography has a long history in research, dating back to the early 20th century. Ethnography concerns the "study of the meaning of behavior, the language, and the interaction among members of the culture-sharing group" (Creswell & Poth, 2018, p. 90). The research ethnographer is more an observer of the studied group than a participant. Bloome and Greene (2018) have described traditional ethnography as writing about the "other."

There are alternative approaches to ethnography with different theoretical orientations that utilize different epistemological approaches in their work (Creswell & Poth, 2018). Creswell and Poth (2018) noted that theory is important when conducting a study, as it allows ethnographers to more easily recognize patterns or have labels for patterns readily available to them. Due to the nature of our study, we gravitated towards an alternative approach to ethnography and have employed critical ethnographic approaches toward language in our work. Critical ethnographies allow us to examine and critique the linguistic position and influence of the English language and literacy practices (May, 2023). Fitzpatrick and

May (2022) have argued that theory and methodology work in unison and that critical ethnography requires active participation, or "being and doing" (p. 97).

For this study, we utilized multiple critical ethnographic techniques, such as engaging with community members in participatory research (Palmer & Caldas, 2016), focusing on social issues that are important to the community, and centering on the community context to move inquiry forward (Fitzpatrick & May, 2022). As the researchers and coaches of a robotics team, we were learning alongside the team members and were in constant dialogue with them during our robotics practices. The collected data during the study included ethnographic field notes and multimodal artifacts created by the team, including mind maps, student-researcher notebooks/whiteboards, prototype sketches of our innovation project, a presentation script, and data charts with visual graphics. Thomas (2021) stated, "Critical ethnography resembles literary criticism in that we look for the nonliteral meanings of our data texts" (p. 43). As researchers, we studied the multimodal texts, artifacts, and discourse within the social-cultural context, examined how language contributed to the construction of lived realities, and explored the power dynamics the participants saw emerge from their own research about farm workers.

Multimodal literacies

A sociocultural perspective on literacy informs this study. A sociocultural perspective situates literacy as a social and cultural practice where language and sign systems mediate our understanding and participation within a particular community of learners (Bruner, 1986; Street, 1995). This study specifically uses social semiotic theory and its construct of multimodality (Jewitt & Kress, 2003; Unrau et al., 2019). Social semiotic theory provides a lens to explain and explore how individuals make meaning using signs and various modes, such as oral or written language, gestures, sounds, symbols, and other visual and linguistic representations, to communicate with others (Kress & van Leeuwen, 1996). Multimodality refers to the many representations individuals use to make meaning and comprehend and communicate information (Kress, 2000). Kress (2000) argued for a theory of semiosis that centers on the "interested action of socially located, culturally and historically formed individuals as remakers, the transformers, and the re-shapers of the representational resources available to them" (p. 155). He called for a view of literacy involving various communicative representation modalities, such as visual and textual representation, collaborative learning, and digital learning. Most of our data are multimodal and include digital images, video scripts, sketches of prototypes, and the actual building of the prototype.

Aims of the study

Our study addressed two research questions. First, in what ways do multilingual Latinx elementary and middle school students use language and literacies to bridge their understanding of real-world STEM topics that impact them, their community, and the Latinx population? Second, how does an OST robotics/ STEM program support the literacy practices of the students? To address these questions, we used a semiotic data analysis approach appropriate for studying a variety of textual meaning-producing experiences and events (Mikhaeli & Baskerville, 2019).

Research context and participants

The robotics learning community in this study used the FLL Challenge framework to position multilingual Latinx students as researchers, robot designers, builders, and programmers. FLL aims to engage children ages 4–16 in STEM concepts by providing a hands-on, project-based approach to learning and researching. The program creates learning opportunities by providing real-world problem-solving opportunities for students. FLL participants are expected to collaborate with their teams to design creative solutions to these real-world problems. The FLL Challenge encourages participants to explore and refine their scientific research skills by interviewing experts, creating and delivering research data, engaging in teamwork, and building and programming a robot to accomplish multiple tasks related to a science topic. The students in this study participated in all aspects of the FLL framework. The FLL Challenge framework for grades four to eight has three main components: (1) Robot Design and Robot Game, (2) Innovation Project, and (3) Core Values. For the first component, participants must design, build, and program a robot to complete a series of missions related to the annual science theme. The Innovation component involves researching a specific problem centered on the annual theme, such as transportation issues for *Cargo Connect* (the theme for 2021). The Core Values component is standardized across the Challenge framework and integral to all aspects of FLL. Teams must display sportsmanship and innovative values that reflect FLL's six Core Values: inclusion, innovation, impact, discovery, teamwork, and fun. All FLL teams must show how they use and embody the Core Values in the robotics arena and their everyday home, school, and community environments. The team collectively works toward a chance to place in the qualifying competition towards the end of the robotics season. If the team is one of the top ten teams, they can compete in the state championship. Team practices are designed so that there is time to work on each FLL component (Robot Design and Robot Game, Innovation Project, and Core Values) during each meeting. All participants have the opportunity to design, build, and program a robot to complete one or more missions on the robot game board, to contribute to the innovation project research, and to participate in core value activities. IRB was obtained for this research study. Assent forms were signed by minors, and consent was obtained from parents and other adult participants.

This study examined the research component of the FLL Innovation Project. The innovation project focuses on the annual STEM theme, and participants are encouraged to think of a problem related to the theme and provide a researched solution. Throughout the project, students examine the theme, pose a problem, and provide possible solutions. Solutions can be modifications of an existing device or new and innovative concepts. The research data for this study focused on the 2021–2022 *Cargo Connect* season, which lasted eight months, from August 2021 to April 2022. The FLL official statement for the *Cargo Connect* theme stated that participants would explore the complexity of modern transportation and how cargo or goods are transported, sorted, and delivered to various destinations. That year, our robotics team comprised seven fourth through seventh-grade students. The team demographic included four females and three males. Five participants identified as bilingual Latinx, one identified as a monolingual Latinx English speaker, and one as an African American monolingual English-speaking student. The team also consisted of two coaches and two undergraduate university mentors. The coaches, who were also the researchers, were a university faculty member and a graduate student. Their roles included leading and facilitating the team while engaging in participatory research and learning alongside the team. The coaches and mentors were all female; three individuals identified as bilingual Latinx and one as Japanese American. While the students came from Title 1 and charter schools throughout the region, the team met and practiced at a center located on a university campus. The meeting site was convenient and strategic for the researchers for several reasons. First, the center provided the students space to bridge and connect their community and home resources with those available at the university that could be used to design, build, and launch their robots and to research, develop, and create their innovation projects. Second, it afforded the students, five of whom had parents without college degrees, a sense of belonging and familiarity with a college environment, as the students mentioned throughout the program. Student comments such as, "When I go here (pointing to the gym), I'll be performing in there (cheerleading)", and "When I go to college here, I know where everything is" demonstrate this sense of belonging. Throughout the season, the team had opportunities to explore different aspects of the campus and the university community. Team meetings occurred two to three times a week after school, usually for two to three hours each. The team spent four months preparing for the qualifier, an additional two months preparing for the championship, and then an additional two months preparing for post-championship advancement. As tournament dates drew near, the team increased meeting times on Saturdays for three-hour sessions each. Each session had time for robot building/programming, innovation project research, and core values activities.

Findings

Our findings suggest that students bridged their understanding of real-world STEM topics through reimagining the brown body as transportation and making connections to their identities, languages, and lived experiences (research question 1), and we describe these below. Research question 2 speaks to our methodological innovation of re-thinking theory, and so we present those findings in the methodological discussion section below.

The *mestiza(o)* body as a bridge

The team's efforts had to correlate with the FLL's transportation theme. The members' brainstorming produced ideas such as smart stop lights for efficient traffic flow, flying cars like the Jetsons, and hover cars on a magnetic highway to transport goods quickly with a low carbon footprint. The generation of ideas was a fun event and allowed for great languaging opportunities and debate among the team members. During this process, one of the coaches shared a cartoon (see Figure 1) she had seen on social media by the Mexican American artist Lalo Alcaraz. The cartoon was labeled "Human Infrastructure" (Alcaraz, 2021) and depicted a Latino farm worker bent over with his arms outstretched while three eighteen-wheeled trucks filled with produce drove over his back like a human bridge.

Figure 1. Human Infrastructure ©
©2024 Lalo Alcaraz. Image appears courtesy of Lalo Alcaraz & Andrews McMeel Syndication

The team studied the picture silently. As team members discussed what they saw in the cartoon, the coach passed out sliced strawberries, pound cake, and cans of whipped cream for the students' snacks. "Imagine where these strawberries come from," she asked. "I know I can't live without my daily dose of berries and fruit." At this point, the United States was trying to return to "normal" after enduring a lockdown and witnessing the horrific toll the COVID-19 Pandemic had on human life, society, and economic infrastructures.

The students began commenting about Alcaraz's picture as they ate their snacks: "They [farm workers] helped put food on the table during COVID." "They kept working while we stayed home safe." "They got sick because they had to work." "They died to feed us." "They're not treated right." One visiting student (i.e., not a permanent team member) said, "I can't eat this anymore (referencing the strawberries and cream); it doesn't seem right." Another team member responded, "You should eat it to support the farm workers. They gave so much. We should respect it."

This discussion was the catalyst the students needed to reimagine the brown body as transportation. The image stuck — they saw the laborer's body as a bridge. They saw their parents or family members, most of whom worked in manual labor, as the body depicted in Alcaraz's cartoon. We all had a visceral reaction to the image. It was impactful for all of us; it resonated with our brown bodies, and the group decided that it was important to move forward and research the body of the farm worker as transportation. Alcaraz's depiction of the brown body created a sense of communion and unity. It filled us with a responsibility to bring awareness to two easily overlooked facts: the indispensability of the farm workers to our economy, and the toll of their toil on the human body.

The students began brainstorming ways to bridge the use of robotics and STEM to help make the farm workers' jobs easier and safer. The team coaches contacted Dr. Ann López, the executive director of the Center for Farmworkers and an expert in farm worker advocacy. Appearing virtually, Dr. López explained that the human body should not be bent over for more than four hours, yet those laboring in the strawberry fields were bent over for eight or more hours a day. The mentors and coaches introduced the work of Dolores Huerta, co-founder of the National Farmworkers Association (now United Farm Workers [UFW]) to the students. Through the research that the students were doing on this topic, a team member discovered a Latinx farm worker who now owned a strawberry farm. The student suggested also writing a letter to the strawberry farm owner, Mayra Paniagua, to learn more about farm labor issues. The coaches and mentors facilitated letter-writing to both Mrs. Huerta and Ms. Paniagua while the students generated the written content. Neither responded, but the students continued their research undeterred by watching UFW videos on farm workers and reading information from the Center for Farmworkers' Families

The team also learned that picking strawberries is a skilled job. Strawberries must be picked precisely with a skilled wrist twist to avoid damaging the berry because blemished fruit is not salable. As such, the brown body was not only a bridge that transports food from farm to table but also a frame that practiced the laborious and specialized skill of strawberry picking — a crucial practice that enabled strawberries to find their way to consumers' tables. Since the strawberry fields are far away in another state, the coaches, a student mentor, and a parent of one of the robotics team members brainstormed ways to simulate working in the fields. We created strawberry fields of crushed brown butcher paper and red plastic strawberries attached with Velcro along the university center hallway to give the students a glimpse into bending over and picking strawberries. The team had to pick the berries without removing both pieces of Velcro from the paper and fill their basket with only "good" strawberries picked correctly. While this simulation was short and not as arduous as working in a field under a relenting sun and other elements, it allowed the team to experience discomforts that were new to them and led them to begin to understand the concept of the brown body as bridge, or human infrastructure, as depicted by Alcaraz's cartoon. They formulated ideas for a solution that incorporated all the knowledge they learned from experts and their research and ways of knowing (*conocimientos*) to present as part of their award-winning Innovation Project.

Our study's findings revealed how the participants produced multimodal artifacts (e.g., written documentation, discussions, video, digital drawings, sketches) and used their full linguistic repertoires to connect their knowledge and understanding of the multiple ways the brown body as bridge (Alcaraz, 2021; Moraga & Anzaldúa, 1983) metaphor applied to not just transportation and farm workers (the STEM project) but to their own identities, languages, and lived experiences.

Bridging identity, language, and lived experiences

The *mestiza(o)* body as bridge (Moraga & Anzaldúa, 1983) and Alcaraz's (2021) work are central to the participants' discourse and understanding of robotics and themselves. Their research ideas on transportation and robotics were spurred by seeing the human body, specifically a *mestizo* body, as transportation infrastructure. The identity label of the *mestizo* body is important to us; it is one we identify with, and we see ourselves as brown/*mestiza(o)* bodies. This concept of the body as transport radically changed the participants' views, language, and understanding of society's injustices, especially during the COVID pandemic. Analyzing Alcaraz's picture made it personal. Seeing the brown body depicted as an actual bridge was visceral and real for all of us. It helped the participants recognize the power imbalances and inequalities that exist for farm workers and brown bodies. One participant observed the picture and asked, "Why is it always us?", saying the quiet part out loud for all of us to absorb. Farm workers are essential workers and should be recognized as such. Anzaldúa frames the *mestiza* consciousness as one that can navigate and question forms of oppression. In the simplicity of his question, "Why is it always us?", our team member voiced the multiple forms of oppression enacted upon brown bodies, including his body and the bodies of his parents. Another participant offered commentary by further detailing an oppressive act inflicted upon brown bodies: "We worked during COVID, others don't have to. So we get sick." The realization that certain groups can exert power over others emerged through this discussion. Anzaldúa's framework centered the participants' lived experiences as we connected with Lalo's picture — embracing and recognizing another brown body similar to our own, and bridging the picture of a *mestiza(o)* body to our reality.

Bridging farm workers toil to fork through multilingual and multimodal literacy practices

During the 2021–22 *Cargo Connect* FLL season, the students discussed how best to design and engineer a robotic arm to make picking strawberries easier. The participants crafted multimodal artifacts to display and share their deep connection and *conocimiento* of the impact of hard labor on the brown *mestiza(o)* body — a body they recognized as their own. The final design was a robotic arm with a color sensor that could detect red to help farm workers select ripe strawberries and stand while working in the field. They collaboratively wrote a script to share their research and knowledge of the difficulty and skill needed to pick strawberries. They produced a video to share with the FLL judges what they learned about the transportation of produce, specifically strawberries picked from the fields and carried across the bridge of brown bodies to our grocery store and, ultimately, our tables. Through the use of video, students adopted a multimodal approach to represent their understanding of the brown body as a bridge. In their production of this video (and other artifacts), they also drew on their entire linguistic repertoires and engaged in translanguaging to negotiate division of labor and representing their understanding of the role of the brown body's toil. We elaborate on translanguaging practices and provide examples in the methodological discussion below related to how the students deterritorialized language.

The findings reveal the participants' understanding of, and connections to, Anzalduan theories. As an acknowledgment of the brown body acts as a bridge in multiple ways and dimensions, Anzaldúa and Keating (2002) have stated,

"Bridges are thresholds to other realities, archetypal, primal symbols of shifting consciousness. They are passageways, conduits, and connectors that connote transitioning, crossing borders, and changing perspectives" (p.1). The artifacts and symbols participants created displayed our "shifting consciousness" and developing perspectives of the multiple ways the brown body performed as a bridge in our world. The experience of the *Cargo Connect* season and Alcaraz's picture had so impacted the participants that in the following year and well into a new season, when asked by a judge to talk about their overall experience in FLL, the same participant who had a year earlier stated she had never considered where her food comes from responded, "I learned so much. Before, I never thought about where my food came from; I still think about it."

Methodological discussion: Rethinking theory for more equitable research

> ...un proceso de crear puentes (bridges) to the next phase, next place, next culture, next reality.
>
> (Anzaldua, 2002, p.574)

Using an Anzalduan framework undergirds our epistemological stance and lens on the theoretical underpinnings of the research process. The next section briefly discusses how Chicana Feminist Epistemology aligns with our understanding of an Anzalduan framework and methodological approaches. We then also overlay Deleuze and Guattari's (1980/1987) characteristics of a *minor literature* with an Anzalduan framework to show how we engaged in rethinking theory for more equitable research that centers on Latinx ways of languaging, knowing, and being, such as those of the participants in our study. It was this rethinking that allowed us to answer our second research question, related to how the program supported students' literacy practice, and we discuss those insights below.

Our *mestizaje*

Chicana feminist epistemology (Calderon et al., 2012; Delgado Bernal, 1998) stems from and aligns with Anzaldúa's (1987/1999) work in that concepts such as *conocimiento, mestiza* consciousness, *mestizaje,* and borderlands are crucial aspects of Chicana epistemology. By centering Chicana Feminist Epistemology, our methodological approach aligns with cultural intuition (Delgado Bernal, 1998). Cultural intuition encompasses personal experience, existing literature, professional experience, and analytical research process.

Personal experience encompasses our lived experiences, family stories of the past, and the knowledge we have gained from our elders; these are all personal experiences that we bring into our work. Existing literature, professional experience, and years of practice in our career field support our understanding of the literature. The last element of cultural intuition is the analytical research process, which includes interacting with the data by asking clarifying questions, engaging in reflection of what was seen and heard, and ultimately making sense of them (Delgado Bernal, 1998). We come to this work acknowledging our Chicana feminist epistemology and the cultural intuition that guides our work, the latter of which informed our critique of integrating language practices and STEM in an out-of-school robotics program. We drew from our own experiences as multilingual learners of English and Spanish who have engaged with out-of-school education programs.

We also understand that our role as robotics coaches/researchers and previous K-12 educators has shaped our experiences in the program, but we also consider ourselves active participants. We learn alongside our students, and we create knowledge together. As we explored the research on farm workers, we learned along with the students about the skills needed to pick strawberries skillfully and efficiently. These are things we did not know prior to this program. We also learned from scientists about the toll the human body takes, bending over for hours in extreme weather conditions. Learning for us extended beyond the science components of the program into the robot-building and programming aspects. Often, students would learn advanced programming techniques and share them with us (the researchers). They figured out ways to modify robots for better performance and taught them to us. Through oral discourse and performative coaching (walking us through the programming blocks and the construction of robot attachments), the students privileged their linguistic practices to communicate their knowledge to teach us (Hurtado, 2020).

Thinking with theory

While engaged in ethnographic research practices, or what St. Pierre (2014) has framed as "conventional humanistic qualitative methodology" (p.3), thinking with theory throughout the study allows for a push against the norms of conventional methodology and facilitates fluidity of thought, practice, and dynamic turns to occur within the research space. The idea of fluidity opens space for using different theories not normally associated with certain data sets. Mazzei (2021) described the process of "thinking with" theory as something that happens as an organic event in the research field as concepts and data merge and develop.

Gloria Anzaldúa was a Chicana, *mestiza*, feminist scholar, and decolonial theorist. Anzaldua theorized the brown body as a bridge, the span used to traverse borders metaphysically, physically, and linguistically. She conceptualized space for new *mestiza* consciousness and *conocimientos* (1990). Language, in all its forms and varieties (e.g., Spanish, Chicano Spanish, Tex-Mex, English), is essential and integral to the identity of the *new mestiza*. Using language in all its forms is also an act of resistance. As Anzaldúa (1987/1999) clearly articulated, "I am my language." (p. 84). We are all our language, and an Anzalduan lens empowered us to reclaim our linguistic heritage and languaging practices. An Anzalduan theory is appropriate for this work, given the researchers' and participants' cultural and linguistic identity as a collective group. Reclaiming our linguistic heritage meant that all participants were free to use linguistic modes and registers to explain, discuss, and describe, or *platicar*, as they felt necessary to communicate their ideas. Sentences could begin in Spanish and end in English. Spanish or English words were interjected as needed. There were no rules that one language must dominate. Several of the students had experienced linguistic racism at school, where they were told not to speak Spanish, and others felt marginalized because they spoke a language other than English at home. These examples of language use move us away from traditional ideas of knowledge and language production, show the complexity of the students' meaning making and the examples detailed above are part of the study's multimodal data and artifacts.

Lather (2007) argued that "the turn that matters in this moment of the post is away from abstract philosophizing and toward concrete efforts to put theory to work" (p. 157). The "post" moves us away from dominant knowledge structures toward recognizing and acknowledging the legitimate ways of knowing of the marginalized other. We put Anzaldúa's powerful theories of linguistic identity, *mestiza* consciousness, the body as bridge, and *Nepantla* to work by showing how her work is critical, dynamic, and inclusive by mapping her theories with Deleuze and Guattari's three characteristics of a *minor literature* (1980/1987, as cited in Mazzei, 2017 and Bogue, 2011). *Minor literature* is postqualitative inquiry that is constructed as "the problems posed in working a concept and problem together" (Mazzei, 2017, p. 198). A *minor literature* is important because it is crafted by the minority to mitigate the majority's colonial or hegemonic language practice. The three characteristics of a *minor literature* are: (1) deterritorialization of language, (2) political immediacy, and (3) collective assemblage.

In describing the first characteristic, Bogue (2011) defined deterritorialization of language as: "When language users subvert standard pronunciations, syntactic structures or meanings, they 'deterritorialize' the language, in that they detach it from its clearly delineated, regularly gridded territory of conventions, codes, labels and markers" (pp. 132–133). This idea of deterritorialization of language allows us to think within Anzalduan concepts and framing of language.

The second and third characteristics, political immediacy and collective assemblage, focus on political and group identity. All things can be seen through a political lens. Also, no single subject, participant, or unit of inquiry provides insight about or speaks for the group but a collective voice and understanding (Bogue, 2011; Mazzei, 2017). These two characteristics provide a path to representing participants' voices and ideas in way that move beyond traditional presentations of individual transcripts and recordings.

Can Anzaldúa's theories stand alone? Yes, but as critical ethnographers, we see the power in "weaving the local with the global and the theoretical" (Fitzpatrick & May, 2022, p. 41). Below, we provide examples of thinking with theory using Anzaldduan concepts that are overlaid on the three characteristics of a minor literature.

Deterritorializing language through enacting the brown body as bridge

Mazzei (2017) has argued that "enacting Deleuzian concepts is a deterritorializing act" (p. 679). We maintain that enacting Anzalduan concepts is an act of deterritorializing language. In *This Bridge Called My Back: Writings by Radical Women of Color*, Anzaldúa (Moraga & Anzaldúa, 1983) introduced the metaphor of the (brown) body as a bridge. She described a bridge as a physical structure used to cross borders and traverse unknown lands, as many *mestiza* bodies of our ancestors, families, and friends have done. It is a structural barrier that can be difficult or dangerous to cross for many brown bodies. It is also a conceptual image representing the body of a people — her/our people who have endured hardships and intellectual, cultural, and linguistic indignities.

We use this conceptual imagery of the brown body as a bridge to move our research inquiry forward and to see data through a new lens. We saw the brown-body-as-bridge depicted in Alcaraz's work as we researched, designed, and produced the robotic innovation solution (robotic arm with color sensor) and created the oral research presentation. After researching how farm labor impacts the human body, the students wrote a script to reenact farm workers picking strawberries in the field under the hot sun. This script was turned into a short video clip they shared with judges during the qualifier and championship. A few lines from the script show how the brown body was always in the forefront of the students' thoughts and ideas. The students wrote this script independently and provided it to me exactly as formatted, except for the pseudonym Anna.

> Hello, This is Anna [*pseudonym*] reporting from the strawberry fields where farmworkers have been laboring under the hot sun all day. The United States produces about 2.9 billion pounds of strawberries a year. We came today to talk to the farm workers who have kept food on our table during the pandemic. Let's interview some of the workers now.
> *Workers picking strawberries*
> *Comes into frame*

Farmworker 1: Picking strawberries takes a lot of practice and skill. You do not just pull the strawberry from the plant you must twist it the right way.

Farmworker 2: Picking strawberries can be dangerous. We pick strawberries all day and can get sunburn, backaches, headaches and some workers have died.

Farmworker 3: We do not get paid much as farmworkers. Most of us are migrants from Mexico and live in poverty here in the United States.

Farmworker 4: We have been told by doctors that it isn't good to stay bent over more than 4 hours but we do it all day.

The body as bridge metaphor showed us one way to deterritorialize language: through physical enactment of the skit, students' bodies and voices highlighted injustices enacted upon the *mestiza* body. By writing and performing this skit, the participants bridged their *conocimientos* to learn about transportation and robotics — home knowledge that their parents are laborers working long hours, too. That their brown bodies are also bridges, providing different services needed by others. The students tapped into the ways of knowing of their families and communities and made clear connections to what we were researching and discovering. While not farm workers, their family members were construction workers, housekeepers, restaurant workers, and other essential workers that kept the economy afloat during the pandemic. The product of collective knowledge-sharing produced many multimodal sources and, ultimately, a research innovation project that they presented to the judges during competitions. Through their physical enactment of a skit, the students reimagined and enacted the brown body as a bridge.

Deterritorializing language through multimodal literacies

Social semiotics and multimodality are central to the study design and the *Nepantla* learning environment. While social semiotic theory is utilized by the researchers, all participants engaged in multimodal meaning-making. Participants were encouraged to communicate and convey information utilizing a variety of forms of media and modalities, such as digital tablets, laptops and desktop computers, video recordings, individual and classroom dry-erase boards, paper, notebooks, pens, crayons, colored pencils, and markers to draw, sketch, write, outline, or doodle their ideas. Supplies to build a prototype, if requested, were also made available for them to create a representation of their ideas. For example, as ideas were generated, one group designed a solar-driven cart to which the robotic arm could be attached. They first sketched their design on the large classroom dry-erase board. Then, they used foam board and PVC pipe to construct a model of the solar cart design. The also team created multiple drawings and used their linguistic repertoires to label their work. Such multimodal engagement both deterritorialized language and allowed students to reimagine the brown body as transportation, similarily to Hsiao-Chin and Sprečić's chapter in this volume, where immigrant students created artwork as a means to express their understanding of their cultural identity

Deterritorializing language through translanguaging

As Spanish speakers, our language is marginalized by the dominant English-speaking culture. Dialects and varieties of Spanish are often delegitimized and considered inappropriate in certain academic and formal settings. Speaking Spanish or a variety of Spanish can result in open hostility towards the speaker. We collected data for this study during Donald Trump's presidential campaign and presidency. We saw and heard on national TV and social media his relentless demonization of immigrants, especially Mexicans and others from south of the U.S. border. As Spanish-speaking people, we have been criminalized, caged, and discarded. It is the personal understanding of the collective that speaking Spanish in the school environment is discouraged. Anzaldúa has termed this linguistic discriminatory practice as *linguistic terrorism*:

> *Deslenguadas. Somos los del español deficiente.* We are your linguistic nightmare, your linguistic aberration, your linguistic *mestizaje*, the subject of your *burla*. Because we speak with tongues of fire we are culturally crucified. Radically, culturally and linguistically *somos huérfanos* — we speak an orphan tongue. (p. 82)

In the process of deterritorializing language as an assemblage, we practice translanguaging (García & Li, 2014) in oral and written structures and visual artifacts created in the program. The artifacts consisted of drawings that included texts in participants' home language and any other languages they chose to explain their work, ask questions, or develop representational products. Translanguaging allows the collective to seamlessly move from one topic to the next, practicing our linguistic *mestizaje*, asking questions in Spanish and answering in English, or whatever combination of languages and language varieties are needed to share knowledge, convey meaning, and deepen understanding. Translanguaging is a conduit for the group to transact, bridge, and move within and beyond the gaps. Words that come easier in Spanish or do not make sense in English or for which there is no true English equivalent are spoken in Spanish, allowing for complete thought processes to occur and flourish.

Translanguaging is encouraged as an act of resistance in our *Nepantla* learning community. It is practiced and encouraged by the head researcher, who is the lead coach and mentor, and who speaks to the group in a mixture of Spanish and English. A common refrain was *"¿Como te fue in school today? To do good?"* Similar to Kim et al.'s (this volume) discussion on translanguaging we support and honor all linguistic repertoires (e.g., Spanish, Spanglish, pochar, academic or nonacademic vocabulary, English). Data were captured in all the languages we speak. Participants talked to each other in Spanish or a mixture of Spanish and English to socialize and recap the weekend or Mexico's football success. *"¿Has visto el partido?"* they would ask as they entered, or *"El juego va empezar a las seis."* So we knew when to turn on the game. They also regaled us with highlights of the game: *"They scored two goals, bien rápido!"* Sometimes they provided details of the game in Spanish so if we missed the game, we could visualize it in our heads. When discussing terms such as hyperthermia and hypothermia during research, there might be a question to ask for more clarity: *"Qué es hyperthermia?"* Alternatively, as they nervously prepared for competition, they might ask, *"Do you know, quien va estar ahí?"*, asking if we know which teams would be at the qualifier. Even the design for their research innovation project had bilingual aspects. The participants wanted to create a body temperature gauge on the cart that would hold the robotic arm, and they sketched the device to read the body temperature in English and Spanish. As mentioned in the findings, language/identity was a theme that emerged from the data and is central to how we used theories to rethink how to center our participants' linguistic skills for more equitable research.

Political immediacy and collective assemblage

As we viewed the digital image of Alcaraz's (2021) "Human Infrastructure" and videos of farm workers laboring in the strawberry fields, we saw the brown bodies working in searing hot weather and cold rainy downpours to collect the produce to feed our families and provide minimum substance to theirs with their meager wages. These videos left a lingering impact throughout the robotics season and beyond.

There were no single interview transcripts that captured group members' thoughts and reactions, but rather, a constant collective voice that spoke to the indecency of our economic structures. These structures placed many brown bodies in peril and highlighted the inhumanity of the political system that neglected and abused brown bodies at home and our southern border. Through digital and video imagery, we immersed ourselves in the research, and the collective grew to encompass not just the robotics team members, but also the brown bodies who labored in the fields and came to represent us all. All data were generated from participants' journals, researchers' fieldnotes, video recordings, and multimodal artifacts.

Depicted below and in Figure 2 is just one example of what a student wrote on a dry-erase board after researching farm workers online, where she found a story that had pictures of young Latinx girls standing in the middle of a strawberry field.

The student brought it to group discussion, where we looked at the information and discussed the validity of the online source before the participants transferred the information to their research journal.

> At ages of 12–13 kids work in the strawberries fields. Over 500,000 of children works in fields. Mostly of these kids don't get the chance to go to school. A lot of people chooses this job because it is legal, a lot of people who works in strawberries fields are undocumented.

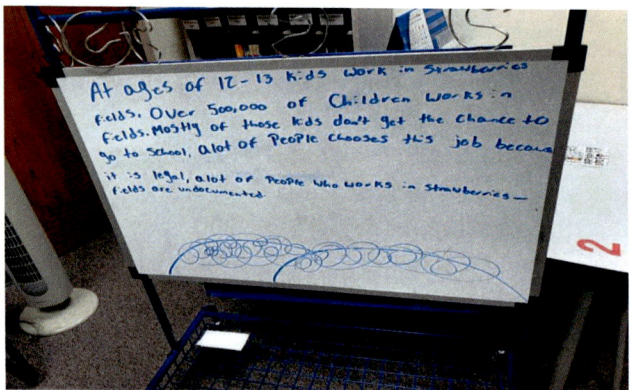

Figure 2. Student's research notes

In the note above, written and shared by a Latinx student, her words give voice to the collective, exposing the exploitation of young children working in the fields, bringing awareness to the group of the political power relations and dynamics that impact the brown bodies in the field and beyond.

Another instance of political immediacy and assemblage can be seen in the following is an excerpt from the head coach and lead researcher's journal:

> January 23, 2022
>
> Competed in the championship yesterday. The event was in person after originally being told it would be held remotely due to COVID. The team did well in the Innovation Project winning the top award for this event. We were also nominated to compete against southern Nevada for the state's Global Innovation Award nomination.
>
> The team did well overall. There were a few issues with the robot game and deciding which robot to use for the last round. The team resolved the issue together but there seemed to be some disagreement about the robot selected for the 3rd round. Miguel [pseudonym] did mention to me at one point during the very long day that he noticed there weren't many people who looked like us. I knew what he meant because he had brought up this topic at other events. He really seemed attuned to the fact that most participants, coaches, refs are white. I asked him if

it bothered him that we were one of the few teams of color. He said, 'a little bit. I just notice it. I am glad when we win something.' I waited to see if he'd say more, but he didn't. 'So they know we can do it?' I asked him. He just nodded but didn't say anything else.

We take our participation in robotics events as political acts — we are brown bodies together in a sea of white. We collectively build a bridge to participate in the annual FLL regional activities, but in our area FLL is presently a white-dominated education program where most teams, coordinators, judges, and referees are white. It is rare to find many teams from marginalized communities who continuously participate in the FLL program. We have learned how to collectively bridge our *conocimiento* along with our *cultura* to cross borders in FLL and find our "in-between space," our *Nepantla*, together. Creating a space for brown bodies to participate in robotics is also political. Using Anzaldúa's framework and Deleuze and Guattari's (1980/1987) characteristic of political immediacy and assemblage provided a lens to see how theory can highlight specific acts of resistance.

Connecting to *Nepantla*

These examples drawn from the concepts of deterritorializing language, political immediacy, and collective assemblage bring us back to Anzaldúa (1993), who used the Nahuatl word *Nepantla*, which means '*tierra entre medio*' or 'in-between spaces'. It is in this in-between space that she claims transformation occurs. All the robotics team members become *Nepantleras*, citizens of a space that allows us to bridge and join forces to transition from one identity to another. *Nepantla* can be a space of discomfort and potential. We see *Nepantla* as a space that allows us to grow as individuals in an assemblage. A place from which we bridge and connect to other spaces to learn and develop — spaces such as robotics events and competitions that take us to other locales that are not familiar. As an assemblage, we have created a safe space to learn, speak our mother tongue, dance to our music, and learn about our heritage — a place that is not school nor home but allows us to be unique, interesting, intellectual, funny, and ourselves.

Nepantla is a place where students teach adults, and adults and students learn together. Students learn the robotic programming language very quickly; they feel free to experiment and create new and interesting programs they teach the adults (researchers) and their peers. They also read and review scientific research online and through informational texts. They interview science experts online and in person to gather information and data about their research problem. They share this knowledge through a multimodal process, producing oral presentations, graphic displays, and digital drawings. We all learn new information and scientific facts through this process. It is in *Nepantla* where our research originates, where Western traditional methodologies dissolve, and a collective *mestiza* consciousness and methodological borderland evolves. *Nepantla* is conceptualized as a place where people living between two or more cultures learn to navigate the complexity of being and negotiating the intersections of language and culture. A form of *Nepantla* has been created at the center where the team meets for robotics practice. It has become a safe space for students to use their linguistic repertoires, ask questions about robotics or life, and challenge themselves to try new things such as programming, robot design, building, and researching science topics. Data that support the creation of *Nepantla* at the center during robotics consists of mostly visual images and short videos that showcase the participants involved in group and individual learning sharing their collective *conocimientos*. There are also images of the students in *comunidad* relaxing, eating, and just talking with each other. Another testament to the *Nepantla* space was the consistent attendance of team members.

Implications for qualitative research on multilingual literacy development

> We die. That may be the meaning of life. But we do language. That may be the measure of our lives. (Morrison, 1993)

Thoughts on ethical reflexivity

Ethical reflexivity, especially in participatory approaches that include children, is integral to our ethnographic work. As researchers working with children from racial and linguistically marginalized groups, we know the ethical issues of power, knowledge, identity, and agency inherent in our work. We position ourselves as members of the assemblage, multilingual Latinx individuals, and active participants in the research context and learning environment. We shared with the participants that we work as a team, learning with and from each other. Moreover, we do exactly that — we learn from them, ask them questions, and get their advice and opinions on projects and designs.

We negotiate power positions in the research context as well. Robotics meetings and sessions are primarily participant-led, and the choice of participating in the different aspects of the program is central. While we work to decenter issues of power inequities, the reality is that there are specific structures we must implement to move the program forward and keep all participants safe. Safety is a group issue and responsibility. In forming collective methodological tools centered on Anzalduan theory, participants are willing to engage in and contribute thoughts, ideas, drawings, scripts, images, and robotics structures to the collective research process. Participants must see themselves in the research and tell and share their stories. Much of the data generated for this study consisted of students visual, digital, and written work products. An Anzalduan framework, as described in this chapter, positions the *mestiza* as the arbiter of their language and their brown body as a site of knowledge.

Reconceptualizing qualitative research

Rethinking how we approach methodology was not exclusive to our methods; rather, it also brought forward reflection and discussion of our epistemological stances as researchers and participants in our work. As researchers, we are often trained in traditional Western methodological approaches, and there is little mention of decolonizing methodologies. The Anzalduan framework and critical ethnography challenged us as researchers to rethink our methodology by thinking with multiple theories that highlighted the identities, linguistic strengths, and practices of the Latinx participants in our study. Thinking with Anzalduan theories centered on Latinx voices and ways of knowing and challenged us to develop our "new *mestiza*" identities as researchers and as an assemblage.

As *mestizas* and academics, we are often expected to center our work on specific methodologies, using formulaic methods to describe and situate our participants in the research. We review the data, voice their thoughts, ideas, and imaginings, and assume to speak their truths. We take participants' lived experiences and paint them with a pen stroke as static entities. We, in effect, are *Nepantleras* living in the in-between space of our culture and language and expected to cross borders to accommodate academic literary norms. Using Anzalduan theory to support a methodological borderland to think with theory allowed for the deterritorializing of methodological language. In our study we deterritorialized methodological language by using our linguistic repertoires and languages. We positioned ourselves as *mestizas*, shared our *conocimientos*, and made a choice to italicize our Spanish because we wanted our language to stand out as spoken word. We acknowledge that others do not agree with this process (Hurtado, 2020). An Anzalduan theory provided an authentic lens that resonated as true with the collective brown body. We are our research, language, and brown bodies — disaggregating is impossible. An Anzalduan theory centered our work and our language.

It is important to provide space for brown voices to speak their linguistic truths as they live them, see them, and experience them in a white world. Brown bodies need space to enact methodologies that open pathways that reveal their linguistic brilliance and elevate their intellect, humor, and languages. As brown bodies, researchers, and participants of this study who have very similar socioeconomic, cultural, and linguistic backgrounds as the student participants, we recognize the importance of existing power dynamics. We shared our stories with the student participants to break down the power dynamics. While power dynamics still exist, such as mentor versus mentee relationships, we work to show the student participants that there is a way forward, there are resources we can share, and we are there to help as much as possible. It is not an easy path to break with methodological norms and conventions, but it is a necessary one. As Latinx, Black, and Indigenous researchers, we need to support each other as we explore and present new methodologies and theoretical and conceptual frameworks that center the needs and accomplishments of our communities. We should promote and adapt these works to showcase the incredible talent among our group and move our research and communities forward.

White researchers entering a research site that is culturally and linguistically different from their own should consider teaming with a researcher from the studied group and make them the lead or co-author in any published works. White researchers should also consider more dynamic forms of inquiry, participate in the community, and listen to the elders and the voices of the young. Asking clarifying questions is vital to this research process.

Some may see our work centered within our cultural and linguistic identities and communities as a limitation. While we do not, we understand that our critical ethnographic work is unique to our research context, participants, and our lenses as Latinx *Mestiza* researchers. Pérez-Torres (2006) posited that *mestizaje* is "an identity of the flesh" inextricably bound within the fabric of our society and politics. We do indeed identify our brown bodies/flesh positioned firmly as bridges across educational, societal, and political structures. Acknowledging the labor-intensive nature of their roles, qualitative researchers acting as bridges across different communities should be aware of the potential for burnout, particularly when there are few individuals that can act as a conduit with vulnerable and minoritized communities.

References

Alcaraz, L. (2021). *Human infrastructure*. Digital image.

Anzaldúa, G. (1987/1999). *Borderlands/La frontera: The new mestiza* (5th ed.). Aunt Lute Foundation Books.

Anzaldúa, G. (1990). *Making face, making soul: Haciendo caras: Creative and critical perspectives by feminists of color* (1st ed.). Aunt Lute Foundation Books.

Anzaldúa, G. (1993). Chicana artists: Exploring nepantla, el lugar de la frontera. *NACLA Report on the Americas, 27*(1), 37–45.

Anzaldúa, G. (2002). Preface: (Un)natural bridges, (un)safe spaces. In G. Anzaldúa, & A. Keating (Eds.), *This bridge we call home: Radical visions for transformation* (pp. 1–5) Routledge.

Anzaldúa, G., & Keating, A. (2002). *This bridge we call home: Radical visions for transformation.* Routledge.

Beltran, C. (2004). Patrolling borders: Hybrids, hierarchies and the challenge of mestizaje. *Political Research Quarterly, 57*(4), 595–607.

Bloome, D., & Green, J. (2018). Ethnography. In B. Frey (Ed.), *The Sage encyclopedia of educational research, measurement, and evaluation* (pp. 618–623). Sage.

Bogue, R (2011). The minor. In C. Stivale (Ed.), *Gilles Deleuze: Key concepts* (pp. 131–141). Routledge.

Bruner, J. (1986). *Actual minds, possible worlds.* Harvard University Press.

Burke, A., Okrent, A., & Hale, K. (2022). *The state of U.S. science and engineering 2022: Executive summary.* National Science Board. Retrieved on 17 November 2024 from https://ncses.nsf.gov/pubs/nsb20221/executive-summary

Calderón, D., Bernal, D.D., Huber, L.P., Malagón, M.C., & Vélez, V.N. (2012). A chicana feminist epistemology revisited: Cultivating ideas a generation later. *Harvard Educational Review, 82*(4), 513–539.

Center for the Advancement of Informal Science Education (CAISE). (2018). *Broadening participation task force: February 2018 update.* Retrieved on 17 November 2024 from https://informalscience.org/broadening-participation-task-force-february-2018-update/

Change the Equation (2017). *Ending the double disadvantage: Ensuring STEM opportunities in our poorest schools.* Retrieved on 17 November 2024 from https://www.ecs.org/wp-content/uploads/CTE_STEM-Desert-Brief_FINAL.pdf

Ciechanowski, K., Bottoms, S., Fonseca, A.L., & St. Clair, T. (2015). Should Rey Mysterio drink gatorade? Cultural competence in afterschool STEM programming. *Afterschool Matters, 21,* 29–37.

Creswell, J., & Poth, C.N. (2018). *Qualitative inquiry & research design: Choosing among five approaches* (4th ed.). Sage.

Deleuze, G. & Guattari, F. (1987). *A thousand plateaus: Capitalism and schizophrenia.* University of Minnesota Press. [Originally published as *Mille plateaux: Capitalisme et schizophrénie II.* Paris: Minuit, 1980.]

Delgado Bernal, D. (1998). Using a Chicana feminist epistemology in educational research. *Harvard Educational Review, 68*(4), 555–582.

Djonko-Moore, C.M., Leonard, J., Holifield, Q., Bailey, E.B., & Almughyirah, S.M. (2017). Using culturally relevant experiential education to enhance urban children's knowledge and engagement in science. *Journal of Experiential Education, 41*(2), 137–153.

Fitzpatrick, K., & May, S. (2022). *Critical ethnography and education: Theory, methodology, and ethics.* Routledge.

García, O., & Li, W. (2014). *Translanguaging: Language, bilingualism and education.* Palgrave Macmillan.

Garza, N. E., Rodriguez, S. L., & Espino, M. L. (2023). Nepantla aquí, Nepantla allá: The borderlands of identity from Mexican-origin women in STEM. *Journal of Hispanic Higher Education*, 22(2), 130–145.

Hurtado, A. (2020). *Intersectional Chicana feminisms: Sitios y lenguas*. The University of Arizona Press.

Jewitt, C., & Kress, G. (2003). *Multimodal literacy*. Peter Lang.

Kress, G. (2000). Design and transformation: New theories of meaning. In B. Cope, & M. Kalantzis (Eds.), *Multiliteracies: Literacy learning and the design of social futures* (pp. 153–161). Routledge.

Kress, G., & van Leeuwen, T. (1996). *Reading images: The grammar of visual design*. Routledge.

Lather, P. A. (2007). *Getting lost: Feminist efforts toward a double(d) science*. State University of New York Press.

May, S. (2023). Critical ethnography, language, race/ism and inequity in education: Charting the field. In S. May & B. Caldas (Eds.), *Critical ethnography, language, race/ism and education* (pp. 31–52). Multilingual Matters.

Mazzei. (2017). Following the contour of concepts toward a minor inquiry. *Qualitative Inquiry*, 23(9), 675–685.

Mazzei, L. A. (2021). Postqualitative inquiry: Or the necessity of theory. *Qualitative Inquiry*, 27(2), 198–200.

McGee, E. O., & Robinson, W. H. (2020). *Diversifying STEM: Multidisciplinary perspectives on race and gender*. Rutgers University Press.

McWhirter, E. H., & Cinamon, R. G. (2021). Old problem, new perspectives: Applying Anzaldúan concepts to underrepresentation in STEM. *Journal of Career Development*, 48(6), 877–892.

Mikhaeli, C. A., & Baskerville, R. L. (2019). Using semiotics to analyze representational complexity in social media. *Information and Organization*, 29, 1–19.

Moraga, & Anzaldúa, G. (1983). *This bridge called my back: Writings by radical women of color* (2nd ed.). Kitchen Table: Women of Color Press.

Morrison, T. (1993, December 7). *Nobel lecture*. Retrieved on 17 November 2024 from https://www.nobelprize.org/prizes/literature/1993/morrison/lecture/

Palmer, D., & Caldas, B. (2016). Critical ethnography. In K. King, Y. Lai, & S. May (Eds.), *Research methods in language and education* (pp. 1–12). Springer.

Pérez-Torres, R. (2006). *Mestizaje: Critical uses of race in Chicano culture*. University of Minnesota Press.

St. Pierre, E. S. (2014). A brief and personal history of post qualitative research: Toward "post inquiry." *Journal of Curriculum Theorizing*, 30(2), 2–19.

Street, B. V. (1995). *Social literacies: Critical approaches to literacy in development, ethnography, and education*. Longman.

Thomas, J. (2021). *Doing critical ethnography* (1st ed.). Sage.

Ung, L., Labadin, J., & Mohamad, F. S. (2022). Computational thinking for teachers: Development of a localised E-learning system. *Computers and Education*, 177, 104379.

Unrau, N. J., Alvermann, D. E., & Sailors, M. (2019). Literacies and their investigation through theories and models in D. E. Alvermann, N. J. Unrau, M. Sailors, & R. B. Ruddell (Eds.), *Theoretical models and processes of literacy* (pp. 3–34). Routledge.

CHAPTER 8

Families' literacies of (in)visibilty

Methodological approaches to understanding precarity without culpability

Melissa Adams Corral & Sarah Gallo

University of Texas, Rio Grande Valley | Rutgers University

In our ethnographic research with mixed-status transborder families who had relocated from the U.S. to parents' hometowns in México, we have sought to better understand what we term *transborder literacies of (in)visibility*, or diasporic people's innovative interactions around texts that prepare them to move across incompatible, racializing mononational institutions divided by borders (Gallo & Adams Corral, 2023). In this chapter we adopt a transborder literacies of (in)visibility framework to trouble and unpack our research methodologies. We turn this lens to our research practices to better understand instances where transborder families' actions challenged us as researchers to think through the colonial roots of our own literacies and thinking.

Keywords: transborder, colonialism, undocumentedness, families, reflexivity, immigration, literacies

Introduction

In our research with mixed-status transborder families who relocated from the U.S. to parents' hometowns in México due to immigration policies, we proposed a transborder literacies of (in)visibility theoretical framework as an approach to center transborder families' innovative practices around texts to facilitate cross-border movements (Gallo & Adams Corral, 2023). Situated within a critical literacies approach that centers interactions around writing as social actions imbued with power relations (Freire & Macedo, 2005; Street, 1984), we defined these literacies of (in)visibility as the set of practices transborder people deploy around texts to facilitate their navigation of the varied and incompatible demands of mononational institutions and their borders. Through attention to the transgressive literacy practices families engaged in as they applied for their U.S.-born

https://doi.org/10.1075/rmal.11.08cor

children's passports from México, we learned how transborder families' unique literacy practices have allowed them to (1) broker across misaligned institutions; (2) accumulate visible documentation of their children's histories and belonging in the U.S. against an elevated burden of proof; and (3) enact measures of invisibility to protect against possible repurposing of information to surveil or deport undocumented parents living in the U.S.

Here we engage the theoretical framework of transborder literacies of (in)visibility to trouble and unpack instances where transborder families' actions challenged us to reevaluate our own literacy practices across the research process and consider how they were shaped by ongoing legacies of colonialism. As researchers working in transborder, multilingual, and other historically marginalized communities, we must confront where our own long-term training in hegemonic Western knowledge has the potential to further colonial goals, including recognizing that training in critical qualitative methodological approaches does not fully prepare us to notice and confront our reification of colonial legacies. Here we argue that the theory of transborder literacies of (in)visibility — engaged individually or within dialogic spaces — offers a lens to better notice, reflect upon, and confront these legacies in our own research practices.

Confronting colonial logics

Here we deploy the framework of transborder literacies of (in)visibility to identify moments when, despite our reflexive practices, we have difficulty understanding precarity without culpability — an idea tied to notions of personal responsibility, where suffering is assumed to represent an individual's failure to correctly navigate necessary institutions. This colonial logic normalizes the idea that people experiencing precarity have, in one way or another, done something wrong that led to their current situation. For example, to defend the Trump Administration's family separations at the border, then-Attorney General Sessions cited scripture and insisted this was the correct response to violations of "orderly" U.S. immigration policies, which he claimed "protect the weak and lawful" (Mullen, 2018). These refrains work to normalize and justify state violence as the fault of flawed individual choices. An understanding of literacies of (in)visibility allows us to make sense of the complexity of families' navigational choices amid oppressive national policies, allowing us to challenge colonial logics that would normalize suffering (Gallo & Adams Corral, 2023; Segato, 2018). The idea of precarity resulting from culpability is one lesson within a larger pedagogy of cruelty that normalizes violence and lessens empathy for marginalized community members (Segato, 2018).

Drawing from empirical examples in various ethnographic research studies across contexts, we consider moments of our own researcher sense-making around stories shared by diasporic families. In these moments, we were challenged by both the stories families shared and our reactions and in-the-moment interpretations of these stories. To better understand these moments as individual researchers, we came together dialogically and decided to turn our transborder literacies of (in)visibility framework onto ourselves to reflect on and challenge our own literacies and their ties to colonial logics.

Extending reflexivity

Applying a transborder literacies of (in)visibility theory to our own research methodologies heightened our engagement in reflexivity. Reflexivity, a core component of ethnography, is a process that has the researcher "unveil their biases and assumptions, negotiate unique socio-cultural and political contexts, and uncover various power dynamics within the research design" (Mao et al., 2016, p.1). If the aim of ethnography is to better understand the complexities of a given reality from participants' perspectives, the ethnographer needs tools to evaluate their own internalized norms to better understand participants' experiences and perspectives (Kirkland, 2014). This is particularly important for researchers benefiting from systemic hierarchies due to their social positions while committing to understanding the experiences of those who have been dehumanized by these systems (Mao et al., 2016; Paris & Winn, 2014). Some ways to engage in reflexivity during data collection include separating observations from evaluations in field notes and data logs, regular memoing, and discussing findings with participants with an openness for change and an eye toward whose understanding of realities should count (Paris & Winn, 2014).

Despite our commitment to reflexive practices, we have found there are still moments when we are unprepared or unable to see our own positionalities and assumptions, and deeper intentionality is needed (see Oliveira & Gallo, 2023). In our search to heighten reflexivity while working with transborder families across contexts, we have sought to catch ourselves when we encounter moments that Jaffe-Walter (2020) has called *breakdowns*: "when researchers struggle to make sense of events because they are not steeped in the social meanings and discourses of a new context" (p.168). During data collection and analysis, we have used this concept to interrogate moments of "profound confusion" (Jaffe-Walter, 2020, p.168), when we are unsure of — and at times find ourselves uncomfortable with — how our ways of seeing the world clash with the unfolding of interactions. Reflexivity requires us to turn our research lens back on ourselves (McDevitt, 2021; Mao et al., 2016). In this chapter we apply a literacies of (in)visibility theory to moments of discomfort and uncertainty in our research process as a tool for researchers to understand participants' complex realities in new ways.

Overview of the study and its findings

Beginning with a transborder lens

Our research partnership grew from a shared commitment to qualitative research centering on the innovative and transgressive ways children and adults in Latin America and the U.S. navigate racializing geopolitical and institutional borders to access their rights and humanity within and across the countries they call home. As scholars in fields called bilingual and immigrant education within the U.S., we choose not to label diasporic families as immigrants, as we see these terms as framings that presuppose directionality, timescales of im/permanence, or goals of assimilation for mononational belonging.

Instead, our research adopts a transborder lens. Transborderness normalizes multidirectional movements across physical and metaphorical borders, actively counters assumptions of mononational and monolingual lives as the norm, and centers the thinking of historically marginalized communities as part of a decolonizing approach to knowledge and an explicit anti-border stance (Anzaldúa, 1987; Cervantes-Soon & Carrillo, 2016; Dyrness & Sepúlveda, 2020; Mignolo, 2000). We also use the term *diasporic* to recognize the varied ways family members may feel tied to certain national communities, regardless of their present location or place of birth (Dyrness & Sepúlveda, 2020). These approaches move beyond recognizing and valuing hybridity; they seek radical reimaginations of ways of knowing and being situated in subalternity and in-betweenness, recognizing that expertise built in life at the margins can offer reconceptualizations of the colonizing hierarchies prevalent within academic settings (Cervantes-Soon & Carrillo, 2016). Although we recognize the prevalence and importance of the immigrant label in unifying a subfield in education that differentiates language-learning from lived experiences of border crossing, we prefer orientations and labels that focus on transborderness to highlight and normalize the knowledges that emerge from multidirectional movements across physical and metaphorical borders.

Overall, a transborder approach recognizes (1) the prevalence and presence of borders at and beyond the physical line demarcating nation-states; (2) the knowledge that comes with the in-betweenness from forced navigation across borders, nations, and governments; and (3) the ways the existence of borders requires a set of dehumanizing logics tied to pedagogies of cruelty that uphold colonial and racial hierarchies (Cervantes-Soon & Carrillo, 2016; Gilmore, 2022; Mignolo, 2000; Peña-Pincheira & Allweiss, 2022; Segato, 2018). As we describe below, this transborder lens was central to how we theorized families' literacies of (in)visibility.

Transborder literacies of (in)visibility

A transborder literacies of (in)visibility approach extends to a retheorizing of what counts as reading and writing. We define these literacies as "diasporic people's innovative interactions around texts that prepare them to move across incompatible mononational institutions divided by borders" (Gallo & Adams Corral, 2023, p.101). We observed how these literacies were developed by parents, who, while living undocumented in the U.S., learned to dexterously maneuver decisions around when and how to be "seen" by authorities (Lugo, 2008) or avoid detection (Minian, 2018). At times, transborder parents needed to deploy their literacies of invisibility to ensure they could continue living and working in the U.S. without access to papeles, avoiding surveillance while navigating requirements for certain kinds of textual evidence of their presence in the U.S. At other points, the same families had to develop a set of literacies of hypervisibility to ensure that their U.S.-born children's citizenship status could be proven and maintained. This meant accessing textual evidence of their child's U.S. citizenship, from apostilled birth certificates (an official government verification) to infant vaccination records (Gallo & Adams Corral, 2023). Literacies of (in)visibility involve brokering across institutions, imagining multidirectional futures into realities, and interrogating disjunctures of inequities. Parents enacted these literacies with and for their children, offering important lessons on how to navigate papeles, institutions, and borders, which we now use to examine our own researcher literacies.

Our research studies

Transborder literacies of (in)visibility provoke specific kinds of challenges to researchers because a decolonial approach extends not only to the ways we interrogate the practices of diasporic families, but also to the ways we interrogate ourselves, our perspectives, and our approaches. Here we draw upon three qualitative studies we have conducted separately with transborder families.

The first takes a critical auto/ethnographic approach (Chavez, 2012; Denzin, 2003), with Melissa studying her students' and her own experiences with a course-embedded service-learning project. The project involved working alongside transborder families recently released from border patrol custody, many of whom arrived to the U.S. after crossing numerous borders, each requiring their own set of navigational literacies (Charles & Iglesias, 2022; del Bosque, 2023; Meko, 2022). Melissa and undergraduate students worked with families to develop explicitly asset-oriented letters of introduction to teachers in their destination states (Adams Corral & Krause, 2022).

The other two studies were ethnographies Sarah conducted with transborder elementary school students (ages 5–12) from mixed-status families on both sides of the imposed border between México and the U.S. The first study was conducted in Pennsylvania as a cohort of Mexican-heritage students moved from kindergarten through second grade and aimed to understand how Mexican fathers engaged in their children's educational lives in contexts of heightened deportations (Gallo, 2017). The second study centered on the educational experiences of 10 students from mixed-status families who had recently arrived to rural Mexican schools due to U.S. immigration policies and explored the intersections of immigration and educational policies in their lives (Gallo & Adams Corral, 2023).

All three qualitative studies utilized similar data collection methods. Melissa engaged in biweekly observations of herself and her students collaborating with families in community spaces. Data collected by Melissa included her own and her students' voice memos capturing their thinking around the work with families, field notes focused specifically on her thinking and her students' expressed thinking, and students' written and video-recorded reflections. No specific identifiable data related to families was collected, as the focus of Melissa's study was the way that she and preservice teachers, all of whom lived in the México/U.S. borderlands and identified as Mexican, Mexican American, and Salvadoran-Mexican, understood, reflected on, and responded to their experiences across the semester.[3] Sarah's studies were ethnographies (Kirkland, 2014) in which she conducted weekly participant observation in transborder students' classrooms over the academic year and engaged in monthly learning with a subset of families in home and community-based settings. Across both of her studies, in-depth interviews were conducted with focal students, their caregivers, and their teachers.[4] Across these three disparate studies, engagement in transborder children's worlds provided insights into the family and school-based ways young people engaged with inequities, such as their migration status, that deeply shaped their lives.

---

3. Melissa's study was approved by her institution's IRB. Students' written consent process was conducted by a colleague who was not one of their instructors and consent forms were not shared with Melissa until after the semester had ended.

4. Sarah's studies were approved by the IRBs of U.S. universities. She also underwent processes of seeking institutional approval from the district and school administration officials in the communities where her studies were conducted in the U.S. and in México. In both studies, adults completed a full written consent process and children completed a verbal assent process. The approved studies specifically focused on issues concerning im/migration and cross-border movements.

Reflexivity in dialogue

To look across these three studies, we engaged in dialogue with one another as part of our research partnership. This partnership, which values trust and transparency as fundamental relational components, involves the use of dialogic space for sense-making. Within this context, we challenged ourselves to unpack and trouble through moments where we needed to confront aspects of our own thinking to work toward dismantling hegemonic research traditions. It is important to recognize that a key component of this space was the fact that the both of us are navigating our own bilingual lives across borders. Understanding who we are can help to provide context for the collaboration that facilitated the emergence and utility of this theory.

Melissa is a Honduran American Latina who grew up between Miami and Tegucigalpa — movements emerging from her own privileged positions, but also experiences that demonstrated multiple ways of living and being. As a young adult, she was a rebellious bilingual elementary school teacher defying language and content mandates and organizing with multilingual and transborder families to navigate an often-hostile school system (Adams Corral et al., 2024). Sarah is a queer English-Spanish speaking bilingual white woman from the U.S. who now forms part of a transborder family in which she and her family members live and learn separated, due to differential access to U.S. papers, across the México/U.S. border. Yet when she began conducting research with families about their transborder lives almost 20 years ago, she knew little about the shifting realities of borders, their exclusions, and the subaltern ways of knowing needed to navigate their textured realities. Even after many years learning from and with transborder families and the intimate ways these themes shape her familia, she knows she benefits from systems of privilege built for her whiteness and U.S. passport, in which she is rarely doubted in her rights to move across borders.

Like many of the ways transborder children and families engage in literacies of (in)visibility via a collective to enact change, our research collectively has become an ofrenda to un-learn the colonizing literacies from our upbringings and their deeply rooted instantiations in our U.S.-based academic realities. In our collaboration, we also developed a practice of thinking deeply about one another's research approaches and prioritized this as a theme in our data analysis discussions. These discussions, and the theory of literacies of (in)visibility, have pushed us to challenge and seek to understand the ways of thinking that can make it difficult for scholars to recognize the deftness of transborder families' navigational literacies.

Within our discussions, we approached one another's and our own experiences thinking, feeling, and being within the communities where we conducted our separate research studies with curiosity. This curiosity is part of the intentional work needed to "make the unconscious conscious" (Pyles, 2021, p.72). There were moments at the individual level where, during our data collection and analysis, we identified breakdowns through locating instances of emotional reactions, including discomfort (Jaffe-Walter, 2020). We shared these moments with one another to create space for dialogue and understanding as part of a mutual commitment to "deep listening, integration of experiences, and connecting the personal and political" (Pyles, 2021, p.72).

In all three studies, we intentionally created space for reflexivity through practices such as separating observations from questions and evaluations in field notes and logs (Emerson et al., 2011) and writing research memos to explore instances that sparked more thinking and questioning. Memos also served as spaces to delve further into our own thinking about what we were seeing, hearing, and experiencing. Memos where we could identify breakdowns were brought into conversation. Individually, we identified breakdowns through their personal impact — we were troubled by these moments because they grabbed and kept our attention and spurred our recognition of how transborder literacies of (in)visibility could call us into self-examination. Within our dialogic space, we each read and considered the other's memos in relation to our conceptualization of transborder literacies of (in)visibility. Together, in a small-scale dialog circle, we discussed the questions and assumptions raised by our experiences in the field and considered how those ideas were shaped by a particular set of literacies (Pyles, 2021). Applying transborder literacies of (in)visibility to our ways of understanding diasporic families brought our attention to our own ideas and interpretations and heightened our awareness of how transborder families' literacy practices might be interpreted by others. Thinking together about our own thoughts, feelings, and interpretations through a literacies of (in)visibility lens, we realized we needed to adapt our practices of reflexivity more intentionally, paying careful attention to how we examine, read, write, understand, and represent our thinking alongside the communities with whom we work.

Methodological discussion: Rethinking theory for more equitable research

Below we use the theoretical approach of transborder literacies of (in)visibility to trouble and unpack instances where transborder families' actions challenged us as researchers to think through our own literacies and the extent to which they are influenced by thought patterns rooted in colonialism. These include moments when — despite our reflexive practices — we have difficulty understanding precarity without culpability when making sense of the decisions of families navigating systems from positions very different from our own. To do so, we explore four examples of how we have sought to confront lines of colonial thinking that reflect perspectives and ideologies we have carried with us for generations. In these examples, some of these ways of understanding the world that we have been steeped in are challenged by the literacies of (in)visibility transborder families have developed to navigate a set of circumstances that defy colonial logics. These examples transverse multiple research sites, contexts, and timescales, demonstrating the ways that attending to our own reactions and ideas are crucial aspects of research with/in multilingual and transborder communities from Melissa's work in bilingual teacher education in the México/U.S. borderlands and Sarah's ethnographies with transborder families in México and Pennsylvania. We highlight these four examples because they involved a range of consequential gate-keeping moments related to crossing geopolitical borders across space, time, and participants that our previous tools of reflexivity, engaged as solitary researchers, were not dislodging. We showcase the ways the theory of literacies of (in)visibility, especially in dialogic space, can mobilize reflexive research practices.

Un-documenting transborder subalternity

In these first two examples from our research, we demonstrate how we read, documented, and navigated whether and how to contest the dehumanizing ways that transborder families experience subalternity. In both instances our traditional researcher literacies misread families' precarity as potentially relating to culpability, but our ways of documenting, unpacking, and confronting it differed.

What we don't write in our field notes

The first example occurred with Sarah in 2011 in Pennsylvania, in a context where local police had just adopted data sharing programs such as Secure Communities — born out of the "show me your papers" lineage of immigration practices that surveilled brown, male bodies in particular. Undocumented family members regularly engaged literacies of (in)visibility to avoid in-print existence in U.S. institutions and to evade the growing number of routine interactions far from the physical border that could lead to their surveillance and potential deportation (Vieira, 2016). During a study with elementary school-aged children and their fathers, Sarah went outside to join students for recess when a second grader she had worked with over the past three years approached her. Sarah wrote:

Field Note: …in tiny, tiny voices Princess tells me in Spanish that the police took her father, and he is going back to México. My ears cannot believe these words. I think I am mishearing. Her cousin is talking about seeing him being handcuffed, his hands behind his back, and put in a police car. This happened right outside their house. I hear the words, but I absolutely cannot believe them. Princess' eyes start to well up with tears, and I pull her in for a huge hug. Later that night her mother explained that he had dropped a soda bottle in front of their house as a police cruiser drove by, leading to the police officers checking his documentation status based on his infraction of littering.

Personal Note: This has really saddened me. I don't have a better way to put it. And I don't think it's just that it happened to a family I know, or a family in the project, but the actual family that it happened to was probably the family that I least expected it to happen to. Why? Because her father has lived here since he was 10 years old? Because he speaks English (and Spanish) fluently? Because of his NY-Puebla style and personality? Because he has talked at length about not being able to imagine going back (to México) to live, how he could never imagine living in México, and I kind of agree? Because on some level I probably thought he might have papers — because of the ease with which he has jobs, his big car, how long he's been here, who knows?

Re-analyzing this interaction from a literacies of (in)visibility theory pushes us to reflect upon what was included and excluded in this field note and personal note. Although qualitative research methodology texts highlight the importance of documenting our thoughts and reactions so we can challenge them (Bhattacharya, 2017; Emerson et al., 2011), we have not sufficiently unpacked the conflicts that emerge when these practices intersect with commitments to humanizing research approaches (Paris & Winn, 2014). This may mean that we seek to suppress or silence thoughts and reactions we recognize as harmful towards our participants, intending to prioritize respect and care for the relationships we are building. This is important — we should attempt to identify thoughts that are not helpful for certain aspects of our research questions and take care to consider which stories are and are not ours to share. Yet, humanizing approaches to research also require recognizing, making space for, and acknowledging our own messy, in-process humanity. This is the very space we wish to engage in with our participants, but one that cannot fully exist without our willingness to share in and turn our gaze to ourselves. In the field note above, Sarah described the first of now many instances in which children told her about a violent government-sponsored family-separation due to exclusions from rights to belonging. In her reflection she drew upon her traditional literacies of observation and rational inference making about people and their lives, unearthing how she imagined Princess' father as less likely to face deportation because of the ways he moved through daily life in the U.S. with familiarity and ease compared with most transborder adults she knew.

Most notable, however, were Sarah's decisions of what *not* to include in her field notes. Thoughts linked to precarity without culpability occasionally crept into her mind, such as wondering if all Princess's father had really done was litter, or if there was potentially something else their family had opted not to share with her, perhaps engaging literacies of (in)visibility with Sarah to protect their family's precarious situation. Back in 2011, Sarah initially knew very little about how deportation-based immigration regimes operated and had internalized the Obama Administration's rhetoric claiming deportations were focused on dangerous criminals. So when Sarah began learning from transborder children's experiences with undocumentedness, she experienced a breakdown across the colonial logics she had subconsciously internalized and the dehumanizing realities being experienced by a family she knew well. Her reaction was to push away thoughts about culpability. Indeed, Sarah remembers feeling ashamed to have thought them at all and did not desire to codify them in her notes or reflections. Yet having these thoughts, and not having a process to truly contest them, closed opportunities to confront the root of her understandings of precarity as the result of culpability. This intentional withholding foreclosed necessary space to help her contest Western norms that blame individuals' actions. In this second example, we see how Melissa began to document, name, and contest this pathologizing logic in her recent research with asylum-seeking families at the México/U.S. border.

Siempre hay una raíz

In the Fall of 2022, after recently beginning the letter-writing project, Melissa had an experience that forced her to examine her own reactions to and ideas about the transborder families she was meeting. As she proactively opened spaces for reflection, she began to unpack her familial and community-based colonial logics, a step required to eventually contest them.

Melissa was meeting families from a range of Latin American countries, including Honduras, one of her homelands. A literacies of (in)visibility framework illuminates the careful textual practices families deploy to be recognized as asylum-seekers — navigating when and how to go unseen or ensure that you are seen. Through this lens, it is possible to recognize how navigating life in communities experiencing high levels of violence involves complex decisions and maneuverings beyond simply choosing not to be involved in violence or seeking support from state institutions (Berg & Carranza, 2018). Instead, transborder families operate from an understanding that existing systems (in Honduras, in México, in the U.S.) were not built for them. As a result, they develop navigational skills designed for navigating hostile institutions from positions at the margins (Rivera, 2013; Loperena, 2017; Obinna, 2021).

One Sunday afternoon, Melissa was on the phone with her mother, who grew up in Honduras, and shared a bit with her about a family she had met in the albergue who had fled Honduras after experiencing a shocking act of violence. During their phone calls, they often shared stories about Honduras — mostly Melissa's mother sharing news and stories from extended family members and friends. On occasion, Melissa shared generalized stories with her mother from the people she met, in a way of adding to the understanding and perspective both she and her mother built from afar. Her sharings never identify names, family roles, or general ages of the people she has met, nor does she include specific details of their location in the country or identifiable specifics about the act of violence they experienced. Melissa's mother does not read her academic writing, so when she asks about her work during their phone conversations, Melissa finds ways to share from her thinking and learning alongside families, following traditional expectations for participant confidentiality, while allowing her mother to be privy to knowledge that too often stays within the walls of the academy.

When Melissa had initially heard this family's story, a fleeting thought ran through her head — a thought she scolded herself for, but that she documented in a personal note as a reminder to take some time to think about the thought's roots. As Melissa shared the family's story, her mother responded with that same thought, saying it aloud, giving it voice, and allowing the roots of Melissa's thought to reveal themselves. "Qué terrible. Pero con algo así, han de haberse involucrado de alguna manera." There it was, an idea Melissa herself had thought and talked back to when it crossed her own mind, announcing itself again, this time reminding her that these are not thoughts that come out of nowhere — they are ideas that we carry, ideas we have heard around us, repeated again and again. When something so terrible happens, we recognize the cruelty of the situation, only to then add a caveat: but they must have gotten involved, they must have done something to bring about their suffering.

Melissa responded to her mother with much the same language she had used to scold herself, challenging the idea that people always have clear cut choices to make, "¿Pero en realidad piensas que uno puede decidir involucrarse o no?" Her mother was open to this line of thinking, pausing and admitting that the situation in their homeland is very complicated and that choice is not always at work in the way we would hope. In a reflective memo (Emerson et al., 2011; Jackson & Mazzei, 2012) written after the conversation, Melissa sought to make sense of why she and her mother both expressed an idea that countered what they knew about life in Honduras. The memo reads:

> This idea — that people make choices that leave them at risk, was one she also probably inherited. Perhaps it's a balm of sorts — one that helps us explain the relative safety of our own family and network of friends living in Honduras. If it's just luck, that could change in any moment. If it's the protection of class privilege, then in some ways it requires facing how we are complicit in the suffering of others in Honduras. But if somehow, those most precarious are culpable, are guilty of making 'bad choices' then we can feel our own innocence....

This note demonstrates an attempt to make sense of how pedagogies of cruelty can both explain and work to normalize violence and diminish empathy. It points to how these ideas can also serve to create distance between oneself and violent systems. By suggesting that precarity requires culpability and feeling one's own innocence, those of us not presently experiencing violence can feel safer, less likely to have to encounter the violence characterizing modern life, while also ignoring the myriad ways these forms of violence police our movements, shape our relationships, and structure our time (Segato, 2018).

The prevalence of violence in many communities is also a result of ongoing legacies of settler colonialism, and the question of making "right" or "wrong" decisions is not a worthwhile approach for understanding people's efforts to navigate and survive in their community or to risk the dangers of migration (e.g., Obinna, 2021). Ultimately, this family used their literacies to analyze the options available to them and chose to leave Honduras seeking asylum, deploying literacy practices that required rendering themselves visible to U.S. institutions — an act demonstrating the ways families must deftly develop and deploy their literacies as they plan for and interact with existing state institutions. The very idea of choice is tied to societal training that there are sources of support or protection available to responsible individuals (Perez & Salter, 2019). When Melissa could pinpoint this thought, she then had a place to re-evaluate these early learnings and to use what is known about the failures of the Honduran and U.S. states (Beltrán, 2020; Loperena, 2017; Rivera, 2013) to challenge her reactions. In conversation with her mother and in reflective writing, Melissa made room for other ways of knowing and being that pushed her to challenge colonial logics that normalize violence or render people disposable (Peña-Pincheira & Allweiss, 2022; Segato, 2018). A literacies of (in)visibility lens on her own understandings provided a pathway for Melissa to better recognize and name her initial reaction and then pull back to question what made her uncomfortable about herself. In doing so, she found roots of these ideas stretching back across generations and space to begin to undo them.

Centering transborder knowledges, challenging colonial logics

In this section we explore how transborder literacies of (in)visibility can push us as researchers to better recognize how families' transborder knowledges can challenge colonial logics and pedagogies of cruelty (Segato, 2018). In the first example we unpack a set of interactions Sarah had with a transborder family in México as they applied for their U.S.-born children's passports to reveal how this theory can push us to center, rather than question, the strengths of families' epistemologies. In the second we return to Melissa's research at the physical border to push us to rethink how we conceptualize systems as rational and consistent as part of a pedagogy of cruelty. Across both examples, we demonstrate how this theory pushes us to critically question the ways we as researchers and educators — and by extension, the border thinkers who demonstrate these knowledges — view ways of knowing as reasonable, trustworthy, and intelligent.

Mis(sed) deliveries

During a year-long study with mixed-status transborder families who had relocated from the U.S. to México due to U.S. immigration practices in 2016, Sarah worked with about a dozen families to secure their U.S.-born children's passports from México. This process included a range of literacy practices with embassies, mail delivery systems that did not extend to rural transborder communities, and the documentation of children's identities and experiences in the U.S. to access the very papers they needed to re-cross the physical border. Six years had passed since Princess's father's deportation, and Sarah had spent this time learning from and with transborder families about deportation regimes. One of the families she worked with in México was renewing their children's passports from México, where their children were currently residing with their mother, Mercedes, while their father, Javier, had returned to the U.S. without access to official documentation to pay off medical debts. Because Javier could not physically be at his children's passport interviews in the U.S. embassy in México City, he had to complete and notarize an official government form documenting his permission for his children to renew their passports. He initially completed and notarized one form and sent it to Mercedes at their address in rural México a month before their embassy interviews. Several months later, Sarah wrote this field note:

Field Note: About a week ago I sent Mercedes a message to see if her daughter's passport had arrived yet.... Last I heard from Javier he had sent the notarized paper to Mercedes, and she had received it, according to him. I noted that he had paid upwards of $100 U.S. to have it sent there, which I could not believe. In the end, the delivery service he used (DHL) does not actually deliver to their small town, so the form never arrived! At first, I misunderstood Mercedes. I thought she had mailed it to México — the embajada — but it never arrived there. I was shocked because I sent her the exact address that the embajada had sent me for the form. She explained that was not the issue. Trying not to be rude, I said I would contact the embajada to see if the family could still send in the form. The embassy responded and explained that nothing could be done. Her daughter's file had been closed and they would have to start the entire process again, including paying and the interview. **Personal Note:** This was one of the moments when I got frustrated with a family for their actions. I could tell that Mercedes was mad at her husband for mailing the form to her, and not to la embajada. It took all my energy to not direct my anger toward her, not to blame anyone when I spoke with her or her daughter, and to seek out the way to be solution oriented. Indeed, I was initially fuming inside, mostly at Javier, and I cannot understand why he didn't just mail the new form to the Mexican embassy, as Mercedes and I instructed.

When this initially happened, Sarah could not comprehend Javier's decisions, and simply documenting and questioning her reactions in personal notes was not enough to unpack the colonial legacies of knowing and being that were implicated in these decisions. She subconsciously positioned him as lacking savviness in navigating U.S. and Mexican government systems, as he had not done what she saw as the U.S. embassy's simple direction – directly mailing them a notarized form. As is evident in this field note – she also moved toward blaming him and his decisions, rather than larger systems.

Yet when both authors began to re-examine Javier's decisions from a literacies of (in)visibility framework, his careful ways of knowing became much clearer. This unfolded when Trump first took office in the U.S., in a context in which his administration was seeking to delimit and rescind U.S. citizenship rights protected under the 14th Amendment. For the notarized passport form, Javier, who was undocumented, had to include his U.S. address, and it is fully reasonable that mailing this form directly to the U.S. embassy felt too risky in the politicized context, so he instead sought out ways to try and get the form to his wife in México where documentedness was not an issue, so she could submit it instead. The very literacy process of hypervisibility to secure his daughter's U.S. citizenship rights required navigating protections of invisibility from government surveillance. Viewed from this theoretical lens, his epistemologies of how systems work were savvy and protective, in ways that Sarah's original colonial literacies could not recognize.

Yet, in noting the breakdown and her own frustrations and engaging with Melissa to unpack it, Sarah drew attention to the existence of a potential missed understanding and allowed new possibilities to be considered. It required a decolonial literacy framework and a collaborative dialogic space for us to begin to question our own assumptions about how systems work, and, by extension, to critically question the epistemologies we value in our research. In the final example below, we extend this to explore how asylum-seeking families pushed us to reconsider the rationality of systems and to find other tropes from Western knowledge working as pedagogies of cruelty to justify the kinds of harm systems can do. The reflexive tools we suggest in this chapter provide a mechanism for researchers to interrogate their own reactions to and reflections of colonization's hegemonic practices.

Navigating institutions and shifting (in)visibility practices

A key factor involved in literacies of (in)visibility includes ways of deciding when to be fully visible to government entities (Gallo & Adams Corral, 2023). These decisions need to be able to shift flexibly alongside immigration policies and practices, even in ways that can seem contradictory. While there are constancies across presidential administrations, the day-to-day operations at the border can shift in subtle ways that may be less noticeable to those with official documents for border-crossing, but that are carefully attended to by those hoping to find pathways towards documented status.

While Melissa worked to establish a service-learning project at the albergue, she continued to encounter families who entered the U.S. through humanitarian parole programs, which offer temporary pathways based on certain compelling reasons for entry (U.S. Citizenship and Immigration Services [U.S.CIS], 2022). During the final months of 2022, practices around humanitarian parole were subject to change while the Biden Administration navigated attention and pressure related to the pending legal status of Title 42, an obscure public health law from the 1940s invoked by the Trump administration to block entry at the México/U.S. border. Still, families Melissa met in late 2022 had been waiting in shelters in México for the opportunity to enter the U.S., often spending months wondering if they would be given a chance (Sandoval, 2022). Recipients of humanitarian parole were given a year-long window to enter the U.S. (U.S.CIS, 2022). At the time, as soon as this window opened, shelter personnel drove families to the border for processing and court date assignation.

As Melissa met families who had received humanitarian parole, she came to learn that it was common knowledge among the community of border-crossing families that some had previously been deported during an earlier attempt to request asylum. These families, deported to third countries (i.e., neither the U.S. or México) had made their way back to México, where they waited in the shelter until being granted permission to enter. The first time a family shared a story like this, Melissa experienced confusion — the very governmental agency that had criminalized, chained, and deported this family had then processed their paperwork and granted them permission to enter the U.S. only a few months later. Despite her initial confusion, Melissa heard this story often enough that it became utterly ordinary, even receiving coverage in major news outlets (Charles & Iglesias, 2022; Rose, 2022). What can make this confounding for those unfamiliar with border-crossing practices is that families, having experienced being detained, chained, and flown to a country they had not seen in years, would return to U.S. immigration officers and attempt a legal entry once more. Melissa's experiences with government systems oriented her to a belief that the same action would lead to the same results, and that expecting different results was illogical.

The transborder families she met held different knowledges formed from very different experiences, and Melissa came to realize their repeated actions had the potential to achieve new results.

Melissa made note of both the prevalence of this story, and her initial disorientation, in her field notes. As this became more common, she used an analytical memo to think through her own confusion, and the knowledge and planning at play in families' decisions, and brought this into dialogic space with Sarah to interrogate it. By taking a perspective shaped by the theory of transborder literacies of (in)visibility, we begin with the recognition that navigating these systems involves a different set of logics — in this case, families choose to do something that, from a U.S. citizen's perspective, makes little sense. They do the same thing that once gave them profoundly negative results and, this time, they face a different outcome. Similarly, families navigating the process of applying for humanitarian parole described regularly adapting to shifting policies and practices, such as having to apply using a newly-launched mobile app. The app requires they learn a very detailed set of navigational skills to request an appointment for humanitarian parole processing at ports of entry along the México/U.S. border (del Bosque, 2023). Discussions of recently arrived immigrants in U.S. news media often point to the very low rates of success in asylum cases (Meko, 2022). Yet, from a perspective shaped by families' transborder literacies of (in)visibility, there may be logics to their decisions and hopes that are less accessible to those operating with a different set of literacies when it comes to U.S. immigration policy.

As researchers, adopting a lens that foregrounds literacies of (in)visibility from the outset allows us to recognize that transborder families may be better positioned to teach us many aspects of how our immigration systems work than official government policies or statements. Moreover, by taking a stance that locates sense, navigational skills, and knowledge within communities seeking official recognition and documented entry into the U.S., and that locates incoherence, confusion, and error within U.S. immigration systems, researchers may be better positioned to shift rhetoric around transborder families, the knowledge they bring, and the systems in place that fail to operate equitably or even coherently. By shifting this mindset, we may be able to draw similar attention to the ways these same dynamics play out within other institutional structures such as accessing health care, education, social services, and employment, thereby deploying knowledge developed at the periphery to point to the central changes needed to counter cruelty.

Implications for qualitative research on multilingual literacy development

Researcher literacies of subalternities

As qualitative researchers working across borders, we are shaped by the legacies of power structures in colonial regimes that imposed and perpetuated social orders that center some and marginalize other communities along racial, ethnic, linguistic, and national lines (Cervantes-Soon & Carrillo, 2016; Mignolo, 2000). These social orders are tied both to who is seen as having valuable knowledge, but also who is 'cosificado' or 'thingified' (Cervantes-Soon & Carrillo, 2016; Cesaire, 2000; Mignolo, 2000; Segato, 2018), a dynamic we see at work in the ways Salas and Lizárraga (Chapter 7, this volume) describe their robotics group's visceral reactions to the dehumanization of farmworkers. But we are also inherently engaged in transborder literacies ourselves — engaging with and creating texts about people's lives across borders — and our findings demonstrate that this requires our own careful navigations of (in)visibility.

We agree with Dolmage's (2018) assertion that "immigration has never been about immigration" (p.1) — these gate-keeping moments are less about nationalities, imaginary lines, and the right set of papeles. Instead, the on-going contested political project of controlling people's movements across imposed geopolitical borders reflects how colonizing powers decide who gets included and who gets excluded. These decisions about people's worthiness have always been made by other people. Who gets to decide, and the logics used, are determined by those in power systems that are structured and upheld by racializing colonial logics (Dolmage, 2018). As qualitative researchers working with children and families whose lives and learning cross borders, we too are entangled in making sense of these realities, and our re-presentations of people's realities are imbued with our ways of seeing, reading, and writing about them (Kirkland, 2014).

As researchers we need to better trouble and unlearn our un-checked logics of colonization around core qualitative research tenants such as: What counts as "true"? Who counts as "trustworthy"? Whose interpretations are worthy of recognition? What logics are embedded in our analysis and triangulation of data that we see as fitting together? Here we ask: What if we engaged our research practices with the same critical interrogations of truth? As a result of these considerations, we seek to call other researchers into dialogic spaces to formulate an intentional methodology using transborder literacies of (in)visibility. As we have shown, our traditional tools of reflexivity — such as separating out our observations from our evaluations of them — do not do enough to question our deep-seated literacies and their applications as we attempt to understand our participants' lives.

To engage this approach, we highlight (1) the ways that the ideas that "pop" into our head have actually taken root there over generations. They are not just passing thoughts, but instead reflect ideologies rooted in the logics of colonialism — logics that are convenient in excusing systemic injustice and quick to blame individuals experiencing harm; (2) our attention as researchers to our own thoughts, as well as those shared by our participants. This is needed if we are to challenge the pervasiveness of colonial logics; and (3) the understanding that pushing back on those ideas can involve inviting in families' literacies of (in)visibility as the lens through which we understand their experiences. We build these understandings by being willing to confront ourselves, but also by building dialogic spaces with other researchers to support one another in our contestations. Together we can better build language to counter the colonizing literacies and legacies that impede people from seeing, knowing, and relating to one another.

To engage literacies of (in)visibility as researchers requires relational approaches in analysis and presentation of research, collaborating with others who share a commitment to dialogical relationships and to recognizing the knowledge within transborder communities. Relationships are key to countering pedagogies of cruelty — and those relationships include collaborative, dialogical relationships among researchers and trusted loved ones. By sharing our data within established trusting partnerships, we allow others to help us see ourselves better. Collaborations can bring other communities to the table or simply act as a mirror that helps us more clearly see ourselves (Pyles, 2021). This may help us to question what may appear natural to us (Peña-Pincheira & Allweiss, 2022). Using a literacies of (in)visibility framework to unpack our own thinking builds our capacities to work with and be answerable to communities experiencing marginalization. It can help us challenge the ways systems operate to exclude, marginalize, or otherwise oppress the communities we claim to support.

In this chapter we have traced one of the logics that facilitate the perpetuation of the violence of settler colonialism, a way of thinking about precarity as requiring culpability that can work to allow researchers to harm the very communities we seek to accompany. This is an example of how pedagogies of cruelty work to "diminish life and reduce empathy for the suffering of others" (Peña-Pincheira & Allweiss, 2022, p. 11). As we learn these ways of thinking, they become much easier to repeat, and violence becomes easier to accept, tolerate, or even ignore. Here, we turned the theory of literacies of (in)visibility on our own researcher practices to challenge some of the insidious *raíces* of colonial thinking within ourselves, and to seek potential escape hatches, or crawl spaces (Moses & Cobb, 2001) where building other ways of researching becomes possible.

References

Adams Corral, M., & Krause, G. (2022). *"How do I work with my newcomer students?": Labels and their implications for teaching* [Webinar]. TODOS: Mathematics for All.

Adams Corral, M., Krause, G. H., & Maldonado Rodríguez, L. (2024). "Va a cambiar"-identifying and rejecting border patrol pedagogies in a Dual Language Classroom. *Journal of Latinos and Education*, 23(3), 1186–1204.

Anzaldúa, G. (1987). *Borderlands/La frontera: The new Mestizo.* Aunt Lute Books.

Beltrán, C. (2020). *Cruelty as citizenship: How migrant suffering sustains white democracy.* University of Minnesota Press.

Berg, L. A., & Carranza, M. (2018). Organized criminal violence and territorial control: Evidence from northern Honduras. *Journal of Peace Research*, 55(5), 566–581.

Bhattacharya, K. (2017). *Fundamentals of qualitative research: A practical guide.* Routeledge.

Cervantes-Soon, C., & Carrillo, J. (2016). Toward a pedagogy of border thinking: Building on Latin@ students' subaltern knowledge. *The High School Journa,l* 99(4), 282–301.

Cesiare, A. (2000). *Discourse on colonialism.* Monthly Review Press. (Original work published 1955).

Charles, J., & Iglesias, J. A. (2022, July 1). Haiti's brain drain: Educated youth are leaving the country as fast as they can. *The Miami Herald.* Retrieved on 17 November 2024 from https://pulitzercenter.org/stories/haitis-brain-drain-educated-youth-are-leaving-country-fast-they-can

Chavez, M. S. (2012). Autoethnography, a Chicana's methodological research tool: The role of storytelling for those who have no choice but to do critical race theory. *Equity & Excellence in Education*, 45(2), 334–348.

del Bosque, M. (2023, February 8). Facial recognition bias frustrates black asylum applicants to us, advocates say. *The Guardian.* Retrieved on 17 November 2024 from https://www.theguardian.com/us-news/2023/feb/08/us-immigration-cbp-one-app-facial-recognition-bias

Denzin, N. K. (2003). *Performance ethnography: Critical pedagogy and the politics of culture.* Sage.

Dolmage, J. T. (2018). *Disabled upon arrival: Eugenics, immigration, and the construction of race and disability.* The Ohio State University Press.

Dyrness, A., & Sepúlveda III, E. (2020). *Border thinking: Latinx youth decolonizing citizenship.* University of Minnesota Press.

Emerson, R. M., Fretz, R. I., & Shaw, L. L. (2011). *Writing ethnographic fieldnotes.* University of Chicago press.

Freire, P., & Macedo, D. (2005). *Literacy: Reading the word and the world.* Routledge.

Gallo, S. (2017). *Mi padre: Mexican immigrant fathers and their children's education.* Teachers College Press.

Gallo, S., & Adams Corral, M. (2023). Transborder literacies of (in)visibility. *Journal of Literacy Research*, 55(1), 101–123.

Gilmore, R. W. (2022). *Abolition geography: Essays towards liberation.* Verso Books.

Jackson, A. Y., & Mazzei, L. (2012). *Thinking with theory in qualitative research: Viewing data across multiple perspectives.* Routledge.

doi Jaffe-Walter, R. (2020). Into the breakdown: Embracing ethnographic confusion in challenging nationalist policy truths. *International Journal of Qualitative Studies in Education*, 33(2), 166–173.

doi Kirkland, D. (2014). Why I study culture and why it matters: Humanizing ethnographies in social science research. In D. Paris & M. Winn (Eds.), *Humanizing research: Decolonizing qualitative inquiry with youth and communities* (pp. 179–200). Sage.

doi Loperena, C. A. (2017). Settler violence? Race and emergent frontiers of progress in Honduras. *American Quarterly*, 69(4), 801–807.

Lugo, A. (2008). *Fragmented lives, assembled parts: Culture, capitalism, and conquest at the U.S.-México border*. University of Texas Press.

doi Mao, L., Mian Akram, A., Chovanec, D., & Underwood, M. L. (2016). Embracing the spiral: Researcher reflexivity in diverse critical methodologies. *International Journal of Qualitative Methods*, 15(1), 1609406916681005.

doi McDevitt, S. E. (2021). "Don't be afraid": Exploring methodological relationships in (re)searching the experiences of immigrant teachers of color. *Multicultural Perspectives*, 23(1), 40–47.

Meko, H. (2022, November 3). Migrants encounter 'chaos and confusion' in New York immigration courts. *The New York Times*. Retrieved on 17 November 2024 from https://www.nytimes.com/2022/11/03/nyregion/ny-immigration-courts-migrants.html

Mignolo, W. (2000). *Local histories/global designs: Coloniality, subaltern knowledges, and border thinking*. Princeton University Press.

doi Minian, A. R. (2018). *Undocumented lives: The untold story of Mexican migration*. Harvard University Press.

Moses, R., & Cobb, C. E. (2001). *Radical equations: Civil rights from Mississippi to the Algebra Project*. Beacon Press.

Mullen, L. (2018, June 15). The fight to define Romans 13. *The Atlantic*. Retrieved on 17 November 2024 from https://www.theatlantic.com/ideas/archive/2018/06/romans-13/562916/

doi Obinna, D. N. (2021). Seeking sanctuary: Violence against women in El Salvador, Honduras, and Guatemala. *Violence Against Women*, 27(6–7), 806–827.

doi Oliveira, G. & Gallo, S. (2023). "I have a story for you: Im/migrant children's politicized funds of knowledge and the role of the researcher. *International Journal of Qualitative Studies in Education*, 36(10), 1966–1980.

doi Paris, D., & Winn, M. T. (Eds.). (2014). *Humanizing research: Decolonizing qualitative inquiry with youth and communities*. Sage.

doi Peña-Pincheira, R. S., & Allweiss, A. (2022). Counter-pedagogies of cruelty across Abya Yala: A move with otherwise present-futurities. *Educational Studies*, 58(5–6), 581–595.

doi Perez, M. J., & Salter, P. S. (2019). Trust, innocence, and individual responsibility: Neoliberal dreams of a colorblind peace. *Journal of Social Issues*, 75(1), 267–285.

Pyles, L. (2021). *Progressive community organizing: Reflective practice in a globalizing world*. Routledge.

doi Rivera, L. G. (2013). *Territories of violence: State, marginal youth, and public security in Honduras*. Springer.

Rose, J. (2022, September 7). *After Del Rio, some Haitian migrants found safety in the U.S. But many have not* [Radio broadcast]. NPR: Morning Edition. Retrieved on 17 November 2024 from https://www.npr.org/2022/09/07/1120775143/after-del-rio-some-haitian-migrants-found-safety-in-the-u-s-but-many-have-not

Sandoval, E. (2022, December 27). *At a crowded border camp in México, frustration and shattered hopes.* The New York Times. Retrieved on 17 November 2024 from https://www.nytimes.com/2022/12/27/us/title-42-border-mexico-migrants.html

Segato, R. L. (2018). *Contra-pedagogías de la crueldad.* Prometeo Libros.

Street, B. V. (1984). *Literacy in theory and practice.* Cambridge University Press.

U.S. Citizenship and Immigration Services (U.S.CIS). (2022). *Humanitarian or Significant Public Benefit Parole for Individuals Outside the U.S.* Retrieved on 17 November 2024 from https://www.uscis.gov/humanitarian/humanitarianpublicbenefitparoleindividualsoutsideU.S.

Vieira, K. (2016). *American by paper: How documents matter in immigrant literacy.* University of Minnesota Press.

CHAPTER 9

Commentary: Advancing theory through multilingual literacy qualitative research

Jim McKinley
University College London

This commentary on Part 2 of *Innovative Qualitative Methodologies in Multilingual Literacy Development Research: Amplifying Voices from Immigrant, Transnational, and Refugee Communities* focuses upon some of the ways in which qualitative literacy researchers have begun to rethink the role of theory in their research methodologies. Insights from the chapters are presented in light of some of the author's own work on innovating and theorizing methods and Applied Linguistics research, focusing on the affordances and challenges of qualitative methodological approaches and their contributions to a more equitable and ethical research landscape

Keywords: qualitative, literacy, multilingual, methodology, theory

Introduction

Qualitative research methodologies in Applied Linguistics research offer invaluable in-depth perspectives through which the intricate dynamics of language use and acquisition can be explored. These methodologies challenge researchers to rethink theoretical frameworks and methodological approaches, particularly in the context of multilingual literacy research. In this commentary on the chapters in this volume by Kim et al. (Chapter 6), Salas and Lizárraga Dueñas (Chapter 7), and Adams Corral and Gallo (Chapter 8), I discuss insights from the chapters in light of some of my own work on innovating and theorizing methods and Applied Linguistics research, focusing on the affordances and challenges of qualitative methodological approaches and their contributions to a more equitable and ethical research landscape. The basis for these arguments were presented in my introduction chapter to *The Routledge Handbook of Research Methods in Applied Linguistics* (McKinley & Rose, 2020).

In the handbook chapter, I underscored a critical need for innovation and deeper theorization within Applied Linguistics research methods, highlighting a

https://doi.org/10.1075/rmal.11.09mck

comparative lack of methodological theorization against fields like psychology. I called for an advanced theoretical understanding to propel the field forward (McKinley, 2020). I noted evolving research designs, including experimental designs, case study research, and various forms of ethnography, each contributing to a broader methodological repertoire capable of addressing the intricate realities of language learning and use. Overall, the handbook advocates for a reimagined approach to research methods in Applied Linguistics, promoting both synchronic and diachronic analyses to generate new knowledge and theorizations. There is a clear push for methodological diversity and theoretical depth in exploring the complexities of Applied Linguistics in a globalized context, highlighting the strengths of qualitative methods. As emphasized by the three chapters in this part of the volume as the focal point of this commentary, qualitative approaches offer great potential to advance theory in multilingual literacy research.

Affordances of qualitative approaches

Multilingual literacy, a field reflecting the intersection of language, identity, and culture, requires research methodologies as dynamic as the phenomena it seeks to understand. Contemporary qualitative research in this area has significantly benefited from innovative, adaptive methodologies responsive to complex linguistic landscapes and global influences. Advancing such methodologies in Applied Linguistics research through innovative theorization has been a concern of mine throughout my academic career, resulting in a number of recent arguments put forward in a range of outputs. Based on the handbook and editorial introduction chapter already mentioned, I extended related arguments in a thought piece, a book review, an empirical research article, and a 'research in progress' report. I will briefly summarize those arguments before moving into my commentary on the three chapters in this volume section.

In an invited thought piece for the *Journal of Second Language Writing* (McKinley, 2022a), I extended the argument by advocating for a mixed-methods approach that incorporates ecological perspectives to grapple with the intricacies of second language (L2) writing (see also Hampson & McKinley, 2023, on more general mixed methods approaches in Applied Linguistics research). I also highlighted as a potential contribution to multilingual literacy theory the concept of 'Ubuntu translanguaging pedagogy,' a model that acknowledges and utilizes the multilingual context in writing to create meaningful connections among diverse readers. This piece was written in tandem with a book review of *Multilingual Literacy* (McKinley, 2022b), in which I emphasized the need for flexibility in research methodologies, focusing on how interactions outside the classroom contribute to multilingual literacy. The exploration of emojis in digital communication probes the potential of these symbols to act as a universal language, suggesting the expansion of translanguaging teaching practices.

I later built on these arguments in an effort to advance reflexive qualitative inquiry in multilingual research. Along with fellow English medium instruction (EMI) research colleagues, we used a reflexive framework to delve into the impacts of our multilingual research practices in EMI in China and Turkey (McKinley et al., 2024). We highlighted the evolution of multilingualism's conceptualization, which has led to changes in research methodologies. Our study illustrates how a translingual mindset equips researchers to navigate the unpredictability of multilingual contexts, with translanguaging emerging as a significant tool in enhancing research quality and participant engagement. The reporting of this study was included in a colloquium on rethinking EMI policy and practice by researching multilingually, reported by Zheng et al. (2024). The colloquium advocated for a redefinition of EMI, highlighting research that promotes an ecological and holistic understanding of 'EMI as lived.'

The works collectively argue for a paradigm shift in multilingual literacy research. The arguments make a case for methodologies that are as flexible and responsive as the linguistic realities they aim to document. The future of multilingual literacy research lies in its capacity to embrace methodological innovation and theorization, adapt to global and technological transformations, and remain inclusive of the myriad ways individuals engage with language. Through such a comprehensive approach, researchers can provide a more representative and nuanced understanding of multilingual literacy, steering clear of simplistic or monolithic representations.

Rethinking theory and methodology

The engagement with theory in qualitative research necessitates a critical stance, as traditional frameworks may not fully capture the dynamic nature of literacy practices across languages and cultures. Thus, researchers develop new perspectives or reinterpret existing theories based on empirical findings, fostering a dialectical relationship between theory and data. In my reading of the three chapters by Kim et al. (Chapter 6), Salas and Lizárraga Dueñas (Chapter 7), and Adams Corral and Gallo (Chapter 8), I found their methodologies and theoretical perspectives illuminating. Each chapter, through its unique focus, contributes to a broader understanding of innovations, connections, equity, ethics, and future directions in the field. I provide an integrated discussion of these chapters with consideration to innovations in rethinking theory, making links between the chapters before then moving onto discussions of equity and ethics in this research. I close with thoughts about where I see this research taking the field.

Innovations in rethinking theory

In Kim et al.'s introduction of the concept of Translanguaging Play-Based Family Literacy (PBFL) (Chapter 6), the researchers integrate the Korean cultural practice of 'suda' into their methodology. This approach avoids traditional didactic literacy instruction in favor of play-based interactions that occur naturally within the context of family dynamics and cultural practices. By doing so, they explain the nuanced ways in which children develop literacy in multilingual settings (in this case, Korean-American children of the researchers who are all transnational mothers and immigrant teacher educators from South Korea), highlighting the importance of cultural context and familial interaction in the learning process. The use of 'suda' is particularly innovative, as it fosters an ethical exploration of children's literacy practices, representing a significant advance in qualitative research methodologies that prioritize the participants' cultural and linguistic heritage.

In Salas and Lizárraga Dueñas's employment of an Anzalduan framework to bridge language learning with STEM education (Chapter 7), the authors focus on the multimodal literacy experiences of Latinx students. Their work is a testament to the potential of integrating sociocultural and semiotic dimensions into literacy research, challenging the boundaries of traditional literacy paradigms. This decolonial framework acknowledges the linguistic identities of students and reconceptualizes literacy as encompassing various modes of meaning-making. The chapter offers a transformative approach that advocates for educational practices that are inclusive of students' diverse linguistic and cultural backgrounds.

In Adams Corral and Gallo's addressing of the literacies of (in)visibility in transborder families (Chapter 8), the authors critique the colonization logics prevalent in conventional qualitative research. They propose a methodological innovation that embraces dialogic and collaborative research practices, aligning with ethical considerations that respect the agency and identity of multilingual learners. By foregrounding the experiences of individuals navigating precarious circumstances, their approach underscores the need for research methodologies that comprehensively capture the intricacies of transborder literacies.

Collectively, these three chapters reflect a move towards culturally integrated research methods that engage participants as central to the research process. They embrace the diversity of multilingual learners' experiences and advocate for ethical research practices that honor participants' linguistic and cultural identities. The proposed methodological reconceptualizations contribute to a broader understanding of literacy, encouraging researchers to adopt expansive views of literacy practices.

Connected themes between chapters

Giving further consideration to tying together the three chapters, I found several strong connections of methodological innovations with shared objectives. These range from embedding cultural norms into research practice to redefining literacy in a manner that transcends traditional academic boundaries.

Kim et al.'s use of the 'suda' approach within a PBFL framework (Chapter 6) signifies a deep respect for cultural narratives and the informal, yet crucial, literacy interactions that occur naturally in family settings. This method represents a paradigm shift in literacy research, pivoting away from rigid, school-centric models and toward those that encapsulate the organic interplay of languages in multicultural homes. This approach resonates with the work of Salas and Lizárraga Dueñas (Chapter 7), who utilize an Anzalduan framework to link language learning with STEM disciplines, thereby recognizing a more comprehensive literacy that includes, but is not limited to, numerical and scientific fluency. Their integration of cultural identity into learning processes foregrounds the role of linguistic diversity as a cornerstone of educational development.

Adams Corral and Gallo (Chapter 8), meanwhile, address the hidden narratives within transnational family experiences, shedding light on the literacy practices that flourish in the interstices of cultures, languages, and nations. Their dialogic approach embraces the complexities of migration and the multifaceted identities of learners, who often navigate multiple linguistic landscapes. This focus on 'invisible literacies' not only underscores the adaptive strategies developed by migrant communities but also the ethical responsibility of researchers to approach these communities' narratives with the distinction and dignity they deserve.

When these innovative methodologies are viewed together, a strong commitment to cultural sustenance and participant-centered research becomes apparent. Each chapter stresses the importance of viewing literacy through a culturally anchored lens that respects participants' lived experiences and linguistic repertoires, much like the researching multilingually framework we used to reflect on our EMI research (McKinley et al., 2024). Such approaches inherently challenge the limitations of conventional literacy paradigms that often neglect the vibrancy and complexity of multilingual environments. In these three chapters, the scholars' work collectively underscores the need for research methods that not only acknowledge but also contribute to the cultural and linguistic assets of communities that are frequently marginalized in academic discourse.

Additionally, these chapters are united by an expansion of the definitions of literacy. Traditional notions of literacy often fail to capture the full spectrum of communicative practices prevalent in multilingual contexts. By broadening the scope to include play-based literacy, as suggested by Kim et al. (Chapter 6), and integrating technological proficiency and STEM literacies, as proposed by Salas and Lizárraga Dueñas (Chapter 7), these authors advocate for a more inclusive understanding of what it means to be literate in the 21st century. Adams Corral and Gallo (Chapter 8) further this expansion by addressing the literacy experiences of transborder individuals, which often involve skills and knowledge that go unrecognized in mainstream education. This expanded conception of literacy implies a shift from a singular focus on reading and writing to an acknowledgement of the varied ways people communicate, learn, and express their identities. It reflects an understanding that literacy is a complex tool for navigating life, inclusive of the arts, sciences, and digital fields. Moreover, this approach recognizes that literacy is not only a medium for education but also a means for social participation and empowerment, particularly for those from immigrant, transnational, and refugee backgrounds.

Equity in literacy research

The combined methodologies presented in the works of Kim et al. (Chapter 6), Salas and Lizárraga Dueñas (Chapter7), and Adams Corral and Gallo (Chapter 8) demonstrate an effort to enrich multilingual literacy development research through equitable approaches. Their strategies highlight the value of integrating home and community contexts into literacy research, reframing educational paradigms to include diverse cultural narratives, and bringing visibility to the literacy practices of marginalized populations.

In emphasizing the richness of translanguaging practices within Korean American families, Kim et al.'s work on PBFL practices (Chapter 6) contributes to a more equitable understanding of literacy that recognizes the full linguistic repertoire of multilingual learners. This acknowledgment of the varied and vibrant linguistic repertoires found in home environments democratizes literacy and challenges deficit perspectives prevalent in research that traditionally privileges monolingual standards. Salas and Lizárraga Dueñas (Chapter7) bring forth an Anzalduan framework in STEM education to center Latinx students' experiences and knowledge, thereby advocating for a curriculum inclusive of linguistic and cultural backgrounds. This move towards inclusivity not only provides equitable access to educational resources but also supports an environment that validates students' identities within the educational system. Adams Corral and Gallo's exploration into the lives of transborder families (Chapter 8)shines a light on the 'literacies of (in)visibility', revealing the intricate literacy practices often obscured by dominant societal narratives. Their approach calls for a methodological embrace of these complex literacies, fostering a research landscape where the voices and experiences of marginalized communities are not merely acknowledged but actively incorporated into literacy research.

These methodological innovations show how multilingual learners' border-crossing and trans/multilingual literacy practices can provide insights into systemic structures and inform social change. By acknowledging translanguaging as a valuable literacy practice, these researchers are paving the way for a reassessment of educational policies and advocating for curricula that represent the authentic language use of multilingual students. Such legitimacy granted to diverse linguistic experiences has the potential to influence educational policies, promoting systemic change that aligns with the multilingual realities of learners.

The collaborative and reflexive research approaches advocated in these chapters underscore the necessity of partnership with multilingual communities. Understanding that literacy development is deeply rooted in sociocultural contexts, researchers are encouraged to engage with participants in a manner that respects and elevates their lived experiences. Together, these chapters extend beyond traditional literacy research, which often overlooks the intricacies of multilingualism. By incorporating a broader scope of research that includes family and community literacies, as well as intersecting language learning with STEM disciplines, the authors redefine what it means to be literate in a multicultural and multilingual world. This expanded view challenges and stretches the research boundaries, offering a more comprehensive perspective on literacy.

Ethical considerations and challenges

Ethical research in multilingual settings necessitates an acute awareness of the power dynamics at play, such as those considered by colleagues reflecting on our multilingual EMI research (Zheng et al., 2024). Researchers must navigate the fine line between observation and intrusion, respect and imposition, understanding and exploitation. Within such a delicate ecosystem, the methodologies chosen have significant ethical implications, as they can either uphold the dignity and autonomy of multilingual communities or perpetuate their marginalization.

Kim et al.'s work (Chapter 6) exemplifies an ethical approach that centers on respecting participants' lived experiences, that is, their linguistic practices and cultural backgrounds. By integrating 'suda' into their PBFL framework, the researchers engage with Korean American families in a manner that respects their inherent linguistic fluidity and cultural nuances. This methodological choice reflects an ethical commitment to valuing participants' lived experiences, allowing the research process to be guided by the natural interplay of languages and cultural practices within family settings. By doing so, the researchers avoid the imposition of external linguistic norms and validate the rich, multimodal communicative practices present in these families.

Salas and Lizárraga Dueñas (Chapter 7) confront the ethical challenges of linguistic racism and the marginalization of non-dominant languages and cultures in educational research. By applying an Anzalduan framework, they advocate for research practices that not only respect but also promote linguistic and cultural inclusivity. Their approach serves as a model for how researchers can actively work against the exclusionary practices that often dominate STEM education, proposing an ethical stance that embraces linguistic diversity as a strength rather than a barrier. This perspective is critical for ensuring that research in multilingual literacy development does not inadvertently reinforce the very disparities it seeks to eliminate.

Adams Corral and Gallo's research into transborder literacies (Chapter 8) directly engages with the ethical implications of colonization logics that often underlie qualitative research methodologies. By emphasizing reflexivity and dialogue, their work represents a concerted effort to adopt an ethical approach to research that disrupts hegemonic traditions. The authors advocate for methods that illuminate the rich literacies developed by transborder communities, which are frequently rendered invisible by dominant societal narratives. In doing so, they assert the ethical imperative to elevate the voices of those communities and recognize their right to narrate their own experiences in their languages and terms.

Across all chapters, a prominent ethical consideration is the representation of multilingual participants. Researchers are tasked with the responsibility of portraying participants' experiences authentically, avoiding misrepresentation or oversimplification. The consent process in such research is specific, requiring clear communication about the aims and potential impacts of the study. Participants must be fully informed and empowered to make decisions regarding their involvement. Likewise, data collection methods must be ethically designed to be non-intrusive and culturally sensitive. The interpretation of data, especially in multilingual contexts, demands an ethical approach that acknowledges the researchers' own biases and limitations. The methodologies highlighted in these chapters suggest a shift towards practices that encourage participant validation of the findings, thus ensuring that the interpretations align with the participants' intentions and meanings.

The methodological innovations described by Kim et al., Salas and Lizárraga Dueñas, and Adams Corral and Gallo offer rich ethical considerations that move the field of multilingual literacy research forward. They set precedents for engaging with participants in ways that respect their autonomy and expertise, challenge oppressive structures within educational research, and advocate for the visibility of marginalized literacies. These approaches serve as beacons for future research in the field, guiding researchers towards practices that not only meet ethical standards but also enrich the knowledge base with culturally and linguistically diverse perspectives.

Looking backward and forward

The chapters by Kim et al., Salas and Lizárraga Dueñas, and Adams Corral and Gallo contribute to the ongoing evolution of qualitative research on multilingual literacy development. These authors build upon established research and theoretical frameworks while also charting innovative pathways that are responsive to the ever-changing sociocultural landscapes of multilingual learners.

Grounded in translanguaging theory, Kim et al. (Chapter 6) offer a nuanced understanding of family literacy practices that reflect the lived experiences of Korean American families. Their work merges with existing research that acknowledges the fluidity of language use in multilingual settings, thereby enriching the body of work on family literacy narratives. They demonstrate how theoretical concepts can be practically applied to capture the complex interplay of languages in everyday life, providing a more holistic view of literacy development. Salas and Lizárraga Dueñas (Chapter 7) take Anzaldúa's decolonial theory into the field of STEM education, opening up new vistas for understanding how language and STEM learning can unite. By doing so, they contribute to a growing body of literature that seeks to dismantle the compartmentalization of language learning and STEM disciplines, advocating for an interdisciplinary approach that recognizes the interconnectivity of linguistic and scientific literacies. Adams Corral and Gallo's emphasis on reflexivity and ethical considerations in research methodologies (Chapter 8) echoes the call within academia for greater sensitivity to the contexts and complexities of transborder literacies. Their proposition for a forward-looking methodology resonates with contemporary discussions on ethical research practices and the need for reflexivity in qualitative inquiry. By doing so, they build on earlier work that highlighted the importance of considering researchers' positionalities and the power dynamics inherent in the research process.

Looking to the future, these chapters underscore the necessity for innovative research practices that align with the sociocultural realities of multilingual learners. They advocate for methodologies that move beyond mere inclusivity to be truly transformative, aiming to effect systemic change within education and broader societal structures. Kim et al. (Chapter 6) propose that research in multilingual literacy development must embrace the everyday realities and strengths of multilingual communities, suggesting a model that values linguistic diversity as a resource rather than a challenge to be overcome. This approach has significant implications for educational policy and practice, advocating for learning environments that reflect and support the multilingual nature of students' lives. Salas and Lizárraga Dueñas' extension of decolonial theory into STEM education (Chapter 7) paves the way for a curriculum that is more equitable and inclusive of all students, regardless of linguistic background. Their work suggests that by integrating language learning with STEM subjects, educators can create a more engaging and representative educational experience for Latinx students and other linguistically diverse populations. And Adams Corral and Gallo's call for a re-evaluation of research methodologies (Chapter 8) offers a plan for future studies that seek to genuinely understand and represent the experiences of transborder families. Their approach encourages researchers to engage in practices that not only acknowledge but also endorse the adaptive and innovative literacy practices that emerge in response to the challenges of migration and transnationalism.

Together, these chapters provide a collective vision for the future of research in multilingual literacy development — a future grounded in the principles of equity, inclusivity, and ethical responsibility. The authors envision a research landscape that is not only responsive to the needs and realities of multilingual learners but also committed to advancing systemic change. This vision implies that researchers, educators, and policymakers must collaborate to create educational spaces that truly reflect the diverse linguistic ecologies of our globalized world.

Conclusion

Reflecting on the collective insights from the chapters by Kim et al., Salas and Lizárraga Dueñas, and Adams Corral and Gallo, this commentary underscores a pivotal moment in the field of multilingual literacy research. In my own advocacy for methodological innovation and deeper theoretical engagement in Applied Linguistics research methods, I intended to provide a critical backdrop for understanding the significance of the discussed chapters. These chapters, through their unique methodological approaches and theoretical perspectives embody the practical application of such advancements in multilingual literacy research.

The essence of my own argument — that Applied Linguistics research must evolve to more accurately reflect and engage with the complexities of language learning and use in a globalized world — was supported in the methodological and theoretical innovations highlighted in the chapters, but also taken much, much further. The integration of cultural practices, such as the Korean 'suda' in Kim et al.'s research, the Anzalduan framework employed by Salas and Lizárraga Dueñas, and the focus on the literacies of (in)visibility in transborder families by Adams Corral and Gallo, exemplifies the type of methodological diversity and theoretical depth research in this area can achieve. These approaches not only challenge traditional paradigms but also pave the way for a more inclusive, equitable, and ethically responsible research landscape in multilingual literacy.

The chapters' collective emphasis on cultural integration, participant-centered research, and ethical considerations in the study of multilingual literacy development aligns with my own vision for a reimagined approach to research methods in Applied Linguistics and offers concrete examples of the advantages of taking such an approach. By foregrounding the lived experiences, linguistic repertoires, and cultural identities of multilingual individuals, the authors contribute to a broader, more nuanced understanding of literacy that transcends monolithic representations. This shift towards embracing methodological innovation and theoretical richness in exploring the complexities of multilingualism not only advances the field but also responds to the critical need for research that is reflective of the diverse realities of language use in contemporary society.

In conclusion, the insights I have attempted to share in my commentary of the three chapters shows a dynamic and evolving field of multilingual literacy research. My reflections highlight the importance of methodological innovation, theoretical engagement, and ethical consideration in advancing our understanding of multilingual literacy. As the field continues to navigate the challenges and opportunities presented by global linguistic diversity, the contributions of Kim et al., Salas and Lizárraga Dueñas, and Adams Corral and Gallo serve as concrete examples, guiding researchers towards a more equitable, inclusive, and comprehensive approach to studying multilingual literacy.

References

Hampson, T., & McKinley, J. (2023). Qualitative and quantitative are data types not paradigms: An MMA framework for mixed research in Applied Linguistics. *LEARN Journal: Language Education and Acquisition Research Network*, 16(2), 1–7.

McKinley, J. (2020). Theorizing research methods in the 'golden age' of Applied Linguistics research. In J. McKinley & H. Rose (Eds.), *The Routledge handbook of research methods in applied linguistics* (pp. 1–12), Routledge.

McKinley, J. (2022a). An argument for globalized L2 writing methodological innovation. *Journal of Second Language Writing*, 58.

McKinley, J. (2022b). Book review: Esther Odilia Breuer, O.D. et al.. (Eds.), *Multilingual literacy*, Multilingual Matters, (2021). *Journal of Second Language Writing*, 58.

McKinley, J., & Rose, H. (Eds.). (2020). *The Routledge handbook of research methods in Applied Linguistics*. Routledge.

McKinley, J., Sahan, K., Zhou, S., & Rose, H. (2024). Researching EMI policy and practice multilingually: Reflections from China and Turkey. *Language and Education*, 38(1), 5–22.

Zheng, Y., Gao, X.A., McKinley, J., Rose, H., Sahan, K., Zhou, S., ... & Lin, A.M. (2024). Researching multilingually to rethink EMI policy and practices. *Language Teaching*, 57(1), 132–138.

PART 3

Interrogating research practices
New explorations of positionality in research on multilingual literacy development

CHAPTER 10

Embodied reflexivity and researching the literacy practices of an adolescent multilingual refugee who is d/Deaf/Hard-of-Hearing

Liv T. Dávila
University of Illinois at Urbana-Champaign

In this chapter I extend recent scholarship on researcher subjectivities in Applied Linguistics by considering affective, spatial, and corporeal dimensions of reflexivity and positionality. I draw from ethnographic research on the multisemiotic language and literacy practices of Madou (a pseudonym), an adolescent refugee student from the eastern region of the Democratic Republic of Congo (DRC) who was diagnosed as having a severe hearing impairment upon his arrival to the United States as a middle schooler. I conclude by presenting implications for how considering positionality as embodied can yield novel analyses and foster relational ethics in research on the literacy development of multilingual learners from immigrant, transnational, and refugee backgrounds, including those who are d/Deaf and hard of hearing (DML).

Keywords: embodied reflexivity, positionality, multilingual, d/Deaf and hard of hearing

Introduction

A growing body of literature examines the communicative practices of multilingual learners who are d/Deaf and hard of hearing (DMLs) (Griffin, 2021; Parks & Calderon, 2021), including translanguaging in deaf education (Swanwick, 2017; Wolbers et al., 2023). Additional research investigates the perspectives of hearing and deaf teachers on deaf students in deaf and "mainstream" learning contexts (Cannon et al., 2022; Scott & Kasun, 2021), and on literacy instruction to DMLs (Scott et al., 2022). In light of this burgeoning line of scholarship and other groundbreaking research on bi/multilingual English learners with disabilities and

https://doi.org/10.1075/rmal.11.10dav

their families (Cioè-Peña, 2021; Kangas, 2021), there is a need for nuanced considerations of positionality of those who conduct research with this linguistically, racially, and culturally diverse student population. This chapter contributes to literature on researcher positionality by considering how embodied reflexivity can enhance research on the literacy development of multilingual learners from immigrant, transnational, and refugee backgrounds, including those who are DML.

Positionality in qualitative inquiry refers to a researcher's standpoint or world view in relation to their research (topic, questions, participants, data analyses; Denzin & Lincoln, 2018). Embodied reflexivity refers to how the researcher negotiates their physical senses and mental interpretation to create meaning (Field-Springer, 2020). In other words, this approach entails seeing researcher corporeality and emotional responses as potential sources of knowledge in research on language and literacy. The aim of reflecting on positionality and embodied reflexivity during the period of investigation is to critically acknowledge that research claims are inevitably embedded in researchers' physical, mental, and affective subjectivities, and to situate research claims in relation to individuals, identities, and knowledges.

Although qualitative researchers commonly include positionality statements in the introductory paragraphs or methods section of an article, book chapter, or monograph, they are often presented as attributes (e.g., I am White, a woman, a professor, multilingual, someone who does not know American sign language [ASL]) that are fixed in space and time (e.g., living in the Midwestern region of the United States) and separate from the analysis of data itself. Although intended to disclose potential biases and make transparent a researcher's relationship to their research site and participants, positionality statements are often just that — statements, or declarations that allow the researcher to subvert questioning and avoid disclosing insecurities or vulnerabilities experienced throughout the research process. In this way, positionality statements can perhaps inadvertently assert epistemological hierarchy and reinscribe authority, and therefore, raciolinguistic ideologies and White privilege.

In contrast to static perceptions and representations of positionality described above, in this chapter I contribute to recent insights on researcher subjectivities in Applied Linguistics (Bucholtz et al., 2023; Canagarajah, 2022) by advancing a notion of reflexivity that:

1. is embodied throughout the research process,
2. acknowledges how researcher positionalities change over the duration of a study as they gain new knowledge about participants and phenomena, and
3. is understood in relation to how researchers are positioned, sometimes in multiple ways, by their research participants.

I situate this understanding of positionality as lived and felt by reflecting on my experiences of conducting research with Madou,[5] a DML high school refugee student in the United States who was from the eastern region of the Democratic Republic of Congo (DRC), and Madou's ASL interpreter, Mrs. Anderson, who accompanied Madou in each of his classes and provided me with background and real-time information about his language and literacy practices.

In reflecting on my research with Madou and Mrs. Anderson, I draw inspiration from indigenous epistemologies that emphasize past-present-future relationships between humans and their social and material worlds (Chilisa, 2019; Leonard, 2021), and from research in the fields of anthropology and Applied Linguistics that push for understandings of positionality that are dynamic and in-the-making, both during and after the research has been conducted (Bucholtz et al., 2023; Rosales & Babri, 2023; Rose, 2020). Acknowledging the "untidiness and humanness" of ethnographic research (Hare, 2020), this chapter highlights the value of viewing emotion and embodiment as integral to, rather than separate from, the research process.

In posteriorly reflecting on my researcher positionality as embodied, I consider how ideologies around multilingualism and (dis)ability, whether asset or deficit-oriented, might occlude our analyses and ultimately our portrayals of how participants deploy language and other modes of communication, and to what ends. I reflexively engage with dimensions of my embodied reflexivity and positionality while collecting and analyzing data for this study and invite a more expansive understanding of researcher identities in relation to inquiry on language and literacy development of multilingual immigrant, transnational, and refugee learners, including DMLs.

Overview of the study and its findings

In this section, I provide background literature as well as an overview of the research context and focal participants, Madou and Mrs. Anderson, the research design, and a snapshot of the findings. I return to these in the section that follows as I re-engage critically with my positionality as rendered through my data — field-notes and photographs taken during classroom observations, document analysis, and segments of interviews I conducted with Madou and Mrs. Anderson together and with just Mrs. Anderson separately.

This research draws on ethnographic data collected for a two-year study of the language and literacy practices of multilingual adolescent English learners

---

5. All participants have been given pseudonyms to maintain confidentiality.

from Central Africa who were attending a public high school in the United States (Dávila, 2019, 2020; 2021; Dávila & Doukmak, 2022; Dávila & Susberry, 2021). My first encounter with Madou took place in his English as a second language (ESL) classroom in March of 2016, after I had received permission from Mrs. Henderson and Ms. Garcia (the ESL/bilingual education teachers) to informally observe their classes as a means of beginning to establish relationships with the teachers and students who eventually became my focal participants, and to learn about the larger school context. I officially began recruiting participants at the beginning of the following school year after receiving Institutional Review Board (IRB) approval.

I had not planned to conduct research on DMLs prior to meeting Madou, and I had no previous experiences teaching or conducting research on DMLs. As I became more familiar with Madou and his classmates in the first months of data collection, I began to develop questions specifically related to Madou's language and literacy development in school. I further refined these questions as I continued to observe Madou in his classes and engage with his peers and teachers in my research. This iterative process resulted in the following two questions that guided this aspect of the research: (1) What are Madou's multilingual visual, oral, and embodied language and literacy practices in school?; and (2) How does he negotiate his literacy development and self-positioning in relation to his peers through his school-assigned ASL interpreter?

Background and theoretical framings

In framing these questions, I consulted several bodies of literature, including recent research on DMLs (e.g., Cannon et al., 2022; Parks & Calderon, 2021; Wolbers et al., 2023) and multisemiotic and embodied literacies (e.g., Ybarra & Saavedra, 2021). My research builds on this work and the work of scholars of translanguaging (García & Li, 2014; Li, 2022) in its attempts to provide nuanced understandings of Madou's translingual, material, sensorial, and embodied literacy practices, as well as the spatial dimensions of his literacy experiences in school.

The research also applies framings of disability in Applied Linguistics, including Canagarajah's (2022) integration of decolonial, disability, and queer studies in the form of crip linguistics. In his work, Canagarajah argued for "relational ethics, vulnerability, and nonnormativity, and nudg[ing] language studies toward a more inclusive and expansive crip linguistics" (p. 11), putting forth an *anomalous embodiment* orientation to crip linguistics, which emphasizes the multiplicity of communication (and therefore identities). This approach to researching multilingual and multisemiotic literacy development articulates with Margaret Mead's (1972) notion of *total communication*, which involves attending to and valuing multimodality in research on communication beyond language and literacy themselves. Non-verbal and embodied literacies entail constructing and communicating meaning that draws on all senses and uses visual, gestural, and spatial resources (Vasuvedan, 2014). From the perspective of scholarship on DML language and literacy, my research explored total communication from a multilingual and multisemiotic perspective by examining Madou's speech, finger spellings, signs, gestures, pantomimes, drawing, writing, and touch, which can be said to meet the needs of deaf people (and presumably all people) (Evans, 1982).

Research context and participants

The school district in which this research was conducted is in a small city of roughly 40,000 inhabitants in the midwestern region of the United States. Students designated as English learners comprised 12% of the entire student population in the district; the majority of whom were from Mexico and Guatemala, followed by the DRC and China. English learners at the high school where this research took place, including Madou, were enrolled in content-focused ESL courses, such as civics, earth sciences, and language arts, some of which were co-taught by ESL and grade-level subject area teachers.

Madou was born and grew up in a city in the eastern region of the DRC. He arrived in the United States in 2014 with his father and was placed in the 7th grade based on his age and years of schooling in the DRC. He attended school in the DRC for five years in a schoolroom with many children, as he pantomimed and vocalized to me in an interview, using his hands to outline the shape of a box. Mrs. Anderson interpreted during this interview and verbally affirmed this point. He did not have a sign language interpreter in school in the DRC and instead learned by copying course content from blackboards and or through other print material. Although I did not directly ask Madou about what and how he was taught in school, school-based assessments in the DRC tend to focus on rote memorization of material written on a chalkboard or provided in a textbook (Depaepe & Kikumbi, 2018). He received much of his former schooling in the DRC in French. Oral communication in the part of DRC where Madou was from occurred in French, Lingala (both of which are official languages of the DRC), and Swahili, which is widely spoken in eastern DRC. His father and mother spoke these languages at home but did not use sign language. Instead, prior to Madou receiving his hearing aid in the summer of 2016, the family communicated using written communication and physical gestures. He was the oldest of five children in his family, and his mother and four younger sisters were in the DRC when Madou and I first met. His father was working on the reunification process to bring his wife and daughters to the United States when I started this study in the fall of 2016, and the entire family had moved to the city where this study took place by the time I had completed data collection in the spring of 2018.

Madou was diagnosed as having a severe hearing impairment after his first month in 7th grade in the United States and was assigned an in-school ASL interpreter in 8th grade. He did not know ASL or English prior to arriving in the United States. He had received a hearing aid in the months leading up to our introduction in his 9th grade ESL/Bilingual Health class, one of the classrooms in which I regularly observed as part of the larger study. Madou was the only DML English learner at the high school during the time of this research. With his hearing aid, Madou began to hear the sounds of English, French, and other languages spoken by his classmates, which he then began to vocalize in his interactions with peers and teachers.

Mrs. Anderson was employed by the school district as an ASL interpreter and only worked with Madou. She is White, in her 40s, and a self-described native speaker of English. She learned ASL in college where she obtained a degree in hearing sciences and licensure in teaching ASL. She had worked with d/Dhh children in the school district for roughly ten years when this study was conducted, and the majority of these students lived in homes where English was the dominant language. She had previously worked with a DML elementary school student whose family was from Mexico. Madou was the first adolescent and African DML student with whom she had worked.

Research design

In this chapter I describe the ethnographic methods employed in the larger study while emphasizing those used in exploring Madou's multilingual and multi-semiotic literacy development. In this research, data collection occurred through *experiencing* (through participant observations), *enquiring* (through interviews), and *examining* (documents, including photographs and written transcriptions of interviews), and by inductively working through empirical evidence to arrive at new understandings (Wolcott, 2008).

Classroom observations

I conducted a total of 63 observations (roughly one two-hour observation block per week) of Madou's civics, health, math, language arts, and science classes. The focus on Madou entailed particular attention to the physical environment and classroom layout, as well as visual cues and learning tools included PowerPoint slides, worksheets, Chrome books, and Madou's smartphone, which he occasionally used for translational purposes. Observations necessitated paying close attention to Madou's physical positioning and communication through finger spelling and signing, eye contact, and verbal gestures with Mrs. Anderson and his teachers and peers, as well as his writing. I took detailed notes on each of these things, often quickly jotting and sketching images in a note pad of what I saw and heard (see Figure 1 and Figure 3).

Mediated and unmediated interviews

I obtained informed consent from the teachers and Madou's parents, and assent from Madou and the students who were part of the larger study by meeting with teachers, parents, and students individually. In these meetings, I explained in writing and orally (in English or French) my motivation for conducting this study including the broad research questions, the time commitment involved on their part, the kinds of data I would be collecting through interviews, classroom observations, and document analysis, and how I would eventually use this data. I also assured participants that data would be de-identified so as to maintain confidentiality.

To gather background on Madou's language and literacy development, I conducted interviews with Mrs. Anderson, Madou's ASL interpreter, who accompanied him to each of his classes; Mrs. Rogers, a speech pathologist and ASL interpreter who also worked with Madou; and his two ESL teachers, Mrs. Henderson and Ms. Garcia (I do not include interviews with or fieldnotes about Mrs. Rogers, Mrs. Henderson and Ms. Garcia in this chapter). These interviews were audio recorded and transcribed afterward. As a hearing and non-signing scholar, I could not conduct one-on-one interviews with Madou; however, I was able to interview Madou on three occasions with the help of Mrs. Anderson and Ms. Rogers. These interviews were also audio recorded and later transcribed. The following excerpt from one of these interviews illustrates my embodied presence during these interviews. This interview took place in a room designated for students receiving special education services and students with disabilities who received individualized instruction from a learning specialist. There were no other students or teachers in the room during this interview, and Madou, Mrs. Anderson and I sat at a round table. Madou made eye contact with me as I asked questions, and then with Mrs. Anderson when she interpreted them.

Liv (to Madou): What is your favorite subject?
Madou: Algebra.
Mrs. Anderson (signing and speaking to Madou): Algebra. Do you like math?

Madou (signing and articulating to Mrs. Anderson, interpreted orally by Mrs. Anderson to me): Yeah. That's good, I'm good. I'm so smart at math, I think about it, and I write it down and I check what the teacher has. And I'm usually right.

Liv: Excellent [giving thumbs up to Madou]

Mrs. Anderson (signing and speaking to Madou): What I've noticed, is that when you've finished your work, and then like Pierre or someone else needs help, you turn around and you help them.

Madou (speaking): Yeah, yeah, I help [my peers].

Noticeable to me during this interaction was my relative outsider positioning by both Madou and Mrs. Anderson, both physically and communicatively, as Madou and Mrs. Anderson conversed. I initiated the questions, but otherwise felt apart from the communicative event, particularly as Mrs. Anderson further probed Madou in the interviews. I elaborate on my embodied reflexivity in collecting and analyzing this data, and on the insights that feeling apart from Madou's interactions yielded in my research, later in this chapter.

In addition to interview data, I also obtained several audio recordings of classroom group interactions that included Madou, during which I took notes on the students' seating arrangement and physical gestures that accompanied their oral responses to another participant. Madou verbalized and used hand gestures as a means of engaging with his peers in these instances. He was also present and contributed during focus group interviews I conducted with other students who were part of the larger study. During these group interviews, I took note of Madou's level of engagement through his posture, physical gestures, and oral responses to his peers' comments.

Analysis of writing

In addition to observations and interviews, I collected and photographed select ungraded written assignments produced by Madou in the classes I observed. I then analyzed these assignments in relation to my observations and interviews (see Dávila & Susberry, 2021, for a detailed description of methods used in the analysis of multimodal texts in this study). In this layered approach to document analysis, I considered (1) where Madou was physically positioned, or how he positioned himself in relation to the teacher, Mrs. Anderson, and his peers the classroom; (2) where Mrs. Anderson was positioned in relation to Madou; (3) Madou's physical disposition; and (4) his written and verbal language (see Figure 4). I also accounted for Madou's positioning of/by and engagement with peers on group writing assignments.

Example of findings: Madou the scribe

Findings of this research center around two interrelated themes related to the research foci: (1) Madou's multilingual visual, oral, and embodied language and literacy practices in school, and (2) his negotiation of his literacy identity and self-positioning in relation to his peers and his school assigned ASL interpreter, Mrs. Anderson. The writing sample shown in Figure 1 offers a glimpse into Madou's socially mediated literacy practices — in this case, during an in-class group writing assignment in which he was asked by his classmates to be the scribe for the group.

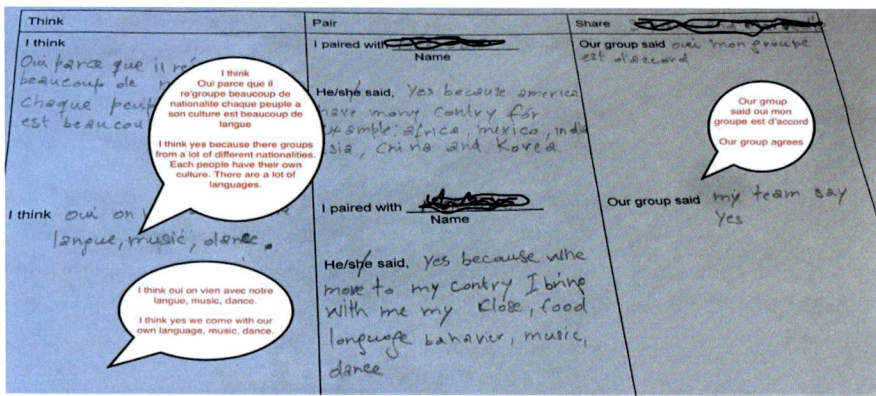

Figure 1. Collaborative in-class writing assignment

This was a collaborative writing assignment given to students in Madou's ESL Human Geography class. Madou worked on this assignment in class with two other students, both of whom were Congolese and who had arrived in the United States at roughly the same time as Madou. Madou and the two other students' desks were pushed together so that they faced one another. I sat in a chair to the right of Madou, where I listened, took hand-written notes, and offered feedback when the students asked for it. Mrs. Anderson was absent from the class on the day I observed, and Madou communicated with his peers through physical gestures and by vocalizing short responses in English. He wore a cochlear implant and was able to hear and process what he heard, and one of the group members spoke with Madou in Lingala, French, and English. The other student did not contribute and instead put his head down on the desk.

I observed other group interactions during which Madou was volunteered by his peers to complete group writing assignments because they believed Madou was a stronger writer than they. On such occasions, I recorded peers uttering, "Madou doit écrire" ('Madou should write'), or "You, Madou," while pointing at Madou with a pen. Using this example as a starting point, a translingual, multisemiotic, spatial orientation to researching and analyzing literacy events such as this demonstrates multifaceted elements of literacy including grammar, words, punctuation, and the messages they impart, as well as the social, physical, and emotive spaces in which reading and writing take place.

This writing sample centers on Madou's multilingual and multisemiotic language and literacy development, his identity and positioning, and his peer socialization; however, it also showcases a potential paradox of Madou's being volunteered by his peers to write for the group. In this instance, although he agreed to take on the role of scribe, he may have felt pressure to do so against his will, or he may have preferred for this to have been a more collaborative writing experience.

This sample and analysis of it is representative of how (1) peers recognized Madou's writing skills (in English) and frequently called on him orally and through gestures to take on writing tasks in group assignments, and (2) how Madou accepted this role, though not always willingly. It captures Madou's view of himself as a sometimes reluctant, yet capable scribe as evidenced by his utterances, body language, and the writing he produced, and it highlights Madou's agency in shaping the terms of his role as a scribe. In other words, in assuming this role, whether willingly or reluctantly, he ultimately had control over the writing process and product.

From the perspective of fieldwork relationships, I reflect on how Ms. Anderson's absence from this class period led me to pay closer attention to how Madou crafted his identity as a writer in the classroom through his unmediated physical and oral gestures. By attending to this interaction, I also considered how my research necessitated a holistic understanding of positionality that shifts throughout the research period and in relation to who was present in any given event. For example, it is possible that in requesting that Madou write for the group, his peers expressed resistance or self-consciousness in response to my presence. To this point, reconsideration of my role in this literacy event provokes a larger question of how students demonstrate agency, whether through physical, verbal, or affective engagement with or disengagement to a researcher who is interested in documenting and understanding their in-school language and literacy practices.

Methodological discussion: Rethinking positionality for more equitable research

Taken as a whole, each of the methods described in the previous section entailed critically re-reflecting on how affect, corporeality, and spatiality were and continue to be implicated in my positionality in ways I had not considered in my previous research or reflected on until writing this chapter. In reanalyzing my field notes, images, and interview transcripts several years after I completed data collection, I awaken to instances in which I took for granted embodied and relational aspects of my positionality during the data collection, unintentionally rendering my identities and ideologies unidimensional and inconsequential in the research. In the first section below, I define the notion of embodied reflexivity. I then explore examples of this reflexivity as it applies to positioning myself and others in the field, writing fieldnotes, and engaging with intermediaries.

Embodied reflexivity

In this section, I consider the application of embodied reflexivity to continuously reflect on positionality as ever-evolving vis à vis relationships and contexts. I do so drawing inspiration from indigenous epistemologies that emphasize relational dimensions of knowledge and knowing (Chilisa, 2019) and that problematize the emic/etic binary in research with marginalized groups (Leonard, 2021; Nero, 2015). The aim is to show how making researchers' presence visible in the research process can reinforce researcher accountability and enhance research on language and literacy development.

Unlike previous research in which I focused more intently on print literacy and verbal communication, researching Madou's literacy practices entailed a particular way of learning and documenting through a DML lens that was new for me. More so than with other facets of the larger research study from which this one is taken, in which I could communicate with students (in English and French, but not Lingala, Swahili, and other African languages they spoke), I saw myself as a cultural, linguistic, and sensorial outsider in relation to Madou. In reflecting on the research methodologies I deployed in my research with Madou and the other participants, I reconsider how I consciously and unconsciously privilege hearing and sound in my own (language) learning and in my research on language and social interaction among immigrant and refugee youth in school, including ideologies around accent, dialect, race, and social class (Dávila, 2008, 2013, 2019).

In my experiences as a language teacher and currently as a university professor, I frequently and intentionally use visual cues such as gestures, writing, and drawings to clarify or emphasize a point, and thus hold an affirmative stance on multisemiotic language and literacy practices and pedagogies. Despite my multisemiotic inclinations in my teaching, I felt cautious approaching Madou without Ms. Anderson's interface, and I kept a physical and communicative distance from him more so than with other students. This was due in part to my fear of making Madou feel as though I was surveilling him or singling him out because of his hearing impairment. I was simultaneously humbled by and self-conscious around Madou because of my knowledge of his trajectory as a DML in school, and because I am a hearing person who does not know ASL. Rather than viewing Madou as being vulnerable, I tended to reflect on my own perceived inability to initiate conversation with Madou or offer my assistance in the classroom as I did with many of the youth in the larger study. This being the case, with his hearing aid, Madou was able to hear many sounds and responded to my greetings with a wave or "Bonjour, Madame", which put me at ease in his presence. I positioned myself as a "vulnerable observer" (Behar, 1997), and through this chapter I write myself into the research in hopes of finding deeper meaning in the study. To Behar, being a "vulnerable observer" means acknowledging emotional constraints of doing ethnographic fieldwork, which for me at times necessitated discomfort and powerlessness, as has writing this research for publication. On a transformative level, this discomfort has led me to engage with and represent broader and more inclusive ways of learning, knowing, and recording what I observed and heard while in the focal classrooms. In the following sections, I elaborate on my embodied reflexivity in collecting and analyzing this data and the insights that feeling apart from Madou's interactions yielded as an impetus to consider later in this chapter.

Positioning in the field: What is seen and not seen

In reconsidering my positionality from an affective and embodied perspective, as in all my classroom research, I attempted to deploy superficial ways of "fitting in," or at least worked to minimize material differences between myself and the participants. I dressed casually (e.g., wearing tennis shoes, jeans, and a sweater), and carried my belongings in a backpack. I purposefully did not remove my laptop from my backpack, and instead took notes by hand. Students expressed curiosity over my hand-held digital recorder, however, and I was open with them about its purpose and sought their permission before using it to record their classroom interactions, or individual and focus group interviews. I also used my phone to take pictures of classroom spaces and documents. In retrospect, I acknowledge how my physical and emotional presence and material positioning impacted participants and myself in this research in a way that was not captured in my earlier research and is undertheorized in qualitative research more generally. For instance, although I have generally considered my physical positioning in most of my research to date, I had not previously reflected on research as an embodied practice in which the data we collect and analyze are conditioned by our physical sensations and affective responses (Field-Springer, 2020). As an example, analysis of photographs taken to document a particular scene or product must also be interrogated from the vantagepoint of the photographer's identity, physical positioning vis à vis their subject matter, and particular focal points. I took one of the few photos I have of Madou (Figure 2) during one ESL civics class period in which I sat with a group of students as they were working on a group assignment.

Figure 2. Photograph of Madou and Mrs. Anderson in the classroom

In this image, Madou is facing the front of the room, where Mrs. Anderson provides ASL interpretation as Mrs. Henderson reads aloud from the PowerPoint slide. In re-analyzing this photo, I consider my physical position and gaze in relation to Madou's and Mrs. Anderson's, as well as Madou's seemingly relaxed posture and his hands that touch, rest on, or perhaps hold open the screen of his school assigned laptop computer. I most often purposefully sat among students or toward the back of the room during classroom observations, which I felt would allow me to gain more spontaneous and holistic understandings of their language and literacy practices than if I were to sit on the periphery. Sitting amongst students also allowed me to assist them with translating and writing when it was needed. Although not in a formalized role, I offered to help the teachers of the focal classrooms as a form of reciprocity for their welcoming me into their classes. They established early in the research process that my help could come in the form of assisting students with in-class activities.

Upon reexamining this photo, I consider ways in which it captures a static impression of Madou's literacy practices in which he is isolated from his peers and passively reads from the PowerPoint slide (or stares into space, as the case might have been). Instead, in this photo and elsewhere in the data I intended to illustrate the classroom as a dynamic and multisemiotic space, where Madou demonstrated agency and creativity in his language and literacy practices, sat amongst his peers rather than apart from them, and engaged his peers and teachers in ways that were simultaneously meaningful and mundane.

The type of positionality advocated for in this chapter and by Arya et al. (Chapter 11, this volume) in their critical examination of the dialogic void in research, in Applied Linguistics research more generally necessitates a sensory embodied reflexivity (Culhane, 2016) that acknowledges and incorporates researcher and participant emotions, embodiment, imaginations, and creativity in ethnographic practice. My exploration of Madou's multilingual literacy development entailed a heightened awareness of the visual, but also other senses, such as the smell of paper, the feel of an eraser, the physical distance between Madou and Mrs. Anderson, the physical positioning of Mrs. Anderson vis à vis other students, and the warmth generated by bodies in a crowded classroom, as well as how these variables may have influenced Madou's engagement in literacy experiences in school. It also called on me to consider how I related to each of these things, as well as my own physical positioning in relation to Madou when I observed him and his peers, or how my physical placement and body language when conducting interviews with Madou and Mrs. Anderson led to or inhibited certain forms of sharing and telling through spoken or written word. In the following section, I consider how embodied reflexivity can inform the research process during and after the data collection has concluded, and how the act of writing whether, in or ex situ, or engages embodied reflexivity.

Writing as witnessing

Writing, whether in field notes, a manuscript, or a book chapter, can in itself be considered an ethnographic method, or *logic-in-use* (St. Pierre, 2018) in that writing entails an analytic process of rendering what is observed into particular words that capture the researcher's perceptions, beliefs, and ideologies. In this vein, Blommaert and Dong Jie (2010) have stated:

> [Field notes] tell us a story about an epistemic process: the way in which we tried to make new information understandable for ourselves, using our own interpretive frames, concepts and categories, and gradually shifting into new frames, making connections between earlier and current events, finding our way in the local order of things. (p. 37)

A sample of my field notes (Figure 3) demonstrates two points to this end. In the scenario depicted here, Madou and Kati, a peer who was also from the DRC, were working on an in-class assignment, and Mrs. Anderson sat next to Kati so that Madou could see her sign language interpretation. I sat to the side of the students with a direct view of Kati, Madou and Mrs. Anderson. In this instance, Kati began talking to Madou in French and Lingala, and Mrs. Anderson interjected, telling Kati to speak to Madou in English. Mrs. Anderson and I then explained (in English and French, respectively) that Kati must interact with Madou in English so that Mrs. Anderson, who does not speak French or Lingala, could interpret. My field notes articulate a narrative around this sequence that is informed by my positionality as a researcher, and in this case, as an interlocutor between Kati and Mrs. Anderson. My notes illustrate how I made sense of the situation.

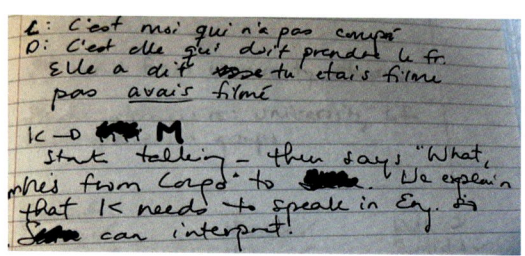

Figure 3. Unedited transcription and translation of sample field notes
Side conversation between two students from the DRC (not Madou):
C: C'est moi qui n'a pas compri ['It is I who doesn't understand']
D: C'est elle qui doit (ap)prendre le fr. Elle a dit 'tu estais filme pas avais filmé'. ['She needs to learn French. She said 'you were filmed not you had filmed''
My notes on conversation between Kati, Madou, and Mrs. Anderson
K ✍️☹️ KKKM
Starts talking (in French and Lingala) — then says, 'What — he's from Congo' to Mrs. Anderson. We explain that K. needs to speak in English so that Mrs. Anderson can interpret (for Madou).

Reviewing the field notes years after they were taken, I note that I purposefully chose to write in the language students were using, and to describe phenomena or events in English, particularly when they included non-French speakers. Re-reviewing the example above, and with one of the editors of this volume's feedback in mind, I see how Mrs. Anderson's English and ASL dominant presence forced a shift in language to English to accommodate her.

In field notes taken during the larger study, I primarily wrote in English and French, as seen in the above example. I also documented words or expressions used by the teachers and students or asked a student to spell words for me in Lingala, Kikongo, or Tchiluba (see Dávila, 2020). In reviewing the transcripts for this chapter, I retrospectively recognize how my positionality, as someone who can read and write in English and passably in French and other European languages (often translingually), is indexed through the students' and my own speech and writing that ultimately shaped the research process and results (Thomas, 2022).

What is also hiding beneath the surface in this and other field notes, and what in many ways led me to focus on francophone African students in the first place, is my affective relationship to the French language — a language I formally studied throughout high school and college, and which I taught as a high school World Language teacher, and as a teaching assistant in graduate school. I invested in opportunities to use French as a means of connecting with students and satisfying my desire to maintain my proficiency in it. My inability to sign equally impacted the research and occasionally created a communicative and relational gulf between Madou, and Mrs. Anderson, and me, as described in the first pages of this chapter. More critically, also embedded in my field notes is an unconscious privileging of Western languages and epistemologies (Chilisa, 2019), seen through World language offerings in schools in the US, and indicative of how language reproduces and is reproduced by colonial power structures that commonly devalue indigenous languages and cultures (Thiong'o, 1986).

The research design and the role of intermediaries

There are several aspects of the research design that equally influenced how I critically reflect on my embodied positionality in this study. For instance, I purposefully did not seek IRB approval to videotape students in this study for two primary reasons. Firstly, I was concerned that videotaping would compromise students' identities. Secondly, when I initiated this research, I was primarily interested in students' oral and written language production, which I captured through audio recorded interviews, focus groups, and classroom interaction, as well as copies and photographs of students' written work. In retrospect, video recordings might have lent themselves to a deeper posteriori reflection on embodied aspects of my positionality as someone who frequently assisted students with writing tasks in the classroom. Including myself — my actions, my words — in an analysis of a videoframe could yield a more three-dimensional understanding of how my presence might have influenced how particular literacy events unfolded. On the other hand, while conducting the research, the use of video could have been perceived by the students and teachers as intrusive or distracting and further distanced me from them. What is more, the absence of video recordings also in some ways forced me to be more attentive to embodied, relational, and spatial dimensions of Madou's literacy development in real time, which I attempted to record in my field notes.

In addition, Madou's assigned ASL interpreters and speech pathologist, Mrs. Anderson and Ms. Rogers, functioned as direct communicative links between Madou and me, and they gave me important insight into Madou's literacy development. This leads me to ask how this research may have unfolded differently had I begun developing this aspect of the research with Madou, rather than with those who in many ways brokered our relationship. If I had done so, I might have designed observation and interview protocols around Madou's lived experiences in school and topics of significance to him. I may have also been better informed about ASL instruction, previous research on DMLs, and education policy that supports these learners' needs. Instead, I relied on Mrs. Anderson and Ms. Rogers to interpret Madou's communication in real time, and on their impressions of his learning and peer socialization. For example, in an individual interview with Mrs. Anderson, I asked about her perceptions of Madou's language and literacy development (in ASL and English) during the beginning of the second year of the study. She shared:

> For Madou, at the beginning of the year, I didn't spell much because he didn't know the [English] words [his teachers used in their classes]. But now he has more vocab knowledge, so I can finger spell more now with him. He will still vocalize the French word, which I don't understand, but he understands from my signs what it is I'm saying.

Mrs. Anderson offered valuable insights from a teacher/interpreter's vantagepoint that may have been expressed differently by Madou. It is also important to acknowledge that I had interacted with Mrs. Anderson on several occasions when this interview was conducted, and that she and I were able to relate to one another as White women who could bridge language and communicative gaps for one another in the classroom and in interviews with Madou — me through my knowledge of French and Spanish, and Mrs. Anderson through her ASL fluency. In short, we had developed a trusting relationship built on our mutual interests in communication and learning in school.

A second unedited example (Figure 4) is taken from my notebook and shows how space and physical positioning was implicated in Madou's literacy development.

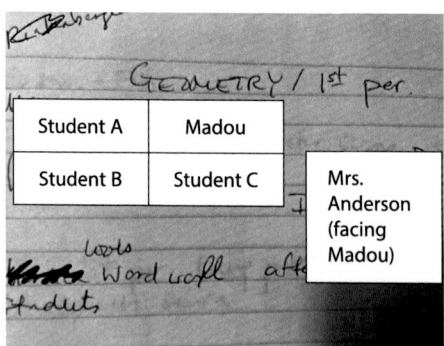

Figure 4. Desk configuration

The students' desks were pushed together, and Mrs. Anderson positioned herself within direct view of Madou as she provided ASL interpretation where possible. The students interacted with one another in English, French, and Lingala, and Mrs. Anderson was not proficient in either of the two latter languages. Thus, in this case, Mrs. Anderson provided access to me by letting me into her process of interpreting for Madou by orally explaining concepts and directions to Madou in English while signing, and then reflecting on her experiences in separate interviews; I in turn provided interpretation to her of what I understood (in French). Although not depicted in this image, I sat across from Mrs. Anderson. This omission of self is perhaps notable in that it indicates that I did not consider my presence to be of importance in this interaction. As I documented in these field notes, Madou seldom made eye contact with Mrs. Anderson in this literacy event and instead focused his attention (gaze, posture, directionality of verbal engagement) on his peers.

In reconsidering the role of Mrs. Anderson in my research with Madou, I am compelled to reflect on our relationship as I came to view it. As a communicative link between Madou and I, she was in many ways a gatekeeper who provided me with access to new understandings of Madou's language and literacy experiences in school and her work in supporting them. Through our interactions — in interviews, spontaneous check-ins, and conversations in the classroom and other school spaces — she also displayed trust in the integrity of my research and in me as a person, which cannot be underestimated. As noted by Christensen and Tian in Chapter 12, the impact of such researcher participant relationships on the research process must be acknowledged and critically explored in qualitative research. A re-examination of my positionality in relation to Mrs. Anderson through the writing of this chapter yielded previously unnoticed analyses that point to the importance of acknowledging ideologies and relationships as evidenced in photographs, field notes, and interview data collected for this research.

Implications for qualitative research on multilingual literacy development

Throughout this chapter, by taking up the notion of embodied reflexivity in my research with Madou, I join other scholars of language and communication to advance an understanding of positionality living, relational and dynamic throughout the research process in ways that are heretofore undertheorized in research on multilingual literacy development (Bucholtz et al., 2023). This positional stance sees researchers' experiences, perspectives, and emotions as they unfold throughout the research process as methodological resources that can yield new understandings and foster researcher accountability.

My research with Madou awakened me to the importance of centering "deaf language" and promoting deaf-centric understandings of language, literacy, and learnings. For instance, in this research I was prompted to think more carefully and introspectively, and to humbly/sensitively interrogate physical spaces in which in-school literacy practices occur in greater detail than in my previous research. Some ongoing questions to myself in relation to this research include: How are desks positioned in a classroom, and how does this shape the literacy practices that take place? How do physical gestures and other forms of body language inform multilingual literacy development? How do students engage various senses as they read and write in school? How are some senses privileged over others in the process of teaching and researching literacy? How might we as a field be better attuned to translanguaging practices that acknowledge multisensorial ways of producing language, and therefore perceptions, knowledge, and understandings? What senses do we most tap into or privilege as we conduct research on multilingual literacy development? How might we reflexively privilege certain kinds of embodied literacies over others? What role does our physical positioning, both in terms of where we sit and our posture, play in shaping the literacy practices we examine? Although these questions are neither novel nor exhaustive, they can provide important insight into more surface-level field observations in qualitative research that may otherwise be neglected.

Considerations for incorporating embodied reflexivity in research on multilingual literacy

In this chapter, I have reflected on my research with a DML as a means of advancing embodied reflectivity as a tool for uncovering new knowledge and leveraging accountability in qualitative research on multilingual literacy development. I conclude by offering guidelines for harnessing its potential.

First, qualitative research on the multilingual literacy development of any learner entails a research design and planning that anticipates the need for different linguistic and semiotic resources that call for collaboration with "expert" community members. For those interested in pursuing a more focused line of inquiry on DMLs than is presented here, planning and undertaking the research and data analysis with interpreters and others who provide support for d/Dhh learners is essential. Careful consideration of these points promotes relational accountability toward and connectivity to individuals and their communities, and not simply to the gatekeeping institutions with which they and the researcher interact (e.g., schools, universities, Institutional Review Boards; Ali & Talbert, 2024).

Secondly, embodied reflexivity in literacy research is a means of deepening engagement, questioning assumptions, and lending transparency to the research process — challenging extractivist research approaches (see Ghiso, Chapter 13, this volume). It also entails reflection on our physical presence in these spaces, including how our presence is taken up by our participants, which can be challenging to do either because of constraints on time and space, or because of the researcher vulnerability it exposes. Stepping away from and returning to data with fresh eyes and seeking feedback on de-identified data from colleagues can generate insights that are often subsumed by more tangential evidence. Returning to and re-reflecting on the data collection process as well as the data itself also serves as a means of seeing one's own development as a scholar.

Finally, embodied reflexivity can open avenues for resisting methodological imperialism, or research practices that privilege dominant voices and ideologies — including methodologies that reinforce "epistemological single-mindedness" (Pallas, 2001. It entails engaging in continuous reflection and ultimately blurring boundaries of research, theory, and practice with the goal of humanizing research that amplifies multiple ways in which we and our research communities experience our worlds.

References

Ali, A. I., & Talbert, R. L. (2024). Accountable to whom?: Relational accountability in social research. *Anthropology & Education Quarterly.*

Behar, R. (1997). *Vulnerable observer: Anthropology that breaks your heart.* Beacon Press.

Blommaert, J. & Dong Jie (2010). *Ethnographic fieldwork: A beginner's guide.* Multilingual Matters.

Bucholtz, M., Campbell, E. W., Cevallos, T., Cruz, V., Fawcett, A. Z., Guerrero, B., Lydon, K., Mendoza, I. G., Peters, S. L., & Reyes Basurto, G. (2023). Researcher positionality in linguistics: Lessons from undergraduate experiences in community-centered collaborative research. *Language and Linguistics Compass,* 17(4).

Canagarajah, S. (2022). A decolonial crip linguistics. *Applied Linguistics,* 44(1), 1–21.

Cannon, J. E., Guardino, C., & Paul, P. V. (2022). *Deaf and hard of hearing multilingual learners: Foundations, strategies, and resources.* Routledge.

Chilisa, M. (2019). *Indigenous research methodologies.* Sage.

Cioè-Peña, M. (2021). Raciolinguistics and the education of emergent bilinguals labeled as disabled. *Urban Review,* 53(3), 443–469.

Culhane, D. (2016). Sensing. In D. Elliot & D. Culhane (Eds.), *A different kind of ethnography: Imaginative practices and creative methodologies* (pp. 45–67). University of Toronto Press.

Dávila, L. T. (2008). Language and opportunity in the "Land of Opportunity": Latina immigrants' reflections on language learning and professional mobility. *Journal of Hispanic Higher Education,* 7(4), 356–370.

Dávila, L. T. (2013). Learning English and "smartness": Refugee students negotiate language, reception, and ability in school. *Journal of Southeast Asian Education and Advancement*, 8, 1–19.

doi Dávila, L. T. (2019). Multilingualism and identity: Articulating "African-ness" in an American high school. *Race, Ethnicity and Education*, 22(5), 634–646.

doi Dávila, L. T. (2020). Multilingual peer group learning in high school ESL classrooms. *TESOL Quarterly*, 54(1), 30–55.

doi Dávila, L. T. (2021). Newcomer refugee youth negotiate language, literacy, and civic education. Special Issue of the *British Educational Research Journal*, 47(4), 855–871.

doi Dávila, L. T. & Susberry, V. (2021). Multimodal and multilingual co-authoring in high school Social Studies ESL classrooms. In D. Shin, T. Cimasko, & Y. Yi (Eds.), *Multimodal composing in K-16 ESL and EFL education: Multilingual perspectives* (pp. 55–71). Springer.

doi Dávila, L. T. & Doukmak, N. (2022). Immigration debated: Central African immigrant youths' discourses of fairness and civic belonging in the United States. *Equity & Excellence in Education*, 55(1–2), 118–132.

Denzin, N., & Lincoln, Y. (2018). The discipline and practice of qualitative research. In N. K. Denzin & Y. S. Lincoln (Eds.), *The Sage handbook of qualitative research* (5th ed., pp. 1–32). Sage.

doi Depaepe, M., & Kikumbi, A. L. (2018). Educating girls in Congo: An unsolved pedagogical paradox since colonial times? *Policy Futures in Education*, 16(8), 936–952.

Evans, L. (1982). *Total communication: Structure and strategy.* Gallaudet University Press.

doi Field-Springer, K. (2020). Reflexive embodied ethnography with applied sensibilities: Methodological reflections on involved qualitative research. *Qualitative Research*, 20(2), 194–212.

doi García, O., & Li Wei. (2014). *Translanguaging: Language, bilingualism and education.* Palgrave.

doi Griffin, D. J. (2021). American Sign Language and English bilingualism: Educators' perspectives on a bicultural education. *International Journal of Bilingual Education and Bilingualism*, 24(6), 757–770.

doi Hare, K. A. (2020). Collecting sensorial litter: Ethnographic reflexive grappling with corporeal complexity. *International Journal of Qualitative Methods*, 19.

doi Kangas, S. E. N. (2021). "Is it language or disability?": An ableist and monolingual filter for English learners with disabilities. *TESOL Quarterly*, 55(3), 673–683.

doi Leonard, W. Y. (2021). Toward an anti-racist linguistic anthropology. An indigenous response to White supremacy. *Journal of Linguistic Anthropology*, 31(2), 218–237.

doi Li Wei. (2022). Translanguaging as method. *Research Methods in Applied Linguistics*, 1(3),

doi Mead, M. (1972). Vicissitudes of the study of the total communication process. In T. Sebeok, A. Hayes, & M. C. Bateson (Eds.), *Approaches to semiotics: Cultural anthropology, education, linguistics, psychiatry, psychology; Transactions of the Indiana University Conference on Paralinguistics and Kinesics* (pp. 277–288). De Gruyter Mouton.

doi Nero, S. (2015). Language, identity, and insider/outsider positionality in Caribbean Creole English research. *Applied Linguistics Review*, 6(3), 341–367.

doi Pallas, A. M. (2001). Preparing education doctoral students for epistemological diversity. *Educational Researcher*, 30(5), 6–11.

doi Parks, E. S., & Calderón, J. (2021). Bimodal multilingual education: Recognizing the linguistic resources of a diverse deaf world. *International Journal of Bilingual Education and Bilingualism, 25*(7), 2699–2710.

doi Rosales, V., & Babri, M. (2023). Harnessing emotions for embodied reflexivity in organizational ethnography. *International Journal of Qualitative Methods, 22.*

doi Rose, J. (2020). Dynamic embodied positionalities: The politics of class and nature through a critical ethnography of homelessness. *Ethnography, 23*(4), 451–472.

doi Scott, J. A., & Kasun, G. S. (2021). It's not enough to move your hands beautifully': Teaching and learning at a school for deaf students in Mexico. *International Journal of Bilingual Education and Bilingualism, 24*(8), 1128–1146.

doi Scott, J. A., Amadi, C., & Butts, T. (2022). *d/Deaf and hard of hearing multilingual learners and literacy instruction.* Routledge.

doi St. Pierre, E. A. (2018). Writing post qualitative inquiry. *Qualitative Inquiry, 24*(9), 603–608.

doi Swanwick, R. (2017). Translanguaging, learning and teaching in deaf education. *International Journal of Multilingualism, 14*(3), 233–249.

Thiong'o. N. W. (1986). *Decolonising the mind: the politics of language in African literature.* James Currey.

doi Thomas, J. (2022). A fish tale about "fieldwork," or toward multilingual interviewing in Applied Linguistics. *Annual Review of Applied Linguistics, 42*, 127–136.

doi Vasudevan, L. (2014). Bodies matter in literacy coaching. *Reading & Writing Quarterly, 30*(3), 237–240.

doi Wolbers, K., Holcomb, L., & Hamman-Ortiz, L. (2023). Translanguaging framework for deaf education. *Languages, 8*(1).

Wolcott, H. F. (2008). *Ethnography: A way of seeing.* Altamira Press.

doi Ybarra, M. G., & Saavedra, C. M. (2021). Excavating embodied literacies through a Chicana/Latina feminist framework. *Journal of Literacy Research, 53*(1), 100–121.

CHAPTER 11

Exploring the 'void' of silent/ced knowledge and expertise of multilingual learners

Diana J. Arya, Fátima Andrade Martínez, Valerie Meier
& Andrew Maul
University of California, Santa Barbara

Grounded in a new sociolinguistic, literacy-centered theory — *dialogic void* — as a way of exploring silences in educational spaces, we explored the expressed cultural, linguistic, and experiential knowledge of 63 multilingual (Spanish/English) elementary students and the contextual factors (e.g., scaffolded questioning from discussion facilitators) that may impact how much knowledge and expertise multilingual students share. Findings show how the questions and methodological decisions literacy scholars make, and the ways findings about multilingual learners in English-dominant classroom contexts are represented can illuminate otherwise hidden knowledge and expertise. We highlight how this methodological innovation may be helpful to qualitative literacy researchers in more deeply exploring their positionality and ways that disciplinary, cultural, linguistic, and professional identities can shape (and potentially obscure) observations.

Keywords: culturally inclusive inquiry, literacy/literacies research, multilingualism, critical reading practices, funds of knowledge

Introduction

Over the past seven years, our team of research faculty, graduate, and undergraduate students have developed literacy-related approaches and material resources designed to center nondominant, multilingual voices, particularly in English-dominant public-school settings. We ground our work in a notion of literacy, or rather literacies, as multiple, multimodal (i.e., print-based, graphical, audio, and video forms of meaning making) communicative practices across sociocultural contexts (e.g., Flewitt, 2008; Serafini, 2015). Further, our view of multiple, multimodal literacies includes notions of critical reasoning, which we define as the

https://doi.org/10.1075/rmal.11.11ary

exploration of potential sociopolitical tensions, hidden agendas, and/or (in)equitable representations in textual media (Arya, 2022; Arya et al., 2022). More specifically, our scholarship features a tool for fostering learning communities' and researchers' dialogic inquiry into interdisciplinary, multimodal textual engagement; place-based and virtual explorative programs for fostering critical discussions and civic action; the development and dissemination of multilingual (Spanish/English) resources for local schools and families; and a new assessment of multimodal, critical reading engagement and practice (Arya, 2022; Arya et al., 2017, 2020, 2022; Cano et al., 2021; Harris et al., 2024; Karimi et al., 2023; Nation et al., 2019).

The summation of our endeavors represents our active stance against colonizing practices that position linguistically marginalized student populations U.S. schools as *lacking* knowledge and skills necessary for meeting institutional benchmarks that prioritize specific notions of academic English. We are particularly interested in research approaches that support mindful exploration into the ways in which we identify, listen to, and document our understanding of what multilingual students in the U.S. (i.e., students who speak a language other than English at home) know and can do. This mindful exploration requires a constant probing into the way that positionality plays a role in what we observe. As such, we aimed to interrogate our approaches and respective positions in order to counter what Tuck (2009) described as "damaged-centered research" that "emphasizes what a particular student, family, or community is lacking to explain underachievement or failure" (p. 413). In so doing, we show how exploring sociocultural phenomena is most inclusive and, hence, impactful when we actively take up and maintain the collaborative interrogation of our respective positionality, which is defined by feminist scholars as the inevitably subjective and incomplete understanding of the world (Simandan, 2019). In particular, we took up the recently introduced theoretical construct called the *discursive void*, defined as unexplored and/or undervalued practices and processes in social spaces, as a framework for making visible what we may overlook or misinterpret based on prior assumptions, of which we may not be consciously aware about the subliminal ways that colonizing research practices can shape what we understand (Arya, 2022; Tuck, 2009). As such, this study is an opportunity to unpack the ways in which we can engage in research that is geared towards acknowledgment of knowledge and abilities that, if celebrated and incorporated in school curricula, support all students to thrive as mindful stewards of our world.

The context of our featured study focuses on our Critical Reading Assessment (CRA), which we designed to position developing readers as knowledgeable others with expertise essential to making sense of and critically analyzing textual phenomena (Arya, 2022). Our study highlights the understanding we gained from a methodological approach that involves mindful awareness of various positional-ities (i.e., identities and roles of researchers as well as identity and role positions of participants) as we explored the expressed views and experiences of commu-nities, which, in this case, included 63 young multilingual students living in an urban coastal community in central California.

We centered our exploration on the social space of paired reading discussions (guided by CRA administration) and the contextual aspects present when multi-lingual participants, positioned as *co-learners* (Arya et al., 2022), share knowledge and experiences. We refer to *all* members associated with this study as co-learners — we learn from one another regardless of age or expertise, and as such, we disrupt traditional views of research-participant positionality. By actively taking up the positions of ourselves as co-learners and our participants as knowledge-able others, we deliberately interrogated the absence of expressed knowledge and expertise that may be due to largely invisible contextual forces — the aforemen-tioned *dialogic void* (Arya, 2022; Harris et al., 2024). Our exploration was guided by the following question: What contextual conditions (e.g., instructional moves, questions, textual artifacts) support deeper understanding of a social space? This is our first full exploration using the theoretical framework of *void* as an analytic tool for making visible how positionality may play a role in what we observe as we attempt to unpack hidden phenomena within reading discussions with young multilingual co-learners.

A study of reading discussions with multilingual elementary students

Context and participants

Our study centers 63 multilingual elementary co-learners attending school within a coastal community in central California. All but three of these students speak at least some Spanish at home; the remaining three speak at least some Mandarin at home. Our acknowledgment of potential multilingual practices (i.e., "at least some") within home contexts is our attempt to decenter school-based labels that can mask the complexities of family literacies within linguistically and culturally diverse communities. According to the 2020 U.S. Census report, there has been a significant recent increase in the number of multilingual families living in the U.S. (U.S. Census Bureau, 2022). Multilingual community members, including young children, have knowledge and expertise as well as hopes and aspirations to contribute to and thrive within our society. In California, 44% of residents who responded to the U.S. Census spoke a language other than English at home. With such a sizable portion of Californians being multilingual and having knowledge and experiences that may be vastly different from teachers, school leaders, and researchers of school spaces, classrooms must be conducive to positions of co-learning.

All 63 young co-learners attended a public elementary school that, like most in the US., exclusively uses English as the medium of instruction and assessments. These co-learners participated in a university-community partnership affiliated with Community Based Literacies (CBL), which reflects the core principles of agency, co-learning, and belonging (Arya, 2022; Arya et al., in press). As such, young co-learners contribute interests and ideas that are in turn taken up in collaborative sessions involving reading and researching topics and issues, share with and listen to others about lived experiences and related knowledge, and connect with one another as members of a community.

Most of the young co-learners (54 out of 63) were fourth graders attending a local elementary school that partnered with our university to provide literacy-related activities, such as reading discussions and blogging about flora and fauna, which preceded and followed field trips (e.g., visits to tidepools and newly restored wetlands). Such activities were crafted from co-learners' expressed curiosities and interests and involved undergraduate activity facilitators and co-learners with their younger peers. The remaining nine multilingual participants, in grades three (one student), four (one student), five (two students) and six (five students), attended our university-housed CBL summer literacy program designed to engage attendees in a variety of place-based literacy activities and collaborative projects such as stop-animation videos that feature new terminology and conceptual knowledge (e.g., sharing new knowledge about the importance of red abalone for supporting the local bay ecosystem).

For this study, we focused on recorded discussions about locally relevant interdisciplinary topics (e.g., the importance of the giant kelp system for supporting habitats within the local channel), each involving one of 63 young co-learners and one of 43 older co-learners. Older co-learners included 40 undergraduates, two graduate students, and one faculty member. More than half of these older co-learners (29 out of 43) spoke a language other than English, with most of these (24) able to speak Spanish. Members of this research team are part of a nearby university recognized as a minority serving institution (MSI). While this study centers the voices of participating young (elementary) multilingual co-learners, our analytic focus is on the social space captured in our recordings. Such a focus aligns with Tuck and Yang's (2014) call to *refuse* traditional empirical practices that position students as objects of study.

Data sources

Our study focuses on 63 audio-recorded reading discussions of locally relevant multimodal texts described above, the content of which was informed and shaped by young co-learners who were asked to weigh in on the importance, clarity, and value of presented texts about locally relevant topics as described earlier (Arya et al., 2022). All participants were enrolled at our local partnership school and were invited to participate during a brief classroom visit. Families received flyers and consent forms in Spanish and English (as per IRB approval from the Office of Research at the University of California, Santa Barbara, under protocol #5–24–0505). In addition to parent consent, we also sought participant consent in accordance with our programmatic principles of agency and inclusivity.

Audio recordings were captured by older co-learners who participated in one-on-one reading discussions with the younger co-learners. These texts are part of the aforementioned CRA, and are designed to reflect the natural purposes and practices of reading. Each audio-recorded discussion lasted an average of 20 minutes and generally took place in or nearby the students' respective classrooms (Arya et al., 2022). Figure 1 is an example of such a text.

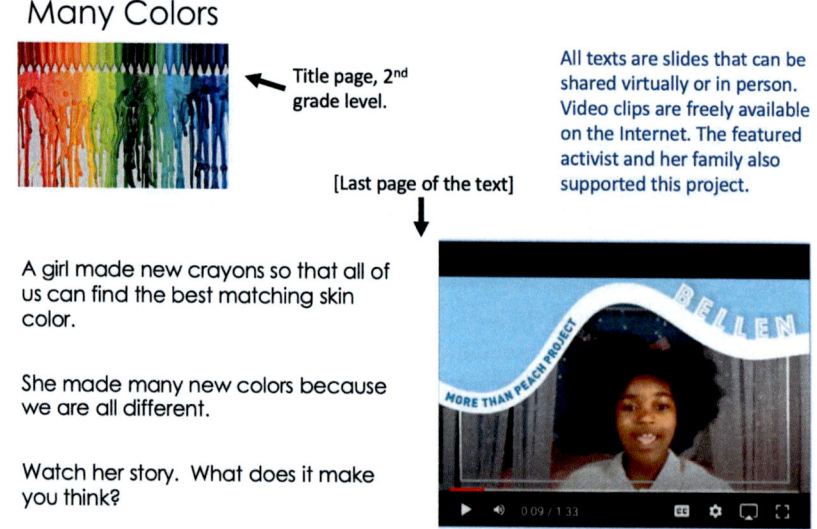

Figure 1. Excerpt of CRA text

All older co-learners received training prior to the reading discussions, during which we encouraged them to connect with young co-learners as knowledgeable others. Hence, listening and learning were key points for the CRA. We emphasized the value of multilingual abilities as important assets for sharing knowledge and, as such, we encouraged the use of other languages during the sessions. We also emphasized the importance of a non-evaluative stance, positioning the young co-learners as cultural guides for clarifying the following questions:

1. *What did you like or dislike about this text?*
2. *What was most interesting or important to you?*
3. *Why do you think the author wrote this?*
4. *Was there anything that seemed missing or unfair?*
5. *Do you have any questions, suggestions, or advice for the author?*

The original purpose of these recorded discussions was to assess and understand the reading abilities of participating young co-learners; for this exploration, we centered our purpose on making visible the often-overlooked knowledge and expertise of young multilingual learners. Such an approach of revisiting audio records for more open explorations benefits both the research and school communities by reducing instruction time taken for research activities while also illuminating partnering school leaders and teachers with important information about their students.

Analytic framework

Guided by the general blueprint of critical discourse analysis (CDA; Fairclough, 2001; Wodak, 1999), we engaged in a systematic, iterative process of describing, interpreting, and explaining observed (a) instances of knowledge and experience by young co-learners; (b) affordances for eliciting funds of knowledge and expertise by young co-learners; and (c) facilitative moves or contextual qualities that potentially silenced young co-learners. Our analysis, including the specific categories used for coding observations (as described below), was informed by previous research (Arya et al., 2022; Cazden & Beck, 2003; Moll et al., 1992). Our process began with parallel, close listening of audio files; two co-authoring researchers listened to and summarized ideas, experiences, and perspectives represented in the young co-learners' responses to textual information. Each summary we produced included observed instances of funds of knowledge (FoK) — linguistic, cultural, interdisciplinary, and experiential understandings (Moll et al., 1992), as well as contextual affordances and silencing. All summaries were discussed and clarified for each recorded session with subsequent interrogations of potential misinterpretations or missed salient moments. Figure 2 presents the kinds of instances of dialogic engagement (FoK, affordances by all co-learners, and potential silences) that we clarified together as most relevant to the purpose of our study.

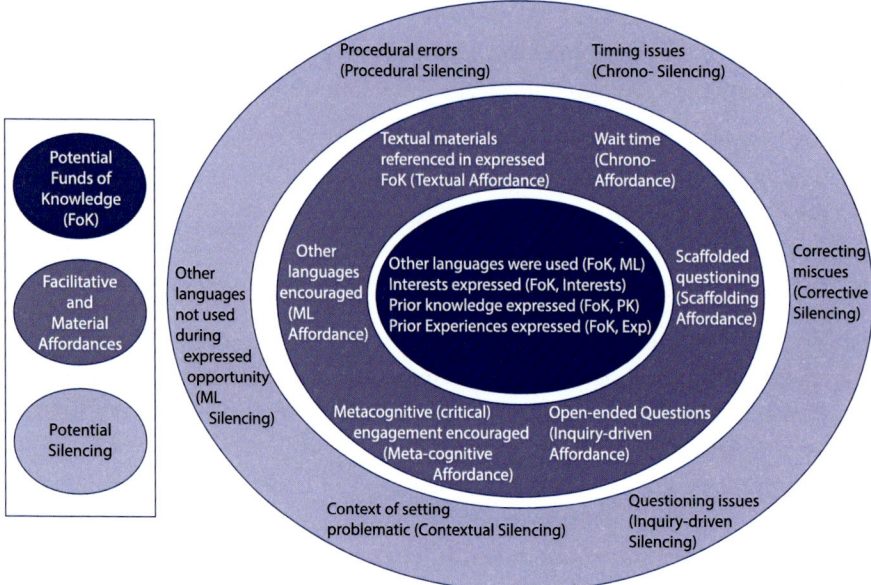

Figure 2. Relevant discursive qualities
Note. "ML" refers to multilingual learner and "PK" refers to prior knowledge.

By targeting these kinds of information, we are positioning our young participants as knowledgeable others while also being aware of the possibility that our own assumptions, our positionality, may hinder our abilities to see and hear what young co-learners know and can do. We then transcribed salient instances in a manner that aligned closely with young co-learners' utterances, maintaining original word use and grammatical choices. The initial descriptive phase of analysis involved iterative discussions among the researchers about interpretations and ways that our respective positions and identities influenced our thinking. Our process of exploration is further described below.

Exploring the void

The identification of factors that potentially silenced young co-learners (point (c) in the previous paragraph) was informed by a previously mentioned theoretical lens called the *dialogic void* (Arya, 2022; Arya et al., 2022; Harris et al., 2024). In brief, the conceptual premise of *void* builds on what physicists call the *known unknown* (Conover, 2016; Weatherall, 2016), referring to the idea that what might initially appear empty or vacuous may truly be teeming with complexities and have much to teach us. We took up this premise of *void* as a potential tool for exploring social phenomena that may seem at the outset to be nothing worth noting. For example, when we found no FoK instances for a particular recording, we focused on what we could glean from the older co-learner and the contextual surroundings. Was there any explicit effort to elicit knowledge and experience from the young co-learner? How noisy was it in the location of the discussion? Was there any sign that time was limited? The philosopher Charles Sanders Peirce (see Frankfurt, 1958) called this process *abducing* — the active, iterative practice of considering multiple plausible explanations for (in this case) a particular observed question or response based on contextual information. Abducing is one way to maintain a mindful approach when interpreting findings, hence connecting directly with one's positionality. The more attuned we are to the possible explanatory signals provided by contextual information, the more we can understand what is happening rather than what we *think* is happening.

Positionality

Scholars engaged in sociocultural research have increasingly emphasized the importance of acknowledging and interrogating differences across research and participant positionalities (e.g., teacher-student; white researcher-participants of color) throughout the empirical process (e.g., Holmes, 2020; Lin, 2015; Manohar et al., 2019). Consistent, mindful questioning in our work involved us continually asking ourselves and each other what I/we might be missing or misinterpreting based on my/our cultural/gender/linguistic/disciplinary identities. Our practice of abduction involved active interrogation into how our respective identities may be shaping what we are, or are not, observing. The researchers represent a culturally and linguistically diverse panel — the first author is biracial, with Southwest Asian/North African and white European roots, and speaks Farsi and Mandarin; the second author has Latinx/Chicanx roots and is biliterate (Spanish/English); the third author has white European roots and speaks Spanish and Italian; and the fourth author has white European roots and speaks Norwegian. Mindful of our multilingual experiences and our commitment to social justice and equity within academic spaces, we positioned ourselves as learners during close listening of recorded exchanges. Analytic discussions were important for interrogating potential blind spots in our observations. In addition to previously mentioned questions related to our positionality, we also asked contextual questions — Was the session cut short? Could the skipped question be a missed opportunity for learning more from the young co-learner, or was the exchange productive for eliciting FoK responses from young co-learners?

In accordance with CDA approaches (Wodak, 1999), such interpretive efforts followed initial descriptions of observed conversational assertions and facilitative moves in iterative fashion. We also considered the positionality of the older co-learner facilitating the reading discussion process, i.e., whether they demonstrated a role of co-learner throughout the session or if they slipped into a role of instructional guide by correcting miscues during reading or explicitly teaching the meaning of concepts. The particular questions that facilitators asked, or the comments they made during these sessions, would have an important role in how young co-learners would respond during the exchange. For example, comments like "You are doing a great job" may seem innocuous but can signal to the young co-learner that they are being evaluated, hence reflecting a teacher-student exchange rather than a discussion between co-learners. Particular verbal cues can signal to the student that they are being evaluated on their reading ability, or that they are invited to share their opinions or weigh in on the quality of the text. We observed that such cues can elicit very different responses from the young co-learners, resulting in either short responses in quick succession (as would be expected in evaluative contexts) or reflexive, winding responses that included narratives of past experiences and relevant knowledge about the world. Such positionality and framing have been noted across disciplinary contexts, particularly educational psychology (e.g., Morita, 2012; Steele & Aronson, 1995) and literacy education (e.g., Hikida, 2018).

Abducing was integrated with efforts to member-check initial and revised understandings of what was happening during recorded discussions. As such, we verified or clarified plausible explanations represented in aforementioned summaries from close listening of audio-recorded exchanges. To the best of our abilities, we took up the practice of synthesized member checking, which is described by qualitative researchers Birt and colleagues (2016) as the effort to provide participants with the opportunity to review and comment on analytic interpretations. For example, we shared excerpted responses along with our interpretive summaries with undergraduate facilitators and partnering teachers and requested feedback in the form of confirmation and/or clarification. While time constraints prevented follow up with young co-learners, including undergraduates and teachers most familiar with the young participants provided greater clarity (and hence validity) in our findings.

Exploring contextual conditions

By abducing potential explanations for salient moments during recorded exchanges, we were exploring the contextual conditions that potentially supported or inhibited expressions of knowledge and expertise by elementary multilingual students. The concentric organization illustrated in Figure 2 (and in Figure 3 below) holds us visibly accountable to our ideological stance that the language produced by multilingual learners is influenced by instructional and contextual factors that may encourage or inhibit expressions of knowledge and the use of languages other than English. For example, if both co-learners can speak Spanish, there may be an increased chance of observing this language in use even though the discussion is taking place within an English-dominant classroom space. As mentioned earlier, our unit of analysis was a given conversation and relevant discursive qualities within each exchange. All observed instances were subjected to open discussions among research team members to resolve differences across separate analyses. Undergraduate co-learners were members of the assessment team and as such, contributed to the contextual ground for our study. While time constraints precluded our ability to involve undergraduates as co-analysts, we followed up with members when clarification was needed. Only one discrepancy (regarding time as an additional potential silence for one of the conversations) needed to be resolved before reaching full consensus on observations. Our connections with the partnering school afforded the opportunity to follow up with available young co-learners (11 in total) to clarify expressed knowledge (e.g., with questions like "Can you share more about your experience of stargazing with your grandfather?") as well as with undergraduate co-learners to clarify notes associated with a recording.

Findings

Instances of relevant discursive qualities

Figure 3 presents our observations across all recorded reading discussions according to the number of conversations (out of 63) that exhibited such qualities.

We observed a total of 72 instances of expressed FoK; the size of graphically displayed instances in the figure varies according to the number of conversations that included respective assertions. Such observations included mentioned interests, which are integral to one's knowledge base (Moll, 2019). Expressions of interest (e.g., "I really like learning about different myths, like the stuff about Greek gods" [related to the text on constellations]) was most frequently observed during recorded discussions. Expressions of prior knowledge (e.g., "I know that donuts didn't come from this country" [on the diversity of American food]) was second most frequent, with expressed experiences (e.g., "We go to food banks, and we give food, too" [on food banks]) as third most frequent. Only one reading discussion involved the use of language other than English (*Es un oso*) [describing a stuffed bear pictured in a text]).

The most frequently observed affordances (i.e., utterances that preceded FoK assertions) included inquiry with an open-ended structure (e.g., "What are some things that you dream about?" [on what people can do], 26 instances); commentary inspired by text (e.g., "I think they should make healthier food cost less than

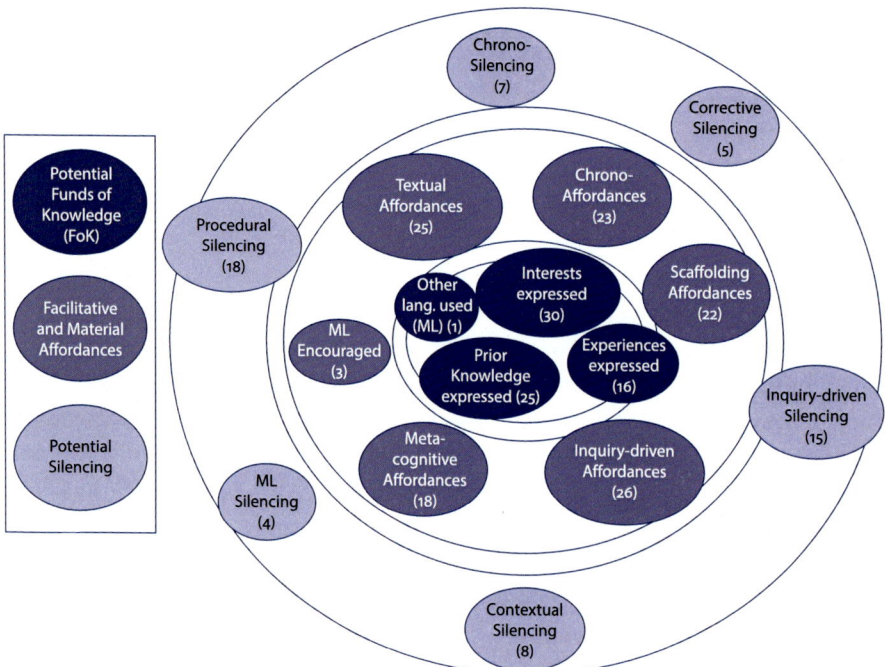

Figure 3. Instances of observed relevant discursive qualities

junk food" [on food banks], 25 instances); conversational space — at least five seconds — allotted through extended wait time by facilitating co-learners (e.g., extended time provided after the open-ended question "Why do you think that the author wrote this?" [on American food], 23 instances); and efforts to elicit engagement through scaffolding (e.g., "Which of these foods have you tried?" [on the diversity of American Food], 22 instances). Noted frequencies of observed affordances play a supportive role in making visible the kinds of discursive moves and textual qualities that seem most able to position the young co-learners as cultural guides in this study. We found that among all observed affordances, open-ended questioning, relevant/familiar textual content, and pointed questions for eliciting perspectives and preferences were most frequently highlighted as relevant contextual factors associated with expressed FoK.

The most prominently observed instances of potential silencing involved procedural errors; during 18 discussions, a question featured within the text was skipped. Rapid successive questioning, particularly during the post-reading portion of the reading discussions, seemed to elicit one or two-word responses from young co-learners; we observed 15 instances of such questioning. Less frequently observed were obvious instances of surrounding distractions (background noise, 8 instances); explicit efforts to increase the pace of the session (7 instances);

efforts to correct miscues during reading (5 instances); and missed opportunities to use other languages (e.g., a young co-learner expressed that they were not certain about how to say something, which was left unexplored).

In order to provide readers with a transparent account of observed silences, Figure 4 illustrates a compilation of all observed *types*, rather than the illustrated frequencies of potential silencing; utterances were transcribed verbatim from different conversations associated with the young co-learners participating in this study.

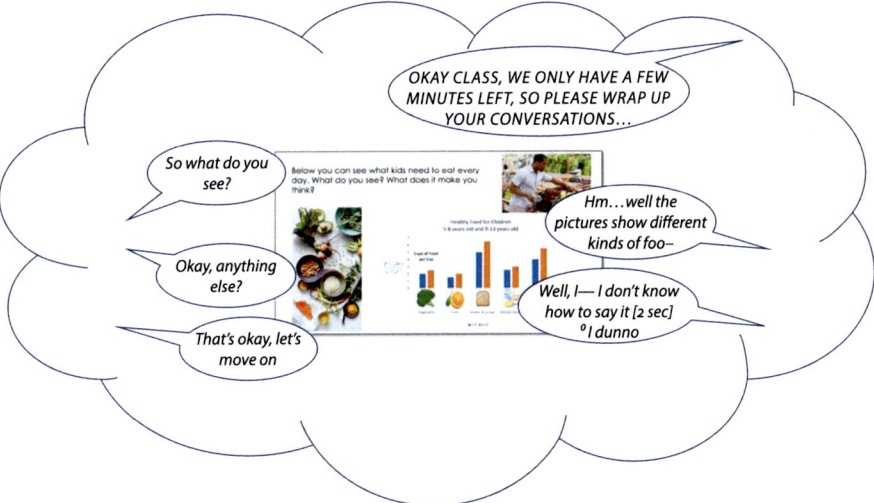

Figure 4. Compilation of potential silences during reading discussions
Note. Featured text excerpted from *Food Bank* (Arya et al., in press).[6]

Contextual factors such as a global announcement from the classroom teacher (top right callout) may have prompted facilitating co-learners to quicken the pacing of their questioning, leading to missed opportunities to connect with and engage their younger peers in reflexive, meta-cognitive discussions about concepts and issues. All such illustrated instances above seemed most relevant to our exploration of the *dialogic void*; perceived efforts to move a young co-learner along during a discussion can curtail what knowledge and experiences might have otherwise been shared.

---

6. Note that all utterances are transcribed excerpts from multiple recorded sessions. The cloud-shape surrounding serves to distinguish this compilation from observed contiguous discourse represented in the discussion below.

Methodological discussion

Positionality and the dialogic void

To research a social space like multilingual engagement during paired reading discussions, one must be committed to the stance that multilingual learners are knowledgeable experts; this is the first position that each research member needed to take up in this study. Such positioning helps us refuse false deficit notions and fosters a sense of trust and belonging among all actors (researchers, facilitators, and community participants) within a research-based program. To be clear, our work does not introduce a new definition of *positionality*, which refers to the cultural, linguistic, disciplinary identities that researchers (Holmes, 2020; Lin, 2015) and other co-learners (Morita, 2012) represent within a social space. By assuming that our young multilingual co-learners are knowledgeable others, and as such *positioning* all actors (researchers, facilitators, and community members) as co-learners, we are able to see more into the void of unspoken knowledge and abilities in classroom spaces. In this way, we are actively taking up positionality as a tool for avoiding unexplored assumptions and clarifying what young co-learners know and can do. As such, the innovation and methodological approach within this study involve the ways in which positionality is a throughline from start to finish; our research questions, data sources, reading materials, reading discussion questions, summaries of recorded sessions, debriefing meetings, and follow-up member checking all converge on our assumption that there is much more than meets the eye, and that we have everything to learn from the undergraduate and young co-learners in our study. Similar to the sentiments expressed by Brooks, author of Chapter 2 on critical questions, we maintained the assumption that young co-learners are knowledgeable, regardless of what labels are given to them in schools.

We are keenly aware that U.S. classrooms and schools — even those serving multilingual communities in relatively progressive states like California — tend to adhere to the unspoken rule that *legitimate* knowledge must be expressed in the dominant language, which is generally presumed to be English, and in a register associated with linguistic accuracy (Council of Chief State School Officers [CCSSO] English Language Proficiency Development [ELPD] Framework, 2023, para. 2). This awareness inspired us to explicitly engage in discussions with our co-learners — younger and older — about the importance of using *all* languages and registers available to us. We (the research team) discussed the different instances in which co-learners used multiple languages and respective registers in their responses. We also kept a mindful eye on the importance of multilingual abilities; however, despite our best efforts, it seemed that the pull to engage in

English was so entrenched that languages other than English were rarely used during the sessions. Even for the three cases in which we observed other languages being used, co-learners quickly demurred with phrases like "I don't know" when they were not understood the first time, as illustrated by the exchange in Figure 5a.

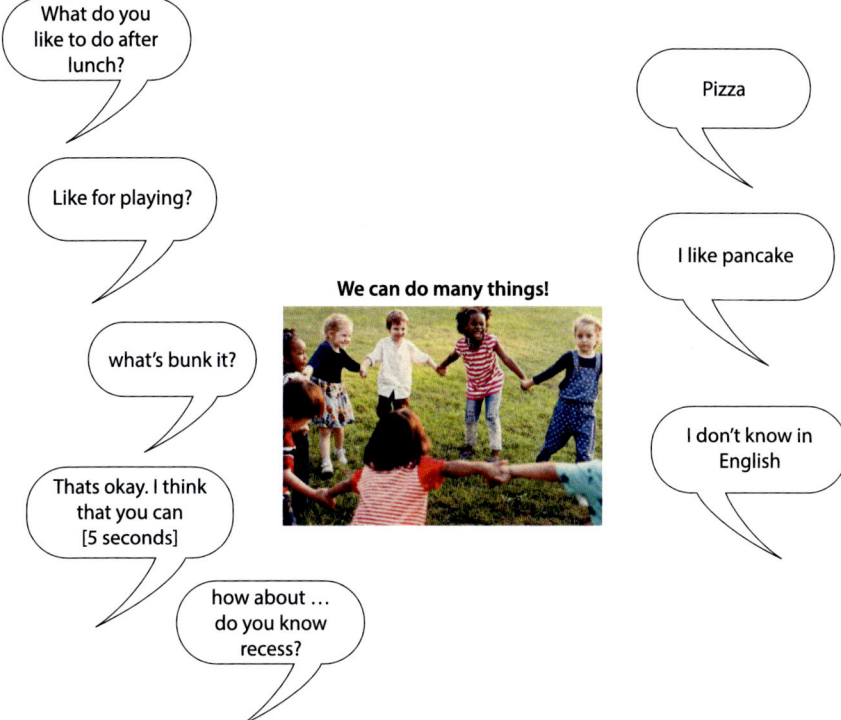

Figure 5a. Initial phase of CRA session
Note. Featured text excerpted from *We Can Do Many Things!* (Arya et al., in press)

This particular moment took place during the first phase of the aforementioned CRA, during which the older co-learner (indicated by callouts on the left) was asking prior knowledge questions to the younger co-learner (right). The purpose of this initial stage of the CRA was to clarify prior knowledge associated with the selected text *We Can Do Many Things*. The young co-learner who identifies as a boy and had arrived from Mexico six weeks earlier initially responded in a way that could be misinterpreted as off-task behavior, hence a position of refusal ("Pizza"). The older co-learner seemed to position themself as a willing recipient of new knowledge ("Like for playing?"). Member checking allowed us to understand that another request for clarification ("What's bunk it?") was a misinterpretation of the younger co-learner's utterance ("Pancake"). The older co-learner then attempted to repair miscommunication by using a more familiar word, "Recess", suspecting that this word was part of the young co-learner's lexicon. As researchers, we kept an attentive eye on all discursive and contextual aspects available to us to see the ways in which young co-learners were positioned and how they were encouraged to share what they know in ways that were familiar.

Positioning young co-learners as knowledgeable others

As mentioned previously, we (researchers) followed up as part of our member-checking efforts with young co-learners who did not have the opportunity to share their perspectives about the multi-modal texts due to time constraints. Such efforts involved us visiting the participating school and asking respective classroom teachers for a few moments to confer with young co-learners. Such exchanges were in addition to the audio recordings and were documented via researcher notes. Further, these exchanges did not explicitly invite alternative or counter-narratives from our participants, which may have made a difference in the kinds of responses that we received. Our invitation was generalized to *any feedback* on graphical representations (this wording was framed as "advice for the authors of the text"), which may not have served as adequate encouragement for expressions of disagreement with or departure from the presented information. In order to get such input from young co-learners, we needed to establish trust and communicate through our actions that we, our facilitating team, wanted to learn what they knew and what they were interested in. Language plays a central role in such alternative positioning of youth. We must show that we welcome all languages, registers, and opinions from our young colleagues if we want to gain a fuller picture of their knowledge, experiences, and perspectives.

Such positioning is true of all actors involved in our study — researchers, undergraduate facilitators, and young community members all have a co-learning role to play and, as such, each of these actors contribute uniquely according to particular roles while also participating as equitable contributors to the social space. For example, one researcher prepared materials for the reading discussions while also being a co-learner within the study. Undergraduate facilitators used these materials during reading discussions with young community members, but their questions (e.g., "What did you think about this text?") positioned them as co-learners. And while young members are potentially learning something new, they are also sharing their knowledge and experiences. Each individual played an important role, but each individual was also positioned to be a co-learner.

Such co-learning positionality also involved encouragement of multilingual engagement. Eight minutes into the exchange illustrated in Figure 5a, the older co-learner encouraged the use of other languages (*español es bueno*), followed by an exchange like the one presented in Figure 5b.

Figure 5b. Encouraging linguistic FoK
Note. Featured text excerpted from *We Can Do Many Things!* (Arya et al., in press)

During a member-checking exchange, the older co-learner clarified that this moment seemed to resolve the confusion described earlier and elicited a smile from the young co-learner, who then took up the opportunity to teach an unfamiliar Spanish word (*ruedas*). Exchanges like those in Figure 5b that involve complementary linguistic and experiential knowledge among interlocutors may increase the prevalence of shared co-learning. Co-learning opportunities like this may be relatively rare in classrooms traditionally made up of one teacher surrounded by students, and hence can be challenging for researchers committed to deconstructing dominant ways of interacting.

Scholars who engage in classroom research may assume that their role should align with general school practices; assuming the position of a teacher aide, for example, may be thought of as a natural, minimally intrusive way to observe within the classroom space. As such, positioning oneself as a co-learner could be viewed as inauthentic to the context and thus may potentially lead to less-than-authentic results. As mentioned in the introduction and study context, our goal was to understand the knowledge and experiences of multilingual students; to gain such information, it was imperative to foster a connection that was very different from what may be typically experienced within the classroom. And yet, it must be acknowledged that complete equity among all actors within a study may be a worthy but elusive goal. The exchange above represents a multilingual interaction that was explicitly encouraged by the older co-learner, but this encouragement could also be perceived as an obligation. All researchers and undergraduates supporting this study are thus in the position of walking a fine line in terms of design and approach; what we ask, what we suggest, and the moments of silence in between can play an important role in the positioning of the young co-learners who were centered in this study and participating in an English-dominant context. To be clear, we have never observed any teacher or administrator from our partnering school actively *discourage* students from using languages other than English. However, neither did we observe proactive encouragement to use such languages.

All texts included in the school's curriculum, including math workbooks, language arts textbooks, and class sets of novels, were in English. Hence, to insert or suggest the use of another language is to depart from the English-dominant context and the student-subject positioning implied within learning contexts. As researchers, we have a responsibility to consider the ways in which we accept and reinforce such dominant practices by positioning ourselves as teachers, teacher aides, or even as learners with a gaze towards young co-learners as multilingual performers. In taking up the culturally affirming, positive approaches of Tuck and Yang (2014), we are committed to engaging in future explorations into linguistic and material affordances that nurture momentary bubbles of co-learning. We believe that such efforts may foster the transformative work that we do with our community partners, so that multilingual learners can thrive in academic spaces. In this sense, we are engaging in a "deconstructive practice" of exploring classroom discourse for transformational ends (Mazzei, 2004, p. 28). Our deconstructive practice is grounded in a mindful, critical awareness of positionality and how the various roles assumed with our respective positions may influence or, in this case, transform a space that allows us to see and hear more from those who may be tacitly viewed as lacking knowledge and expertise.

Young co-learners are not only knowledgeable others, but they also have aspirations worth learning about. The young co-learner within the highlighted exchange from Figures 5a and 5b seemed more comfortable with sharing about himself during the last five minutes of the session, when he shared his desire to become a pilot. In a multilingual space, this desire was further clarified through scaffolded questioning, as represented in Figure 5c.

Figure 5c. Final phase, dreams of possibility
Note. Featured text excerpted from *We Can Do Many Things!* (Arya et al., in press)

The translanguaging moves between the two co-learners in the above exchange seemed to be aided by the shared cognates between Spanish and English; the older co-learner picked up the last word of the young co-learner's comment (*piloto*) and used it in their follow-up question. The suggested qualifiers to the desired profession ("Government? Military?") seemed to provide a scaffold for the young co-learner to use. It was at this point that the older co-learner felt a shared understanding that the goal of this session was to share their interests. The young co-learner seemed to understand that he was not being tested in English, and that the text was an anchor to learn more about one another. The shift from "I don't know English" to *Quiere ser piloto* could be interpreted as a move from examinee to co-learner, albeit it is also possible that the older co-learner misinterpreted the young co-learner's statement. Nonetheless, the young co-learner seemed to respond enthusiastically, and Spanish played a key role in this shift.

The kinds of questions that researchers take up have an impact on the positioning of participants. For example, what was less observed in this exchange were instances of open-ended questioning as exemplified by the initiating question in Figure 5a ("What do you like to do after lunch?"). The older co-learner later reflected that the use of scaffolding during questions seemed more productive than the use of purely open-ended questioning:

> I could tell that open-ended questions were not going to help, so I was trying to think of possible words that are similar in Spanish. I wasn't sure about the words I shared, but [young co-learner] was able to help me by pointing out the word that fit best.

Providing a space for active engagement was useful for positioning the young co-learner as one who had agency to choose which word fit best. The older co-learner in this multilingual exchange used wait time throughout the session, and this strategy seemed productive for eliciting more information from the younger co-learner. When we reviewed data sources in aggregate, we needed to be mindful of how one's position, as demonstrated in Figures 5a–c, might shift during an event.

Researcher assumptions and positions can also shift during an empirical exploration, which is why constant questioning and discussion about assumptions and interpretations of observations throughout the study are warranted. From such meta-cognitive engagement, researchers may uncover relevant phenomena (e.g., knowledge, expertise, histories) that would otherwise stay silenced and thus be excluded from the knowledge base that researchers are committed to enhancing through their scholarship.

Researching moments of silence

It is relatively easy to observe what is explicitly said and done within a social space. If we can see it or hear it, we can do our best to (re)present actions as they unfold and the kinds of positioning that occur. Explicit directives from teachers, for example, clearly signal the role that they assume as instructors of action and learning. What is more challenging is making sense of the spaces between such explicit actions and the positionality reflected in the silence. Was it a strategic move to encourage additional commentary from interlocutors? Or was it a moment of internal reflection? Each of these possibilities could reflect a particular position — for example, that of a teacher plotting next steps, or an active listener taking in what they just learned. Similarly, the young co-learner in silence may be contemplating what they want to share next, or may be frozen with anxiety. To explore moments of silence, it is important to take into account whatever is available about the context in order to clarify the positionality of interlocutors. The location, the activity, the participating members, and even the general vibe of the social space established through interactions can have an impact on positionality during moments of silence. For example, a moment of silence (five-second pause) from the older co-learner in Figure 5a was interpreted (and later clarified through member checking) as a moment of decision-making about the next discursive move to connect with the young co-learner; the question that followed was indication of this effort.

In a 2022 special issue of *Linguistics and Education* (volume 68), the authoring scholars explored the complex landscape of what silence can mean in different socio-educational contexts and showed how not speaking can be many things, such as a result of actions that suppress participation, or an attempt to resist the compulsion to participate. What we have introduced with our chapter is a methodological approach that may help mitigate the former type of silence/ing. We also showed a way to explore phenomena that can be invisible by positioning ourselves as learners and our participants as knowledgeable others that have resources to share. Our approach is mindful questioning about our curiosities, of assumptions about the population of interest, and of our own histories and positions as researchers. From the featured study, we learned about which communicative moves were most useful for understanding the FoK resources of our young multilingual co-learners. We observed, for example, that the use of wait time following open-ended questions was likely to be more associated with expressions of interest and of prior knowledge than other discursive qualities. Simply put, it seemed that the more space young co-learners had to think about their preferences and connect with textual content, the more able they were to share such thinking.

Less facilitative forms of silence were also observed, as illustrated in Figure 4 (i.e., "That's okay, let's move on"). Such suppressive instances of silencing included abrupt redirections through questioning or correcting a young co-learner's reading or language use, or a quick succession of questioning that prompted shortened or partial responses. When we closely read the social space, we can begin to recognize how various forms of actions shape what transpires and what remains in the void. However, we can never see and hear everything — nor should this be the goal of researchers.

None of us are fully aware of what would be collectively relevant at a given space and time. Moreover, the goal of unpacking *everything* that happened, or even the goal of unpacking as much as possible, assumes a position of privilege on the part of the researcher. By exploring the potential relationship between instances of silencing and observed (or missing) expressions of interest, prior knowledge, and meta-cognitive reasoning, we are exploring the relationship between moments of silence and moments of linguistic action, and how this relationship may help explain the ways in which multilingual learners are positioned (and hence supported) in English-dominant classroom contexts. But this study, like any study, is an incomplete account of what multilingual learners were thinking and feeling. This is what it means to explore the void — it is our humble dip into a fathomless ocean of stories to be shared and told. To engage in equitable research, researchers must acknowledge how relatively little is known about a topic and population, regardless of how many decades of research is represented across scholarly archives. The void of multilingual youth experiences represented in our study holds knowledge and histories that cannot fit into a single study and, as such, to engage in equitable research practices is to acknowledge this fact along with our need to position ourselves as co-learners with those who honor us by participating in our studies.

We also acknowledge that the ways in which we presented our findings, similar to all the authors who contributed to this volume, is a departure from traditional approaches. Specifically, Kuo and Sprečić, authors of Chapter 4's Communicating Selves, share our affinity for seeing what can be accomplished within social spaces by presenting artwork of multilingual students. We use graphical representations to help readers see the interactions that took place within such spaces. We address our graphical decisions in the following section.

Positionality and graphical (re)presentations

A common practice across many research traditions is to display lists and tables that neatly organize data such as demographics, performance scores, and timestamps. The presentation of such information comes with the best of intentions — clarity and replicability, which may be considered part of the cornerstone of reliable and ethically-conducted research. What may seem distinctive to readers about the present chapter is the absence of such traditional formatting. We aimed to make visible the multiple layers of social phenomena relevant to our study and in doing so, we made visible the void of multilingual students' funds of knowledge and expertise while maintaining our positions as co-learners. For example, in Figure 2, the reader sees the rings of influence on how or whether multilingual learners' funds of knowledge and expertise is expressed within an English-dominant classroom space. In Figure 3, we indicated the number of observed instances of each relevant discursive quality across the dimensions, based on our interpretations of what we heard and learned about from each recorded discussion and follow-up member checking. Our iterative approach of describing, interpreting, and clarifying with knowledgeable others began from previous work about young students and their families (e.g., Moll et al., 1992), our previous scholarship about what counts as 'academic' in academic language (Harris et al., 2024), and guidance on how to disrupt the deficit-oriented gaze of dominant practices in educational research (Tuck & Yang, 2014). What we learned about multilingual literacy development from creating these graphical representations is how dominant structures — assumed roles and responsibilities of classroom engagement, teacher talk, English-driven curricula, and the like can influence what one can see and hear from multilingual students. As exemplified by Figure 3, we also learned how visual representations of what we have been calling the void of multilingual FoK can provide tangibility to what may otherwise feel like an elusive phenomenon. We can see, for example, the layers of affordances associated with what co-learners shared. Such visual representations may have a communicative power about the relationship among discursive qualities of interest.

We were also inspired to rethink the ways in which we represented the recorded exchanges. Taking up the notion of individually uttered message units within the event of an exchange (Bloome et al., 2004), we configured excerpted exchanges into a display of speech bubbles as they unfolded during the recording, with the pointer (or tail) indicating the location of the young co-learner (right) and the older co-learner (left). These sequential speech bubbles surround the excerpted text viewed at the time of the exchange. Such graphically constructed accounts seemed appropriate based on our intention to make visible the experiences and perspectives of our young multilingual learners. We also intend to share our work with community members who represent varying levels of experience with reading research publications (particularly in English). The illustrated exchanges involving our young co-learners may help foster a shared understanding about our young multilingual learners and ways that we can support or inhibit communicative engagement in the classroom.

Positionality and exploration within social space

Using the void as an analytic lens helped us in maintaining our awareness that there is much hidden from eyes and ears, and observed actions across the contextual layers (e.g., responses from young co-learners, reflections from older co-learners, background noise) can help illuminate some of what is hidden. In a world filled with inequities and social injustices, there are systems in place that prevent us from seeing the realities of marginalized populations who are silenced on a daily basis. Such a reality requires that we commit ourselves to making visible the hidden mechanisms that prevent multilingual learners from full membership of academic communities — the lack of time and space, the constant corrections, the need for talk to *sound academic* in order to *be academic*. Such expectations were consciously avoided in the present study, which helped to strengthen our positionality as co-learners. Traditional classroom discourse represents a dominant positioning of teachers who provide directives and clarifications within a language that meets school standards. The irony of such positioning is that the language of learning actually aligns more closely with the language of professionals when engaged in knowledge building (Arya & Maul, 2016, 2021). The forms of language within English-dominant public-school contexts may inadvertently prevent students from authentic engagement in subjects like science and reading if students are required to use certain words or phrasings during discussion. Positioning multilingual learners as co-learners necessarily involves adhering to the language(s) that the young co-learner deems most useful during discussions.

Implications

If literacy researchers position themselves as learners guided by knowledgeable others (who, in this case, are multilingual learners in an English-dominant classroom), they will be better positioned to create a space to learn more about the interests, stories, lessons, experiences, and perspectives of research participants. As we emphasized earlier, we do not mean to provide readers with a new or different definition of positionality; rather, we attempted to demonstrate how much we can learn and how much we can bring to light if researchers maintain a mindful awareness of assumptions and beliefs about a given population. By positioning our participants as co-learners with knowledge and experiences that researchers do not have, we are best positioned to explore phenomena that are largely invisible in a society that privileges White, English-dominant voices and experiences. We explored the presence, or absence, of various contextual aspects — the location, unspoken classroom rules, established classroom routines, and in vivo facilitative moves — during instances of expressed knowledge and expertise from young multilingual co-learners. We also reflected on the ways in which we positioned ourselves in this research, sharing what we have learned and how other educational researchers may benefit from the ways that we presented our findings in ways that were less tabulated and more graphically representative of hidden contextual phenomena within a social space. In our positioning of multilingual voices as knowers and creators that have much to teach, we departed from deficit frames and stories of suffering (Tuck & Yang, 2014). Hence, we showed how positioning can be a powerful tool for both research and practice.

Findings from our exploration may be helpful to language and literacy researchers who are committed to the transformative educational practices that are needed now more than ever. Based on our work described in this chapter, we offer a series of questions that may be helpful to researchers' reflexivity and mindful awareness of positionality:

1. What beliefs and assumptions do we have about the co-learners centered in our literacy research? How do such beliefs and assumptions shape our ability to learn from others?

2. What kinds of literacy-related activities are best for centering the funds of knowledge of young co-learners?

3. In what ways can we follow up with participants to ensure accuracy in our reporting? What are we potentially missing or misinterpreting?
4. How does our literacy research uplift our multilingual and other traditionally marginalized communities? In what ways are we engaging in transformative work *with* our communities?

These questions offer space for reflexivity not only as researchers but also as human beings who support equitable and ethical social practices. Being an adult in an interaction with a child involves power dynamics that need to be accounted for; thus, we need to continuously work toward encouraging and engaging younger co-learners as knowledgeable. Such questions can allow for reflection on what it is that we value and make space for during the various phases of research — the questions we ask, the theoretical claims we make, the analytic approaches we use, and the ways in which we interpret our findings. Future research that is aimed at making visible the ways in which students, teachers, and community members are positioned during literacy activities may benefit from utilizing the notion of the dialogic void as a starting point for exploration. Starting, for example, with the assumption that there is always more than what initially meets the observing eye, researchers are better positioned to make visible the potential biases that prevent us from fully understanding what multilingual students know and can do.

References

doi Arya, D. J. (2022). Into the void of discourse. *Linguistics and Education*, 68, 100964.

doi Arya, D. J., Clairmont, A., & Hirsch, S. (2020). Interpreting and explaining data representations: A comparison across grades 1–7. In T. Phillips & R. Dippre (Eds.), *Approaches to lifespan writing research: Generating murmurations towards an actionable coherence* (pp. 177–193). Colorado State University Press & the University Press of Colorado.

doi Arya, D. J., Harlow, D., Hansen, A. K., Harmon, L., McBeath, J., & Pulgar, J. (2017). Innovative youth: An engineering and literacy integrated approach. *Science Scope*, 40(9), 82–88.

doi Arya, D. J., & Maul, A. (2016). The building of knowledge, language, and decision-making about climate change science: a cross-national program for secondary students. *International Journal of Science Education*, 38(6), 885–904.

doi Arya, D. J., & Maul, A. (2021). Why sociocultural context matters in the science of reading and the reading of science: Revisiting the science discovery narrative. *Reading Research Quarterly*, 56(S1), S273–S286.

doi Arya, D. J., Pihen González, E., Christman, D., Ozgen, D., Cano, J., Muller, A., Shackley, M., Meier, V., & Mottus, R. ((in press). Rising with the tides of change through community based literacies. In M. Mahmood, J. Cano, & M. Orellano Faulstich (Eds.), *University-University-community partnerships for transformative education: Sowing seeds of resistance and renewal.* Palgrave Macmillan.

Arya, D. J., Sultana, S., Galisky, J., & Katz, D. ((in press). *The Critical Reading Assessment.* Xóchitl Justice Press.

doi Arya, D. J., Sultana, S., Levine, S., Katz, D., Galisky, J., & Karimi, H. (2022). Raising critical readers in the 21st century: A case of assessing fourth-grade reading abilities and practices. *Literacy Research: Theory, Method, and Practice,* 71(1), 418–436.

doi Birt, L., Scott, S., Cavers, D., Campbell, C., & Walter, F. (2016). Member checking: A tool to enhance trustworthiness or merely a nod to validation? *Qualitative Health Research,* 26(13), 1802–1811.

doi Bloome, D., Carter, S. P., Christian, B. M., Otto, S., & Shuart-Faris, N. (2004). *Discourse analysis and the study of classroom language and literacy events: A microethnographic perspective.* Routledge.

Cano, J., McBeath, J., Pulgar, J., Arya, D. J., & Durán, R. (2021). Narrativas digitales para fomentar el interés en el aprendizaje de ciencias [Digital storytelling to foster interest in STEM learning]. In C. Ricardo Barreto, M. Borjas, J. Cano Barrios, & C. Astorga (Eds.), *Ambientes de aprendizaje mediados por TIC en educación infantil* (pp. 113–136). Editorial Universidad del Norte.

Cazden, C. B., & Beck, S. W. (2003). Classroom discourse. In A. C. Graesser, M. A. Gernsbacher, & S. R. Goldman (Eds.), *Handbook of discourse processes* (pp. 165–197). Lawrence Erlbaum Associates.

Conover, E. (2016, November 13). 'Void' dives into physics of nothingness. *Science News.* Retrieved on 18 November 2024 from https://www.sciencenews.org/article/void-dives-physics-nothingness

Council of Chief State School Officers (CCSSO). (2023). *English language proficiency development (ELPD) framework.* Common Core State Standards. Retrieved on 18 November 2024 from https://csaa.wested.org/resource/framework-for-english-language-proficiency-development-standards-corresponding-to-the-common-core-state-standards-and-the-next-generation-science-standards-2/

Fairclough, N. (2001). Critical discourse analysis as a method in social scientific research. *Methods of Critical Discourse Analysis,* 5(11), 121–138.

doi Flewitt, R. (2008). Multimodal literacies. In J. Marsh & E. Hallet (Eds.), *Desirable literacies: Approaches to language and literacy in the early years* (pp. 122–139). Sage.

doi Frankfurt, H. G. (1958). Peirce's notion of abduction. *Journal of Philosophy,* 55(14), 593–597.

Harris, S., Meier, V., & Arya, D. J. (2024). Reconstructing the academic in academic language: Radically listening to hidden worlds of knowledge building. In A. Tomlin & O. Silverman Andrews (Eds.), *When we hear them: Attuning teachers to language diverse students* (pp. 57–72). Information Age Publishing.

doi Hikida, M. (2018). Holding space for literate identity co-construction. *Journal of Literacy Research,* 50(2), 217–238.

Holmes, A. G. D. (2020). Researcher positionality: A consideration of its influence and place in qualitative research: A new researcher guide. *Shanlax International Journal of Education*, 8(4), 1–10.

Karimi, K., Sañosa, D. J., Hernandez Rios, K., Tran, P., Chun, D. M., Wang, R., & Arya, D. J. (2023). Building a city in the sky: Multiliteracies in immersive virtual reality. *CALICO Journal*, 40(1), 24–44.

Lin, A. M. (2015). Researcher positionality. In F. M. Hult, & D. C. Johnson (Eds.), *Research methods in language policy and planning: A practical guide* (pp. 21–32). Wiley Blackwell.

Manohar, N., Liamputtong, P., Bhole, S., Arora, A. (2019). Researcher positionality in cross-cultural and sensitive research. In P. Liamputtong (Ed.), *Handbook of research methods in health social sciences* (pp. 1601–1616). Springer.

Mazzei, L. A. (2004). Silent listenings: Deconstructive practices in discourse-based research. *Educational Researcher*, 33(2), 26–34.

Moll, L. C. (2019). Elaborating funds of knowledge: Community-oriented practices in international contexts. *Literacy Research: Theory, Method, and Practice*, 68(1), 130–138.

Moll, L. C., Amanti, C., Neff, D., & Gonzalez, N. (1992). Funds of knowledge for teaching: Using a qualitative approach to connect homes and classrooms. *Theory into Practice*, 31(2), 132–141.

Morita, N. (2012). Identity: The situated construction of identity and positionality in multilingual classrooms. In S. Mercer, S. Ryan, & M. Williams (Eds.), *Psychology for language learning: Insights from research, theory and practice* (pp. 26–41). Palgrave Macmillan.

Nation, J., Harlow, D., Arya, D. J., & Longtin, M. (2019). From becoming to being scientists: Developing STEM programming for girls using design-based implementation research approaches. *Afterschool Matters*, 29, 36–44.

Serafini, F. (2015). Multimodal literacy: From theories to practices. *Language Arts*, 92(6), 412–423.

Simandan, D. (2019). Revisiting positionality and the thesis of situated knowledge. *Dialogues in Human Geography*, 9(2), 129–149.

Steele, C. M., & Aronson, J. (1995). Stereotype threat and the intellectual test performance of African Americans. *Journal of Personality and Social Psychology*, 69(5), 797–811.

Tuck, E. (2009). Suspending damage: A letter to communities. *Harvard Educational Review*, 79(3), 409–428.

Tuck, E., & Yang, K. W. (2014). Unbecoming claims: Pedagogies of refusal in qualitative research. *Qualitative Inquiry*, 20(6), 811–818.

U.S. Census Bureau. (2022). *U.S. Census Bureau: 2020 Census Results*. Retrieved on 18 November 2024 from https://www.census.gov/programs-surveys/decennial-census/decade/2020/2020-census-results.html

Weatherall, J. O. (2016). *Void: The strange physics of nothing*. Yale University Press.

Wodak, R. (1999). Critical discourse analysis at the end of the 20th century. *Research on Language & Social Interaction*, 32(1–2), 185–193.

CHAPTER 12

Critical collaborative autoethnography

M. Sidury Christiansen & Zhongfeng Tian
The University of Texas at San Antonio | Rutgers University — Newark

This chapter explores the transformative potential that applying critical collaborative autoethnography can have in the path towards decolonizing academic writing, a particular type of literacy practice. Traditional research methodologies, both quantitative and qualitative, are critiqued for marginalizing non-Western perspectives. We propose a paradigm shift towards decolonizing methodologies, foregrounding our own positionality as multilingual researchers navigating the complexities of academic publishing. We re-introduce the concept of *critical friend* as a unique method for conducting autoethnographies. Thus, we advocate the use of *critical* collaborative autoethnography to foster collective exploration of research subjectivity and power-sharing among researcher-participants. This approach moves us beyond simply acknowledging positionality to embracing of relationality in research, advocating for more collaborative inclusive research and multilingual literacy practices in academia.

Keywords: collaborative autoethnography, critical friend, decolonizing methodology, academic writing, positionality

Introduction

In recent years, qualitative research methods have confronted the reality that many of the traditional approaches have colonial roots, originally designed to study colonized or *othered* communities. These traditional approaches deeply rooted in Western perspectives have further marginalized or even silenced non-Western ways of knowing or points of views. The hegemony of traditional approaches is also evident in many literacy practices, especially *essayist* literacy. Essayist literacy, also known as academic writing, can be characterized by the share of rhetorical features represented in English and its Anglo-American seemingly linear, direct, and unmediated style of writing (Trimbur, 1990). Essayist literacy has indirectly silenced populations, branding any deviation from what is considered "standard" (aka white, middle class, European English) as deficient,

https://doi.org/10.1075/rmal.11.12chr

inappropriate, or incorrect. By this hegemonic definition, the writing done by transnational multilingual scholars, which is rich in syntactical and rhetorical structures, has also been considered problematic, and has long been seen in need of remediation by educators and institutions alike (You, 2018). Additionally, academic writing is often considered to be a solitary endeavor (Karell, 2002), a practice that privileges a traditional paradigm of research.

To counteract this problem, humanistic methodologies have emerged to give visibility to multilingual communities and their practices. We aim to contribute to this paradigm shift in academic research and its literacy practices by engaging in collaborative autoethnography because it transcends solitary confines of research subjectivity. In this collaborative space, we introduce the concept of *critical friend*, which can serve as a catalyst to challenge conventional solitary methods while actively engaging in the process of self-reflection to understand better how as researchers we influence the research process. Collaborative autoethnography is an established research method (Chang et al., 2016), but adding the innovative component of a critical friend can serve as an exercise to engage in reflecting on our own positionality that can help researchers not only in their autoethnographies, but also in the positionality section of any qualitative research paper.

A researcher's positionality, which is often seen in a positionality statement within a research article, is a research practice that has sought to make the process more transparent, reflexive, and ethical. It is a way to acknowledge and make explicit the researcher's own positions, personal biases, and possible influences on the research process and outcomes. Many times these statements lack criticality because they have been treated as a way to state a researcher's background, identity, claims of authority, and relationship to the communities being studied. However, these statements need to be crafted in a way that reflect how researchers interrogate the power structures in the context of the research, address privilege and oppression, and change the traditional way to generate research with their knowledge making processes (Boveda & Annamma, 2023; Secules et al., 2021). To know one's positionality in the research implies an exercise in self-reflection to understand how the researcher's own subjectivities influence the way that they perceive and interact with participants, data, and the writing and dissemination of this data (see Chapters 10 and 13 of this volume).

In this chapter, we offer critical collaborative autoethnography as a way to challenge conventional research dissemination practices, foster equitable dialogue, and acknowledge researchers' privileges and adherence to hegemonic writing norms. We describe our recent work to propose multilingualism as an asset not only to diversify language practices, but also literacy practices — particularly academic writing. Rather than romanticizing the process as the mere inclusion of multilingual practices in publication, we argue that achieving essayist literacy diversity requires time, academic effort, and emotional work. We hope to use this new approach to take steps toward systemic change. To achieve this, we first summarize our study, our approach to multilingual practices in essayist literacy, and our methodology and findings. We then engage in a methodological discussion on how the approach we present helps better address our positionality within our research and yields more equitable research practices. Finally, we present some implications and recommendations for employing this approach so that more critical researchers and educators can be cultivated to transform the ways that multilingual learners engage in literacies.

Overview of the study and its findings

To describe what critical collaborative autoethnography is, we will provide a summary of a recent study in which we applied this methodology. Our study, *Critical language awareness in L2 writing: Starting por la autorreflexión,* 自我反省 (Christiansen & Tian, 2023), is part of a special issue of the *Journal of Second Language Writing* that focused on critical language awareness (CLA). CLA is an "approach to study the intersections of language, identity, power, and privilege with the goal of promoting self-reflection, social justice, and rhetorical agency among student writers" (Shapiro, 2022, p. 4). The goal of the special issue was to assess the past, present, and future directions in Second Language Writing in response to changes in academia that called for new ways in which equity and inclusion through language can be enacted in the dissemination of research. The editors framed their invitation for authors to "look backward, outward, and forward" in the field to enact systemic changes in how we conceive writing and the teaching of writing. Our main argument claimed that to critically do so, we must start *inward* by situating ourselves (positionality) within the field. We in that article illustrated how this introspective exercise helped us question our own assumptions, acknowledge our privileges, and gauge how to best advocate for more equitable linguistic practices in academia.

Even though the special issue was pedagogically oriented, we focused on the writing that we ourselves engage in based on the premise that as multilingual, transnational scholars who write about issues of translingualism (in the field of composition) or translanguaging (in the field of language education), we do not always make visible or discuss our own translingual writing practices, nor do we engage in translanguaging in our articles. Therefore, at the research level, our literacy practices appear to be monolingual, favoring the variety of English imposed on us by our position as outsiders (linguistically and epistemologically) to 'western' and U.S. academic contexts. Below, we describe key elements of the critical collaborative autoethnography we conducted and published in the special issue.

Literature review

In academic settings, a strong preference for the "standard" variety of English often eclipses other varieties from being part of writing. This practice perpetuates an ideology of native speakerism (Holliday, 2018), characterized by the belief that "native speakers" represent a monolithic western culture that does not include other non-western cultures, speakers of "vernacular" varieties (e.g., African American English, Latino English), or the English of minoritized communities, even if they speak the so-called standard. Thus, the norm of publishing in "standard" English favors certain types of writing and perpetuates personal biases from editors and reviewers. In the article, we explain that there have already been efforts to pluralize linguistic practices in the dissemination of research by calling for the decolonization of both language and research itself (Cushman, 2016). Scholarship on translingual writing shows the potential for decolonization practices across various domains, including the classroom, teacher education, composition programs, and the workforce — and even extending to academic publishing (e.g., Blommaert & Horner, 2017; Canagarajah, 2013, 2023). These studies highlight how translingual and plurilingual pedagogies prioritize the requirements and strengths of culturally and linguistically diverse writers from all parts of the globe.

However, the uncritical adoption of these new pedagogies may result in superficial engagement with languaging practices that results in the exoticization and alienation of language differences. Therefore, in the article we discussed a critical engagement with translingualism or translanguaging (we see these two terms, while rooted in different disciplines, as interchangeable because of their shared critical orientation to decolonize academic monolingualism) in L2 writing as a means to challenge power structures. We highlighted the need for self-reflexivity in translingual/translanguaging pedagogy and emphasized the importance of "walking the talk." We argued that collaborative, self-reflective practices are essential to challenge the norm of writing as an individual endeavor, linking CLA to action in the effort to decolonize "standard" English and language use in writing and teaching.

In the article, we also described how scholarship on translingual writing has potentially decolonized linguistic practices across various contexts — including classrooms, teacher education, composition programs, and academic publishing — in different ways. We explained that a translingual approach promotes the acceptance of non-standard language in published texts; at a different level, it allows for epistemic, rhetorical, and methodological diversity. While translingual writing is essential, it must be approached critically — that is, considering inequalities, injustices, and social categories such as race, gender, and social status — as language varieties are shaped by complex power dynamics in relationship with other varieties.

Reflecting on the translingualism that each one of us can bring to our writing practices is a critical step to combat the linguistic injustice known as *epistemic ethnocentrism*. This linguistic bias promotes certain worldviews while excluding and devaluing others. One striking example is that traditionally, only those methods used in the natural sciences — including a hypothesis, experiment, quantitative analysis, and conclusion — have been regarded as rigorous (until recently), while qualitative methodologies are seen as subjective, biased, and lacking rigor because they are not designed to be replicated nor do they rely on formulas. Raciolinguistic perspectives (Flores & Rosa, 2015) further characterize the work of scholars targeted by racism as lacking validity. Even when multilingual authors conform to conventional writing standards, their language use is often unfairly scrutinized (Heng Hartse & Kubota, 2014).

One issue that many multilingual writers face is the limit in the acceptance of different English varieties due to many stakeholders' own language ideologies. This is the case of many editors or reviewers, some who may find it difficult to differentiate between developmental stages in writing and personal style of the prose of multilingual speakers (Heng Hartse & Kubota, 2014). Novice scholars, both "native" and "non-native" speakers of English, often face similar challenges in scholarly publication, including requests for "native speaker" proofreading (Fazel, 2019; Mur-Dueñas, 2019). To navigate these issues, many novice scholars conform to "epistemic ritualism," or the uncritically abiding by the established hegemonic structures, discourses, and rules in academia (Habibie, 2022, p. 61) as a survival strategy, especially until they gain more empowerment post-tenure.

To address linguistic inequalities and decolonize academic discourse, scholars have employed pedagogical techniques like textual hybridity, code meshing, and strategic language mixing (see Canagarajah, 2013, 2022, 2023 for specific examples). These practices have allowed writers to use alternative languages alongside "standard" English conventions. However, these efforts alone are insufficient for challenging hegemonic discourses. Therefore, scholars advocate for self-study and self-reflection as a means to promote CLA. Becoming self-aware opens space for challenging established ways of thinking, writing, and teaching. The use of self-reflection helps scholars grow their CLA, question their hurdles and privileges, and transform the way they construct, write, disseminate knowledge, and advocate for translingual practices — ultimately working to decolonize academic discourses. We chose a critical collaborative autoethnographic approach in our study to systematically engage in self-reflexivity and recognize the turning points in our own language histories that empowered us to question hegemonic practices.

Methodology

By using a critical collaborative autoethnographic approach, we first examined our journeys as multilingual writers, focusing on learning English and navigating academia as scholars who primarily use English for scholarship. We critically reflected on our educational and professional experiences in academic English writing in the context of CLA. We contend that CLA benefits both students and instructors by promoting self-reflection, social justice, and rhetorical agency. Our self-reflection encompassed personal backgrounds, contexts for teaching and publishing, and the impact of cultural, linguistic, and educational backgrounds on our academic paths, recognizing our own identities, power, and privilege as transnational, multilingual scholars.

Self-reflection then became a means for critically engaging with multilingual writing before we considered how to move the field forward. As scholars, we have the privilege to advocate for pluralizing language norms and can propose a utopian vision of a diverse language. We are aware that in order to achieve this, as scholars and reviewers we need to meticulously analyze our roles and responsibilities and consider the consequences of our musing about these translingual possibilities — something Canagarajah (2023) skillfully explained in a special issue that presented different ways to disseminate research beyond the traditional academic paper. Collaborative self-reflection, often missing in CLA literature, is key, and the current chapter is an attempt to advocate for non-traditional formatting of scholarship.

Autoethnography is a popular qualitative research method used widely in anthropology, sociology, and, more increasingly, in education. In this method, "a researcher draws on their own experiences to investigate a social phenomenon" (Piller et al., 2022, p.6), and engages in self-reflection, connecting their experiences to broader cultural or social issues. Thus, reflexivity is the core of this practice, which helps researchers become more transparent about their subjectivity and biases. Specifically, in the Second Language Writing scholarship, for example, *critical* self-reflection is encouraged for developing greater social and linguistic responsibility (Britton & Lorimer Leonard, 2020). This process prompts multilingual writing instructors and researchers to reevaluate their past experiences and reassess their validity in the present. Autoethnography is particularly useful for exploring personal topics with social and cultural significance to contribute to a richer understanding of human behavior.

Despite systematic reflexivity, individual autoethnography has faced criticism for being perceived as relying too much on anecdotal evidence, being "self-absorbed," and lacking analysis (Chang et al., 2016, p.21). To counter this perceived bias, researchers participate in self-reflection through activities like journaling, engaging in discussions with peers, and engaging in profound contemplation of educational phenomena (Piller et al., 2022). That is, an alternative to individual autoethnography empowers researchers to pool their experiences and collaboratively evaluate, compare, contrast, and interpret them (Piller et al., 2022). Collaborative autoethnography tackles problems related to epistemic injustice and facilitates epistemic transformation in the way teachers and researchers envision themselves as critical educators, challenging the conventional practice of individual thought and writing. The idea is that self-examination of one's learning, teaching, and writing experiences can be challenging, and seeking input from colleagues (Costa & Kallick, 1993; Schuck & Russell, 2005) can enhance the reliability of the research while providing mutual support (Britton & Lorimer Leonard, 2020). For collaborative autoethnography to achieve *criticality*, this form of self-reflection requires confronting personal limitations and shortcomings; doing so leads to increased critical awareness, social responsibility, and empathy. Additionally, criticality is also engaged when recognizing both the positive and negative consequences (Heng Hartse & Kubota, 2014) of the theoretical, empirical, and pedagogical approaches resulting from the collaborative self-reflection.

To negotiate meaning, scholars embarking on autoethnography first write narratives that facilitate the engagement of external and purposeful negotiations between their readers and themselves.

We began the entire process with informal discussions about translanguaging. When we formalized our paper idea, we worked on a living document, continually commenting and responding to comments for a year. Although we had initially focused on specific topics (e.g., literacy, autoethnography, addressing questions about our English learning experiences), we engaged in freewriting (the practice of writing all of one's thoughts without pausing and thinking about writing rules), which allowed us to understand each other's processes. We then exchanged drafts with over 50 comments, focusing on key experiences that revealed CLA. We each wrote initial narratives about our own individual experiences, which ranged from 2,500–5,000 words. After we exchanged them and engaged in the role of critical friend, these narratives were ultimately condensed to 1,400–1,500 words each and were included in the publication. To read the full narratives, refer to Christiansen and Tian (2023).

We engaged in the following steps for a critical collaborative autoethnography:

1. We crafted a dynamic narrative document in Google Docs, which evolved from our initial discussions to manuscript preparation. In this document, we synthesized our discussions for each meeting as preparation for the critical asynchronous dialogue through the comment features used before our following meeting.

2. We each critically reviewed the dynamic document, leaving comments via the commenting feature. For example, if there was a comment about deficit perspectives in our language use, we ask in the comment for more information so we could determine where the deficit ideology came from. We then addressed these comments in writing and during scheduled meetings to identify patterns. We repeated this process three times, creating a space for dialogue to reflect on our experiences as transnational scholars and gain insight into our translanguaging practices. This process exemplifies both our role as critical friends and the process of addressing each other's comments.

3. We convened for a final meeting to analyze the narrative documents and discussions, identifying patterns and organizing key themes across narratives.

4. We engaged in several informal instant messaging (IM) conversations via Messages on our iPhones, where we sought clarifications, provided additional insights, and held discussions on all related topics. Open dialogue and communication are a crucial part of a critical friendship role. Communicating over IM allowed for micro-dialogues and micro-commenting that enhanced the criticality of our comments in the document and the future meeting we had scheduled.

Findings and discussion

After analyzing the autoethnographic data (personal narratives), we identified three overarching themes that highlighted the collective process of our epistemic transformation and how CLA helped us become more critical educators and scholars: (1) our ingrained monolingual and purist language ideologies; (2) our turning points; and (3) our continuous journeys to embrace translingualism in academic publications.

First, despite our various professional development journeys, we both came to realize our deep-rooted ideologies toward monolingualism and native-speakerism and the driving factors behind them. For Sidury, her striving for linguistic purism was reinforced by her English learning experience, which prioritized strict language separation to avoid "contamination" across languages, her undergraduate program training, which emphasized a full immersion approach with limited use of students' L1, and the job market in México, which favored "native English speakers" and people with "less accent." For Zhongfeng, these similar ideologies got formulated due to the circulating xenocentrism in the Chinese society when he grew up, his English learning experience, which focused heavily on "perfect grammar," and his college training in an English-Medium Instruction (EMI) institution, which perpetuated Anglo-dominated academic cultures. Both of us suffered from linguistic inferiority complexes (Piller, 2016) even though we could use English in speech and writing fluently, which is indicative of the impacts of neo-colonialism on language teaching and learning.

Next, we both revealed our turning points where we started to be aware of these deficit ideologies and problematize them. For Sidury, her working experience with multilingual students helped her realize the benefits of using her L1 to promote deeper language and content learning; meanwhile, her encounter with the concept of *multicompetence* (Cook, 2008) shed light on her view of linguistic repertoire as an ecosystem consisting of interconnected languages to mutually support one another (instead of seeing L1 as an interference). For Zhongfeng, his engagement with the notion of translanguaging (García & Li Wei, 2014) during his PhD program prompted him to reposition himself as a proud multilingual speaker and rethink more equitable and humanizing ways to work with culturally and linguistically diverse learners, debunking the myth of English-only as the one and only path to successful English development. These iterative processes of un-/re-learning represented our growing CLA and laid a foundation for our later advocacy work for the linguistic rights of multilingual speakers.

Lastly, as our CLA continued to grow, so did our frustration with our scholarship presented in English only. We both hoped to take concrete steps to "walk the talk" in academic publications, moving beyond shifting mindsets to see bi/multilingualism as a resource. We shared our different small moves to embrace translingualism in our own literacy practices, such as providing bilingual abstracts and choosing not to italicize words in languages other than English. While acknowledging the symbolic importance of these strategies, we confessed that our adoption of translanguaging seemed like add-on rhetorical devices and we were still bounded by monolingual expectations and the gatekeeping mechanism in the publishing industry. However, by engaging in this introspective exercise and linking CLA to action, we further solidified our unwavering commitment to decolonizing multilingual writing, and we would continue to seek creative and critical ways to actively blur the fronteras 边界 (biān jiè) in our linguistic and scholarly practice and advocate for our natural languaging processes to be normalized and legitimized in academia through collaboration with more like-minded scholars.

Methodological discussion: Positionality for more equitable research

Addressing positionality

Traditionally, scientific inquiry rooted in positivist epistemologies emphasizes objectivity and seeks to detach the researcher from the research itself (Smith, 2023). Although this is nearly impossible to achieve, quantitative research relies on structured design in an attempt to minimize the impact of researcher bias on the study. In many ways, while quantitative research design emphasizes objectivity, qualitative research brings subjectivity to the foreground (Glesne, 2016; Lather & St. Pierre, 2013). Qualitative research requires the researcher to explain how their own background, experiences, and values may influence the research process and interpretations (Hesse-Biber, 2017). This reflexive exercise is integral to the credibility, transparency, and validity of the study, providing a richer understanding of the topic at hand.

Quantitative and qualitative research approaches were developed via Eurocentric traditions of thought. That is, their development and their application contribute to colonial and/or oppressive practices. Both quantitative and qualitative traditions can employ frameworks that marginalize, silence, and invalidate non-Western perspectives. Both mine information from marginalized and vulnerable populations without necessarily taking the researched population into consideration as participants in the research; both have inadvertently, and in some cases purposefully, imposed cultural assumptions on research processes and participants, resulting in their oversimplification and stereotype. In fact, the purpose of qualitative methods such as ethnography was to study the peoples in the colonies who were deemed different, and often, less civilized (Smith, 2023). Ethnographic methods were founded on the ideas of studying "other" cultures (Marcus, 1998).

In response to these earlier research practices, scholars have recognized a lack of trustworthiness and ethics in them and attempted instead to center the voices and perspectives of minoritized communities, moving to embrace decolonizing approaches that, ideally, empower minoritized communities to study and represent themselves in the research they do (Smith, 2023). Decolonizing and humanizing methodologies are grounded in the perspectives and experiences of minoritized communities (Paris & Winn, 2014). The goal is to showcase what is gained by listening to the insights of minoritized people studying their own cultures, instead of outsiders giving an etic account of what they see minoritized people do. Examples of these approaches include oral histories, community-based participatory research, indigenous research and methodologies, intersectionality, storytelling and narrative analysis, and autoethnography.

We chose collaborative autoethnography (see other ethnographic approaches in Chapters 3 and 8 of this volume) for two reasons. One was to decolonize research and academic writing by treating it as a collaborative rather than solitary task. Writing has traditionally been seen as an individual task that people need to master in a composition class. Collaborative writing is seldom taught or advised; in fact, the opposite is true. Collaborative efforts are often considered cheating in evaluative contexts — such as tenure reviews in some disciplines, for instance —

and not representative of a person's ability to write, despite the numerous articles, books, and other academic work co-authored and done in working groups. In this way, collaborative autoethnography decolonizes research and the writing of it at the same time.

The other reason why we chose critical collaborative autoethnography was the opportunity it provided to add criticality and center our positionality in our research. This type of autoethnography offers the unique advantage of using the researchers' own knowledge and experiences as a window to observe and analyze society. We both are transnational, multilingual scholars from Global South countries (México and China), and we both have experienced *epistemic ritualism* — uncritically abiding by the rules of academia. We both were trained in the U.S.; thus, in part, we learned colonized perspectives and the *epistemic ethnocentrism* of the U.S. — the performance, promotion, and validation "of certain world views while excluding, marginalizing, discrediting, and devalorizing others" (Habibie, 2022, p. 60). We both exist within the "publish or perish" culture and have had to change our multilingual language practices to conform to the standard "English only" policies of academic publication. Thus, understanding how our life experiences shaped our thinking and our views of English was important to recognize what aspects and in which ways we have been determined to decolonize this practice. As Heng Hartse and Kubota (2014) explained, self-reflection can help us "recognize the positive and negative consequences of our theorizing" (p. 80), thus taking more responsibility in how we promote the decolonization of language in research and publication. Discussing this process with a trusted colleague (the critical friend component) to make sense of how these deeper thoughts affected our view of the research topic, and our choices to write and disseminate such research, is adding criticality to the research. This collaborative exercise is the core of positionality. For example, positionality statements (in any type of qualitative research, not just ethnographic research) should go beyond stating one's background, identity, claims of authority, and professional proximity to marginalized communities; crafting a positionality statement should help the researchers reflect on how they will transparently deal with interrogating multidimensional power structures, dislocating privilege and oppression, and changing traditional knowledge production (Boveda & Annamma, 2023; Secules et al., 2021).

Methodological innovations

As a research methodology and data collection method with reflexivity as its core, autoethnography and reflexive positionality have been discussed in ethnographic research (Consoli & Ganassin, 2023). For instance, in ethnography, reflexivity has been described as the "self-critique, the personal quest, playing on the subjective, the experiential, and the idea of empathy" (Marcus, 1998, p. 193). In this sense, reflexivity merges the theoretical and practical questioning in an attempt to change ethnographer's view of themselves and their work. An early critique is that reflexivity, when not done well, even if collaboratively, can fail to challenge the paradigm of traditional ethnographic research (Marcus, 1998). This risk is why proponents of humanizing methodology advocate for building a rapport, connections, and links with your participants (Paris & Winn, 2014) as a way to understand the context in which we need to understand people's experiences. Because an autoethnography is a solo endeavor, to gain different perspectives, researchers can engage in collaborative work to understand themselves and their experiences in relation to others.

Collaborative autoethnography (and duoethnography, co-ethnography, or collective autoethnography) surged as a way to collaborate in combining both analytic and evocative research agendas not limited to a particular approach or style, but shaped by the needs of the community to understand social structures (Chang et al., 2016). There are five benefits for collaborative autoethnography: "(1) collective exploration of researcher subjectivity; (2) power-sharing among researcher-participants; (3) efficiency and enrichment in the research process; (4) deeper learning about self and other; and (5) community building" (Chang et al., 2016, p. 25). We focus on benefits 1 and 4 below because we can highlight the innovative approach of adding the role of a critical friend to enhance the exploration of subjectivities and biases, and in doing so learn more about our positionality as researchers (as well as our colleagues).

The concept of "critical friend" is the idea that someone trustworthy can ask "provocative questions, provides data to be examined through another lens, and offers critique of a person's work as a friend" (Costa & Kallick, 1993, p. 50). This person should be deeply invested in the same work one does and should be an advocate, encouraging the researcher for the success of the project (Schuck & Russell, 2005). The concept dates back at least to the early 1990s in the literature about learning organizations, explained as team learning (Senge, 2006), but it has been used in areas such as in teacher education (Britton & Lorimer Leonard, 2020; Pinnegar & Hamilton, 2009; Schuck & Russell, 2005), which rely on self-study and feedback to develop pedagogical and classroom management skills. A critical friend can help another person grow while simultaneously benefiting in the process. The first step is to establish trust; the second is to establish the logistics of meetings (frequency, length, format) and interaction protocols (manner of requesting and providing feedback); the final step is to establish time for reflection and dialogue (Costa & Kallick, 1993). The way in which the steps are to be carried out varies, and the process is not as linear as it seems; rather, it is iterative.

In our case, for our 2023 journal article, we started developing a critical friendship even before we knew what we were doing. As stated in our published article, we began talking regularly about topics of translanguaging and academic writing. Our point of departure was Sidury's skepticism towards the uncritical use of terms such as *translanguaging* and *translingualism* in the fields of education and Applied Linguistics, and Zhongfeng's realization that many transnational, multilingual scholars do not engage in translanguaging or translingual practices, even if that is the point of our research. Initially, we began listening to each other, clarifying what we meant by translanguaging, translingualism, multilingualism, and transnationalism. We encouraged each other to explain more and in detail without fear of being criticized or judged. We wanted to understand each other. We would only offer judgments or clarifications if we asked for them. In doing so, we began building trust in each other. We were able to create a space where we knew we could tell each other "like we saw it" with no filter, no worry. We realized we started giving each other new perspectives, and ideas began to flourish. We decided at that early stage that we would want to collaborate on a manuscript that would synthesize our conversations; thus, we began writing down ideas, thinking points, and summaries of these conversations.

Once we formalized the process of critical friendship, we agreed to (1) keep our weekly talks, (2) synthesize our discussions in notes, (3) write our autoethnographies separately, and (4) exchange our autoethnographies, reading and commenting on parts that were unclear and needed explanation/clarifications, were similar to us, or that looked different from our perspectives or experiences.

The following is an example of the synthesis notes from our conversations that shows how we discussed an issue and provided critical feedback in an amicable and collaborative manner. These conversations took place before the writing of our 2023 article, and none of these synthesis notes was published in the 2023 article, but are shown here for illustrative purposes. This example below was written by Sidury after we had composed the abstract we sent for the special issue in which our article was published:

> June 15, 2022
> One thing we discussed was that our approach to writing the abstract followed Smitherman's translanguaging use (presented in Suresh's article). That is, we wrote in English and then chose carefully how best to integrate our words where it would make rhetorical sense. We also discussed how little by little some scholars are including words in another language in their publications but it always happens in the context of speaking about translanguaging. So far, neither one of us has noticed much change in other journals. Although there are a few articles reporting that some less frequently forms used by NES are increasingly been used by NNES in English as a medium language journals (Martinez, 2018) and that

when the journal is predatory (which are usually not based in English language medium), the language is less 'standard' (Soler & Wang, 2019) which may speak to the overlook of any standards in general including language, but which shows that the linguistic diversity could be greater if there was a choice for those conventions.

There is no recording of the conversation we had that led to this synthesis note. However, we can see that there are a few instances of criticality in our own writing. For instance, we both noticed that we did not engage in translingual practices ourselves (we both only wrote in English), and we discussed that one reason is that we were forced to keep our languages separate, so a natural process had been suppressed. The other reason was to find common ground, since we do not speak each other's "native" language(s). We also critiqued our own insertion of Spanish and Mandarin words, and noticed it was for rhetorical purposes. At that stage, we were not thinking of creating a new way to produce research; we were focused on departing from English-only ideologies that had permeated so deeply into our writing practices.

Once we engaged in the writing of our 2023 article itself, in order to provide critical comments on our autoethnographies, we used a Google Doc with the comment feature. We agreed to do two iterations of responses before discussing again; after we had read and responded to comments twice, we reflected on what we were asked and on the responses to the narratives. Figure 1 shows part of this iterative process:

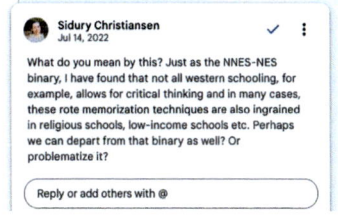

Figure 1. Example of iterative process

The advantage of collaborative tools such as Google Docs is that the process of critical friendship can be done asynchronously, leaving both researchers more time to engage with the text sent and the response given to them. As the comment on Zhongfeng's draft shows, Sidury is requesting clarification of terms used, which later prompts Zhongfeng to rethink about the "eastern vs. western-oriented" binary and to use more nuanced ways to represent his complex learning situation at the undergraduate level. In a way, she is also challenging what she perceives as a generalization, which, though perhaps unintended, allowed us both to engage in a dialogue about our views. Being a sociolinguist, Sidury keeps in mind the diversity in each community. Thus, she felt the need to point out a generalization that we later discussed, and she then understood the point Zhongfeng was trying to make. Sidury also realized that many assertions she made were equally at fault for erasing diversity. Thus, having someone point these out and then engage in dialogue about where these ideologies come from was advantageous to the development of our argument for the manuscript.

This collaborative self-reflection helped us realize that as multilingual scholars we are constantly using our full linguistic repertoire. That is, we engage in translingual practices when writing, whether it is at the invention stage (planning, outlining) or at the composition stage (actual drafting of the manuscript); however, the editing and the final stages are only in English, but we helped each other realize we are both trying to push back in one way or another. Sidury, for example, publishes in journals where diverse linguistic practices are already welcome, and Zhongfeng advocates for the inclusion of diverse linguistic practices in spaces where traditionally that has not been the case. Both of us agreed that while superficial, adding words in other languages to English writing is a necessary step towards the decolonization of our own academic writing.

These two excerpts from our collaborations are examples of how engaging in a systematic process of collaborative autoethnography enriches the analytic experience in two main aspects of collaborative autoethnographies as described by Chang et al. (2016): collective exploration of researcher subjectivity, and deeper learning about self and other.

Collaborative self-reflection calls for a perspective of transformation that invites researchers to merge matters of justice and fairness to personal struggles and desires for social change (Britton & Lorimer Leonard, 2020; Canagarajah, 2002). Thus, after our discussions, we identified the ways in which we would want to decolonize our own language practices and what we could do to move the field of academic writing towards accepting more linguistic diversity. Additionally, collaborative autoethnography addresses epistemic injustice and supports the development of critical educators by challenging individual thinking in academia and enhancing research trustworthiness.

Focusing on equity

In our critical collaborative autoethnography, we strived to foster an equitable way of dialogue and listening in which we learn *alongside* each other, drawing upon our collective experience, knowledge, and perspectives, and centering epistemic openness and heterogeneity (Bang & Vossoughi, 2016). Throughout the process, we realized that while we both are Global South scholars, we somewhat benefited from the mastery of hegemonic codes in academic writing and continued to participate in standardized ways of performing academic literacies without fully leveraging our own translingualism and transnational perspectives in our respective scholarly work. These honest, emotional, and introspective conversations pushed us to critically think about the "access paradox" question (Janks, 2004, p.33) and how to equitably advocate for the linguistic rights of minoritized communities and strategically pluralize and decolonize academic writing.

To enact systemic change and amplify voices from immigrant, transnational, and other marginalized communities in academic writing, we call for deliberate and gradual shifts in language and discourse that have dominated academic language, including its genre forms, practices, and onto-epistemologies, in order to advocate for and propose different forms of writing from within (Canagarajah, 2023). Based on our interdisciplinary positionalities in bilingual education, writing and composition, and applied linguistics, we propose translingual or translanguaging practices as one viable action step to engage in this subversion of language and discourse use. Interestingly, this also prompted us to have genuine conversations to understand the interrelations between the two terms *translingual practice* (Canagarajah, 2012) and *translanguaging* (García & Li Wei, 2014), tracing their roots, histories, and research to date. These discussions further enriched our re-conceptualizations of equitable academic literacies from a cross-disciplinary perspective: we eventually saw these two notions as interchangeable because regardless of the disciplines from which they originated, they both share a critical orientation to perceiving communication as going beyond monolithic labeled languages and treating communication as drawing from diverse semiotic repertoires (including multiple languages and modalities). In our view, a translingual or translanguaging approach to writing includes engaging in various registers and languages in a manuscript, being aware of established linguistic and genre conventions at the institutional level while embracing diversity at local scales, diversifying discourses and rhetorical moves, refining grammatical and syntactical structures, and creating spaces for non-dominant ontologies and epistemologies (García et al., 2021) to flourish. We believe such a literacy approach has the potential to empower all writers and challenge the power structures in academic publishing (Canagarajah, 2011, 2022; Horner et al., 2011).

Furthermore, in our collaborative autoethnography we reminded each other that our goal was not to display a utopian future of academic writing; instead, we, as two multilingual, transnational scholars in relatively privileged positions, should start practicing how to "walk the talk" ourselves and modeling how to work within and against the hegemonic discourses in our own academic writing. Overall, thanks to this dialogic and safe space, we both engaged in deep reflective and reflexive work, learning to reconcile with our own assumptions, bias, and privileges and moving beyond our individual positionality to an embrace of relationality centering on our collective knowledge and agency to promote equity in research.

Implications for qualitative research on multilingual literacy development

In this chapter, we have discussed the transformative potential of critical collaborative autoethnography. It not only serves as a promising way to decolonize traditional research methodologies that are deeply rooted in Eurocentric perspectives, centering on non-Western ways of knowing, perspectives, and experiences, but also provides a humanizing space for researchers (especially those who are from minoritized backgrounds) to collectively engage in positionality reflection, transcending solitary confines of research subjectivity (Boveda & Annamma, 2023; Secules et al., 2021). The aim of this decolonial approach is to advocate for a shift from individual positionality to relationality — a more dynamic understanding of the relationships and interactions that shape one's research (de los Ríos & Patel, 2023) — fostering a more collaborative inclusive research process.

In our case, drawing upon our collective personal and professional experiences, knowledge, and perspectives, both of us were able to look inward critically to question our own assumptions, acknowledge our privileges, and gauge how to best advocate for more equitable literacy practices to support multilingual writers in academia. This introspective exercise helped us reimagine the ways of conducting and disseminating research. We therefore invite future researchers and educators to adopt and adapt this qualitative methodology based on their contextual affordances and constraints to better support multilingual learners from immigrant, transnational, and refugee backgrounds to develop and mobilize literacies across languages. Below, we offer five lessons we learned as important components to consider when embarking on and navigating this journey. We would also like to emphasize that critical collaborative autoethnography can involve more than two people.

1. It is important to start by building trusting relationships among the researcher-participants involved in collaborative autoethnography so that all parties feel comfortable and safe to share their knowledge, stories, and experiences. This can be achieved through multiple ways, such as finding common ground for dialogues, being willing to share feelings and listen to each other without making assumptions, demonstrating the ethic of genuine care and respect during communications, and asking clarification questions if needed.

2. It is beneficial to establish an agreed-upon structure or routine that is constrained enough to enable efficient and effective group reflection (such as developing a timeline and a set of guiding questions) while having wiggle room for adjustments if needed. Meanwhile, it is highly recommended to take advantage of collaborative digital tools (such as Google Docs or Zoom recordings) or other means to document ongoing questions, reflections, and communication moments in systematic ways.

3. This research methodology requires an openness to changing philosophy and practice. During the critical dialoguing process, the two (or more) parties may ask difficult questions to push one another to problematize their original ideologies and expand ways of thinking, knowing and onto-epistemologies. It is essential to commit to a stance of ongoing (re-/un-)learning with open mindsets and learn to embrace ambiguity, uncertainties, and constant shifts, which may eventually lead to personal and collective growth.

4. This methodology also involves complex emotions because of its deep introspective nature. The researchers may experience frustration, confusion, anger, anxiety, epiphany, or awakening moments when sharing, unveiling, facing, and discussing their assumptions, bias, perspectives, privileges, inner fears, and so forth. It is critical to acknowledge the emotional labor as part of the decolonizing research methodologies and academic literacies work. Critical friends play an important role in supporting one another's affective growth, paving the way for engaging in ethical and responsible practices to initiate systemic change.

5. Lastly, critical collaborative autoethnography is an iterative instead of a linear process that involves multiple cyclical steps of reflective and reflexive work about positionality occurring at different temporal-spatial scales. Researcher-participants may go through different learning trajectories due to their varying backgrounds and experiences. Some key questions may need to be revisited, and reversion is a normal part of the process.

Ultimately, this methodology aims to cultivate collective forms of "transformative agency" (Haapasaari et al., 2016, p. 233) in which different parties are attentive to one another's desires, needs, and feelings, listen to and leverage one another's (conflicted) voices and stories, and co-create a change-enhancing context without being impositional (Lather, 1991). With these lessons in mind, we hope the use of critical collaborative autoethnography can cultivate more critical educators and better inform equity-oriented instructional practices aimed at supporting multilingual learners' literacy development across settings.

References

Bang, M., & Vossoughi, S. (2016). Participatory design research and educational justice: Studying learning and relations within social change making. *Cognition and Instruction*, 34(3), 173–193.

Blommaert, J., & Horner, B. (2017). Mobility and academic literacies: An epistolary conversation. *London Review of Education*, 15(1), 2–20.

Boveda, M., & Annamma, S.A. (2023). Beyond making a statement: An intersectional framing of the power and possibilities of positioning. *Educational Researcher*, 52(5), 306–314.

Britton, E.R., & Lorimer Leonard, R. (2020). The social justice potential of critical reflection and critical language awareness pedagogies for L2 writers. *Journal of Second Language Writing*, 50, 100776.

Canagarajah, S. (2002). *A geopolitics of academic writing*. University of Pittsburgh Press.

Canagarajah, S. (2011). Codemeshing in academic writing: Identifying teachable strategies of translanguaging. *The Modern Language Journal*, 95(3), 401–417.

Canagarajah, S. (2012). *Translingual practice: Global Englishes and cosmopolitan relations*. Routledge.

Canagarajah, A.S. (2013). Negotiating translingual literacy: An enactment. *Research in the Teaching of English*, 48(1), 40–67.

Canagarajah, S. (2022). Language diversity in academic writing: Toward decolonizing scholarly publishing. *Journal of Multicultural Discourses*, 17(2), 107–128.

Canagarajah, S. (2023). Decolonization as pedagogy: A praxis of 'becoming' in ELT. *ELT Journal*, 77(3), 283–293.

Chang, H., Ngunjiri, F., & Hernandez, K.-A. (2016). *Collaborative autoethnography*. Routledge.

Christiansen, M.S., & Tian, Z. (2023). Critical language awareness in L2 writing: Starting por la autorreflexión. 自我反省. *Journal of Second Language Writing*, 60, 101008.

Consoli, S., & Ganassin, S. (Eds.). (2023). *Reflexivity in applied linguistics: Opportunities, challenges, and suggestions*. Routledge.

Cook, V. (2008). *Second language learning and language teaching* (4th ed.). Routledge.

Costa, A.L., & Kallick, B. (1993). Through the lens of a critical friend. *Educational Leadership*, 51(2), 49–51.

Cushman, E. (2016). Translingual and decolonial approaches to meaning making. *College English*, 78(3), 234–242.

De los Ríos, C., & Patel, L. (2023). Positions, positionality, and relationality in educational research. *International Journal of Qualitative Studies in Education*.

Fazel, I. (2019). Writing for publication as a native speaker: The experiences of two anglophone novice scholars. In P. Habibie & K. Hyland (Eds.), *Novice writers and scholarly publication* (pp. 79–95). Springer.

Flores, N., & Rosa, J. (2015). Undoing appropriateness: Raciolinguistic ideologies and language diversity in education. *Harvard Educational Review*, 85(2), 149–171.

García, O., & Li Wei. (2014). *Translanguaging: Language, bilingualism and education*. Palgrave Macmillan.

doi García, O., Flores, N., Seltzer, K., Li Wei, Otheguy, R., & Rosa, J. (2021). Rejecting abyssal thinking in the language and education of racialized bilinguals: A manifesto. *Critical Inquiry in Language Studies*, 18(3), 203–228.

Glesne, C. (2016). *Becoming qualitative researchers: An introduction* (5th ed.). Pearson.

doi Haapasaari, A., Engeström, Y., & Kerosuo, H. (2016). The emergence of learners' transformative agency in a Change Laboratory intervention. *Journal of Education and Work*, 29(2), 232–262.

doi Habibie, P. (2022). Early-career scholars and scholarship: A social justice perspective. *Annual Review of Applied Linguistics*, 42, 55–63.

doi Heng Hartse, J., & Kubota, R. (2014). Pluralizing English? Variation in high-stakes academic texts and challenges of copyediting. *Journal of Second Language Writing*, 24, 71–82.

Hesse-Biber, S. N. (2017). *The practice of qualitative research: Engaging students in the research process* (3rd ed.). Sage.

doi Holliday, A. (2018). Native-speakerism. In *The TESOL encyclopedia of English language teaching* (pp. 1–7). John Wiley & Sons.

doi Horner, B., Lu, M.-Z., Royster, J. J., & Trimbur, J. (2011). Opinion: Language difference in writing: Toward a translingual approach. *College English*, 73(3), 303–321.

Janks, H. (2004). The access paradox. *English in Australia*, 139, 33–42.

Karell, L. K. (2002). *Writing together/writing apart: Collaboration in Western American literature*. University of Nebraska Press.

doi Lather, P. (1991). *Getting smart: Feminist research and pedagogy within the post modern*. Routledge.

doi Lather, P., & St. Pierre, E. A. (2013). Post-qualitative research. *International Journal of Qualitative Studies in Education*, 26(6), 629–633.

Marcus, G. E. (1998). *Ethnography through thick and thin*. Princeton University Press.

doi Martinez, R. (2018). "Specially in the last years...": Evidence of ELF and non-native English forms in international journals. *Journal of English for Academic Purposes*, 33, 40–52.

doi Mur-Dueñas, P. (2019). The experience of a NNES outer circle novice scholar in scholarly publication. In P. Habibie & K. Hyland (Eds.), *Novice writers and scholarly publication: Authors, mentors, gatekeepers* (pp. 97–115). Springer.

doi Paris, D., & Winn, M. T. (2014). *Humanizing research: Decolonizing qualitative inquiry with youth and communities*. Sage.

doi Piller, I. (2016). Introduction. In I. Piller (Ed.), *Linguistic diversity and social justice: An introduction to applied sociolinguistics* (pp. 1–8). Oxford University Press.

doi Piller, I., Zhang, J., & Li, J. (2022). Peripheral multilingual scholars confronting epistemic exclusion in global academic knowledge production: A positive case study. *Multilingua*, 41(6), 639–662.

doi Pinnegar, S., & Hamilton, M. L. (2009). Questions of practice. In S. Pinnegar & M. L. Hamilton (Eds.), *Self-study of practice as a genre of qualitative research: Theory, methodology, and practice* (pp. 47–65). Springer.

doi Schuck, S., & Russell, T. (2005). Self-study, critical friendship, and the complexities of teacher education. *Studying Teacher Education*, 1(2), 107–121.

doi Secules, S., McCall, C., Mejia, J.A., Beebe, C., Masters, A.S., L. Sánchez-Peña, M., & Svyantek, M. (2021). Positionality practices and dimensions of impact on equity research: A collaborative inquiry and call to the community. *Journal of Engineering Education*, 110(1), 19–43.

Senge, P.M. (2006). *The fifth discipline: The art & practice of the learning organization*. Doubleday.

Shapiro, S. (2022). *Cultivating critical language awareness in the writing classroom*. Routledge.

Smith, L.T. (2023). *Decolonizing methodologies: Research and indigenous peoples* (2nd ed.). Bloomsbury Academic.

doi Soler, J., & Wang, Y. (2019). Linguistic differences between well-established and predatory journals: A keyword analysis of two journals in political science. *Learned Publishing*, 32(3), 259–269.

doi Trimbur, J. (1990). Essayist literacy and the rhetoric of deproduction. *Rhetoric Review*, 9(1), 72–86.

doi You, X. (Ed.). (2018). *Transnational writing education: Theory, history, and practice* (1st ed.). Routledge.

CHAPTER 13

Commentary: Challenging extractive epistemologies through positionalities of relation and community accountability

María Paula Ghiso
Teachers College, Columbia University

This commentary on Part 3 of *Innovative Qualitative Methodologies in Multilingual Literacy Development Research: Amplifying Voices from Immigrant, Transnational, and Refugee Communities* focuses on how qualitative literacy researchers have begun to rethink positionality in ways that challenge extractivist epistemologies and create new opportunities to work alongside and in the service of multilingual, transnational, and/or immigrant and refugee communities.

Keywords: qualitative, literacy, multilingual, methodology, positionality

Educational research about and with multilingual, transnational, and/or immigrant and refugee communities is at an inflection point. Research-partnerships, community-based research, and participatory methodologies — approaches that foreground collaboration, the democratization of knowledge production, and the direct benefits of research to impacted communities — have unsettled entrenched paradigms and raised critical questions about the ethics and practices of research (Caraballo et al., 2017; Ghiso & Campano, 2024; Perauch et al., 2022). The chapter authors in this section of *Innovative qualitative methodologies in multilingual literacy development research* take up the call to envision more relational and dialogic forms of research by exploring self-reflexivity as a methodological underpinning. Together, through concrete examples of their methodological choices vis-à-vis their positionalities, Dávila (Chapter 10), Arya et al. (Chapter 11), and Christensen and Tian (Chapter 12), illustrate what it means to go beyond the positionality statement to embody self-reflexivity across their research. They offer pathways for making visible and contending with the dilemmas, tensions, and contradictions of positionality in research.

https://doi.org/10.1075/rmal.11.13ghi

Taking positionality seriously as an epistemic practice is a challenge to extractivist approaches to research and necessarily entails an analysis of power. Linda Martín Alcoff (2022) describes extractivist epistemologies as having inter-related impulses that map onto the global capitalist project of coloniality, including: "extract[ing] epistemic elements from their original surroundings and in this way from their political, ethical, and institutional context of articulation", "defining the value that is extracted in non-relational way" (p. 4), and "seeking exclusive appropriation and control over intellectual items such as knowledges and processes" (p. 16). Alcoff argues that these dimensions of extractive epistemologies allow "knowledge-seeking institutions or individuals to avoid being held accountable to the ethical, political, and economic demands of indigenous groups or other local communities whose resources are being extracted" (p. 5). Seeking greater accountability to the communities our research engages is paramount if we are to interrupt the oppressive conditions many youth and families from immigrant, transnational, and multilingual backgrounds experience in the education system.

Extractivist epistemologies have long been the foundation of much university-based research. We can see these reverberations in the hierarchies between those who carry out research and those whose experiences, perspectives, or outcomes are "researched," the ways that scholarly rigor is often characterized by abstraction and generalizability, and the lack of attention to participants' own desires for and relations to the research enterprise. These are not only philosophical critiques, but actual demands by communities to have research be aligned to their goals and by refusals (Simpson, 2014) to participate in extractivist knowledge projects. In the Communities Advancing Research in Education (CARE) Initiative, the long-term community-based research partnership I have had the privilege to help cultivate (Campano et al., 2016; Ghiso & Campano, 2024), immigrant families have been vocal about their critiques of university-based research. One Mexican elder and community activist recently noted in a presentation, "no somos ratas de laboratorio" [we are not lab rats] and advocated instead for research that is community-led and relational, where collaborators work together to develop trusting bonds rather than be used transactionally for the benefit of others (Rusoja et al., 2024). As my colleague Gerald Campano and I have noted in our work with members of CARE,

> [w]hat community members have taken issue with over the years is any form of epistemic objectification, where they are "theorized" rather recognized as theorists and intellectuals in their own right. Often there is even a double form of exploitation: Community members are objectified *and* their knowledge is often appropriated, lifted out of context, and circulated as a commodity or form capital by others".
> (Ghiso & Campano, 2024, p. 54)

Communities are being vocal about the need for accountability, reciprocity, and equity in research processes. It is an urgent time for university-based researchers to interrogate the work they do, to consider how they might be perpetuating extractivist epistemologies (in an academic system that values and rewards such stances), and how they can use their own positions to advocate for and enact more just methodologies.

In this regard, self-reflexivity of one's positionality is central. This is not an intellectual exercise, a type of disembodied reflection to be conducted from the Ivory Tower or contained by one section of a published article. In the remainder of this response, I think alongside chapter authors Dávila (Chapter 10), Arya et. al (Chapter 11) and Christiansen and Tian (Chapter 12), to argue that one's positionality in research is best lived as an embodied, affective, and material practice. It is a type of reflexivity that involves showing up, thinking alongside, feeling alongside, and working together to create more horizontal conditions for joint inquiry. Engaging in non-extractivist work necessitates that researchers step out of the realm of the spectatorial and enact more dialogic and situated ways of producing knowledge in community with others.

Christiansen and Tian (Chapter 12) describe positionality as a means to foster methodologies that are "more transparent, reflexive, and ethical" and which "acknowledge and make explicit the researcher's own position, personal biases, and possible influences on the research process and outcomes." (p. 236). These principles are central in how we conceive of ourselves in our research and in how we are in relation with others (participants, collaborators, broader academic fields, and the contexts our research seeks to influence). Through their study, Christiansen and Tian turn the methodological lens inward to report on a critical autoethnography of their translingual/translanguaging academic writing practices. This internal focus contests extractivist colonial logics through the critiquing and remaking of academic research dissemination, through the collaborative inquiry practices themselves, and by challenging the presumed dichotomy between "researcher" and "researched." Multilingual and immigrant-origin learners are often the subjects of study, whether our attention be on their perceived deficits or on a strengths-based perspective that foregrounds their funds of knowledge (González et al., 2006). Christiansen and Tian, by analyzing their own multilingual writing practices as researchers, disrupt "us"-"them" binaries and make visible the ways that they are part of — rather than separate from — immigrant and transnational communities. These actions recognize that researchers are not decontextualized beings who make claims "from a detached and neutral point of observation (that Colombian philosopher Santiago Castro-Gómez (2007) describes as the *hubris of the zero point*)" (Mignolo, 2009, p. 160) but are entangled in specific sociopolitical contexts and producing knowledge from within these systems. Such situatedness punctures the presumed universality of the researcher lens, what Mignolo (2009) characterizes as "epistemic disobedience": a "delink[ing] from the illusion of the zero point epistemology" (p. 160).

Throughout their inquiry process, the critical friendship that Christiansen and Tian (Chapter 12) enact becomes a form of collective witnessing and shared consciousness-raising, as the Global South researchers develop trust with one another, tell their stories of navigating a Eurocentric and English-only academic sphere, and challenge each other to question their affective investments and complicity in these systems. As a multilingual academic myself, their words struck a chord. I vividly recall an early publication experience when my colleague and I submitted an article revision and inadvertently retained a comment we had made to each other in Spanish within the submitted English text. The reviewer spent a full paragraph on this inadvertent inclusion: first translating our aside into English and then subsequently using the lens of language (in)competence to call into question other aspects of the writing which were merely stylistic choices or typographical errors, minutia that would otherwise have gone unmarked. That rogue sentence had called attention to our linguistic "otherness" and in the process made starkly clear both the unspoken norms of the genre and the role of other academics as arbiters of appropriateness. Through their collective inquiry, Christiansen and Tian (Chapter 12) bring such normativity and surveillance to the surface, in the process inviting all researchers to contend with their relationship to academic writing norms and the presumed monolingualism of its writers, and to challenge and remake these assumptions. One powerful dimension of Christiansen and Tian's reflexive inquiry on positionality was their commitment to "practicing how to 'walk the talk' [them]selves" rather than "display[ing] a utopian future of academic writing." This intentional lingering on the at-times-uncomfortable process of autoethnography, including the impulse to "abide by the rules of academia" and the possibly limited impact of our efforts, neither brackets nor romanticizes that it might look like to interrogate one's positionalities in research.

While Christiansen and Tian's work spotlight researcher inquiries into their positionalities in representing and disseminating autoethnographic scholarship, the other chapters in this section grapple with self-reflexivity within classroom-based research projects with other non-author participants, inviting us to dig beneath the surface of our initial findings and routinized ways of doing things to reconsider how research might be made more relational, situated, and less extractive. Dávila (Chapter 10) revisits her data, particularly her fieldnotes, from a classroom study of adolescents' language and literacies. The unexpected presence of Madou, a student from the Democratic Republic of Congo who was part of the Deaf and Hard of Hearing community, and the reliance on an ASL interpreter as a mediator for the research, becomes a catalyst for Dávila to interrogate her positioning in the research more broadly. Methodologically, Dávila powerfully describes how the ASL interpreter's presence and lack of understanding of French curtailed the possibilities for direct engagement with Madou's expansive literate repertoire by asking directly that communication be conducted in English rather than in French, a shared language with other students in the class. This practical consideration is a stark reminder of how multilingual youth are often made to assimilate to the established school system or the established research protocols.

Dávila (Chapter 10) notes how the interpreter would often take the lead in following up on interview questions independently, in a sense directing the exchanges and amplifying Dávila's outsider status. These additional layers of relations both introduce something new into the research dynamics but also help to show how our interpretations and influences as researchers are always already present, with Madou in the picture or not. Dávila's reflections on the partial or incomplete nature of her observations, what she was attending to or ignoring, and how her presence influenced her readings of Madou's literacies remind us how all research is interpreted. All our research is also being shaped institutionally and personally through the resources made available, the structures of the research process, and our habituated ways of attending. The methodological reflections about positionality modeled by Dávila invite us into "reconsideration[s] of [our] role[s]" — into looking anew, and differently, at what might have otherwise gone un-interrogated.

Dávila's consideration of the relational, embodied, and affective dimensions of research, and her ongoing questioning of methodological choices through these lenses, destabilize extractivist research paradigms. She sheds light on the entangled relationships among those involved in the research: Madou, his friends, the classroom teacher, the ASL interpreter, and Dávila herself. At times different synergies or exclusions surface, with some conversations amplified and others curtailed or narrowed, thus emphasizing research as a relational and dialogic endeavor. Dávila, for example, at once points to the ways she sought to cultivate trust with Mrs. Anderson, the interpreter, and to the limits of such relations. She powerfully asks "how this research may have unfolded differently had I begun developing this aspect of the research with Madou, rather than those who in many ways brokered our relationship." This retrospective call to action raises important methodological issues that don't have easy resolution, including: How can our methodological approaches be responsive to and formed in dialogue with the people whose language/literacy practices are the focus of inquiry? What might a Deaf and Hard of Hearing-centric or Madou-centric research design look like? How might processes of interpretation be made more collective? How can institutional structures be better attuned to flexibility and relationality as research necessities?

The chapter by Arya and colleagues (Chapter 11) takes the idea of analyzing what may be overlooked or misinterpreted because of our positioning and provides a framework for how to intentionally think with the silences of research — what they refer to as a "discursive void." Through this lens, silences do not constitute a "lack" (in participants' perspectives, contributions, or input), but are potentially the product of the research design itself. Arya et al. undertake several innovative and non-extractive methodological moves in thinking with their positionalities as "a throughline from start to finish." They intentionally name their positionality as that of "co-learners" alongside multilingual children and design their study to foreground children's funds of knowledge. The authors align their work with Tuck and Yang's (2014) admonition against reproducing damage-centered research that promotes deficit paradigms and position communities as objects of study. Importantly, the authors note that "complete equity among all actors within a study may be a worthy but elusive goal." Even the shift to "co-learner" cannot erase power dynamics and could even be used to paper over hierarchies that are salient to participants in our studies or the communities we research alongside. In my own research, community members have reminded me that in my efforts to center their knowledge and voices I don't forget that I am also a participant with something to contribute, that not speaking up can be disingenuous, and that power can be exercised in the service of others and of the collective.

One way in which Arya and colleagues in Chapter 10 engage the goals of co-learning while attending to power is through their examination of the research invitations themselves. The authors revisit previously collected data from a study of reading abilities to understand "the social space" within which those recordings took place. Their gaze is not on the children's funds of knowledge but on how the interactions can create the conditions for sharing or suppressing those insights. The focus on the "dialogic void" thus puts the onus not on students (whose insights would then be categorized and evaluated, such as by their presence or lack thereof) but on the built environment of the research design itself, which created the conditions for some knowledges to surface and not others. The framework identifies types of potential silencing: corrective silencing, procedural silencing, contextual silencing, multilingual silencing, inquiry-driven silencing, and chrono silencing. These textured potentialities very concretely demand that researchers engage with the silences their methodological decisions create. As university-based researchers, we are heirs to and complicit in academic social spaces that are extractivist and which participate in silencing through language hierarchies, imposed timeframes, bureaucratic and exclusionary procedures, and circumscribed modes of inquiry and publication. We can also commit to doing research that works within and against these academic histories and norms. Engaging productively with the discursive void created through our research decisions suggests ways of mobilizing self-reflexivity not as a social identifier or disclosure to be contained within a specific section of one's work, the prevalent genre in educational research (de los Ríos & Patel, 2023). Rather, self-reflexivity becomes a continual process of questioning how we shape opportunities for multilingual and transnational learners to engage in and with our work, engage in and with the field, and engage in and with our methodological decisions.

The arguments laid out by all the chapter authors in this section emphasize how even once a research project is "done," a methodological re-reading through positionality offers new possibilities for future work. As we sit with their critical questioning and with their learnings, it behooves us to consider how these provocations can shape future work. The chapter authors showcase processes that peel back and think through the influence of our situated lenses on the research process. As we commit to working towards more relational and non-extractive methodologies, one impulse is to consider how each of our future projects might engage in collaboration with participants themselves, including in the research design, interpretations, or or writings. The authors' efforts also invite us to name the ethical principles that arise from non-extractive research positionalities: being in relation through research, resisting the commodification of knowledge, and striving for accountability through research that benefits multilingual, transnational, and immigrant communities directly, not as filtered through our academic lenses.

In one of his seminal works on literacy, Juan Guerra (2004) argues against the underlying assumption that critical consciousness is a linear progression from naiveté to a discernment, culminating in a clear end point where we pull the veneer from others' or our own oppressive circumstances. Methodological self-reflexivity is more like Guerra's "nomadic consciousness," a self-reflexivity that "follows no predetermined sequence" (p.10) and is "unsteady" and "unpredictable" (p.11). Guerra writes that, "[n]o one among us ever achieve such a heightened state of consciousness that we no longer have any place to go" (p.10). In 'walking the talk' of engaging positionality across all aspects of the research process, the chapter authors showcase how this undertaking is unsteady, may have us wander down unintended paths, and involves steps backward as much as forward progress. This is where the journey is made stronger by the company of others who can walk alongside and can take the lead or clear the path when we are unable to, and for whom we can do the same.

References

Alcoff, L. M. (2022). Extractivist epistemologies. *Tapuya: Latin American Science, Technology and Society*, 5(1), 1–23.

Campano, G., Ghiso, M. P., Welch, B. (2016). *Partnering with immigrant communities: Action through literacy*. Teachers College Press.

Caraballo, L., Lozenski, B. D., Lyiscott, J. J., & Morrell, E. (2017). YPAR and critical epistemologies: Rethinking education research. *Review of Research in Education*, 41(1), 311–336.

Castro-Gómez, S. (2007). The missing chapter of empire: Postmodern reorganization of coloniality and post-Fordist capitalism. *Cultural Studies* 21(2–3), 428–48.

de los Ríos, C. V. & Patel, L. (2023). Positions, positionality, and relationality in educational research. *International Journal of Qualitative Studies in Education*, 1–12.

Ghiso, M. P. & Campano, G. (2024). *Methods for community-based research: Advancing educational justice and epistemic rights*. Routledge.

González, N., Moll, L. C., & Amanti, C. (Eds.). (2006). *Funds of knowledge: Theorizing practices in households, communities, and classrooms*. Routledge.

Guerra, J. (2004). Putting literacy in its place: Nomadic consciousness and the practice of transcultural repositioning. In *Rebellious reading: The dynamics of Chicana/o cultural literacy*. Chicano Studies Institute, UC Santa Barbara. Retrieved on 18 November 2024 from http://escholarship.org/uc/item/52q817fq

Mignolo, W. D. (2009). Epistemic disobedience, independent thought and decolonial freedom. *Theory, Culture & Society*, 26(7–8), 159–181.

Peurach, D. J., Russell, J. L., Chen-Vogel, L, & Penuel, W. R. (Eds.). (2022). *Foundational handbook on improvement-focused educational research*. Rowan & Littlefield.

Rusoja, A., Portillo, Y., Vazquez Ponce, O., Ponce, O., & Hernández, M. (2024). "Espérate, vamos a echar chisme": Latinx immigrants co-designing participatory action research through communal research literacies. Paper presented at the AERA Annual Conference, Philadelphia, PA.

Simpson, A. (2014). *Mohawk interruptus: Political life across the borders of settler states*. Duke University Press.

Tuck, E., & Yang, K. W. (2014). Unbecoming claims: Pedagogies of refusal in qualitative research. *Qualitative Inquiry*, 20(6), 811–818.

CHAPTER 14

Conclusion: Innovative research on multilingual literacy development
New directions for methodology

Amanda K. Kibler & Fares J. Karam
Oregon State University | University of Nevada, Reno

In this concluding chapter to the volume, *Innovative Qualitative Methodologies in Multilingual Literacy Development Research: Amplifying Voices from Immigrant, Transnational, and Refugee Communities*, we argue for the importance of responsive, inclusive, and ecological epistemologies in guiding researchers engaged in critical and equity-oriented qualitative research in multilingual contexts. We close with implications for qualitative literacy researchers as they rethink data, theory, and positionality in their work.

Keywords: qualitative, literacy, multilingual, methodology, innovation, equity

Introduction

Across the nine empirical-methodological chapters and three commentaries in this volume, authors have presented multiple approaches to rethinking data, theory, and positionality in order to create more equitable and insightful research into multilingual immigrant, transnational, and refugee learners' literacy development and use across languages. Central to this challenge is the notion that literacies are always "on the move" (Stornaiuolo, Chapter 5), as people, things, and literacy practices themselves move across physical spaces, digital and other media (Karam & Kibler, Chapter 3; Kuo & Spreçic, Chapter 4), languages (Kim et al., Chapter 6; Salas & Lizárraga Dueñas, Chapter 7), and temporal dimensions, among others. Global migrations and disruptions have further highlighted this dynamic reality for those whose lives cross borders and languages (see Adams Corral & Gallo, Chapter 8). Engaging in equitable research with these populations requires new approaches, and the authors in this volume attempt to show how researchers can methodologically innovate in response to these dynamic contexts.

https://doi.org/10.1075/rmal.11.14kib

The value of responsive, inclusive, and ecological stances
for equity-oriented research

Because literacies and their users are always on the move, rethinking methodologies is a constant process rather than a single decision or study design element. In this way, equitable literacy research methodologies can be better understood as a responsive stance, or epistemology. Such work includes but extends beyond critical reflexivity, requiring qualitative literacy researchers to fundamentally reconsider their empirical endeavors.

Critical and equity-oriented literacy research that aims to document or support social and/or systemic change must have at its core a focus on ethics, and on "context specific research ethics" in particular (Cinaglia et al., 2024, p.2). Ghiso (Chapter 13) explains that this work requires a rejection of "extractivist epistemologies" (see Alcoff, 2022) aligned with colonial and hierarchical traditions that distance researchers from those who they study, objectify rather than partner with those participants, and value abstraction and generalizability. Instead, ethical and equitable qualitative literacy research should be grounded in epistemologies that "foreground collaboration, the democratization of knowledge production, and the direct benefits of research to impacted communities" (Ghiso, Chapter 13, p.256). This can be done in community, walking alongside those whose literacies we seek to understand, and engaging with those participants to ensure that ethical choices in both our research design (which De Costa et al. [2019] describe as macro-ethics) and our day-to-day decisions (or micro-ethics) are guided by inclusive rather than extractivist epistemologies. Authors in our volume highlight a range of approaches to doing this work in methodologically rigorous and systematic ways. They also show us the value of re-reading data after our initial studies have concluded, and how such reflexive re-visits can lead to new insights into literacies, their users, and ourselves (Brooks, Chapter 2; Dávila, Chapter 10). They also highlight the value of collaborative and critical engagement with fellow researchers (Christensen & Tian, Chapter 12).

Across the chapters in this volume, it is also clear that responsive and inclusive epistemologies are grounded in ecological approaches to research. As qualitative researchers, we stand at the nexus of several interconnected ecologies. From one perspective, we are situated in methodological ecologies that include multiple research approaches and paradigms, some of which are contentious and irreconcilable, while others — like those from indigenous and Global South communities and researchers — have been systematically excluded from the canon of qualitative methods, a trend that is changing somewhat but has yet to be meaningfully integrated into mainstream qualitative methodologies (McKinley, Chapter 9). Disciplinary, professional, and institutional ecologies in which researchers are situated also influence how multilingual literacy research is approved, funded, conducted, and received. Methodological innovations and equity-oriented research may not be universally welcomed in these spaces, and those undertaking such work may be tasked with educating and persuading colleagues, supervisors, funders, and editors of the value of their work. Recent institutional restrictions in some conservative U.S. states on diversity, equity, and inclusion (DEI) related activities have also shown how much our institutional ecologies are influenced by political discourses and rhetoric. Arguing for the importance of research on literacy development in multilingual immigrant, transnational, and refugee communities can thus be a political act for researchers rather than simply a scholarly one.

Another set of ecologies in which we as researchers are situated includes the spaces in which we conduct research, and at the center of these ecologies are the research participants themselves. In rethinking data, theory, and positionality in multilingual literacy research, we must consider whose stories and narratives are centered in our work, and whose are silenced (Arya et al., Chapter 11), as well as which literacies we prioritize or value in our work. Further, no single person or community has a single story, and so researchers' choices of which of the many possible stories to tell are consequential.

Two characteristics of ecologies – their interconnected and their dynamic nature – are also valuable for qualitative literacy researchers to consider. The notion that each element of an ecology is interrelated and inextricable means that we cannot fully understand an individual without understanding the contexts in which they are embedded, nor can we assume that making particular changes to learning environments or research methods will have singular or intended effects. We can assume, however, that what we study is constantly changing, and so our methodologies must also be responsive, dynamic, and holistic. Such a perspective can help us more fully understand the nature of multilingualism and literacy development in the context of literacies that are on the move. As researchers, we simply cannot be the ones standing still: doing so risks the relevance and value of our work and the impact it can potentially have.

The ethical motivation to be literacy researchers on the move

Bringing responsive, inclusive, and ecological stances to multilingual literacy research provides us with an ethical motivation to innovate. Professionally and methodologically, it calls us to move out of our comfort zones and engage in the new approaches and perspectives that are needed to fully capture multilinguals' dynamic and ever-changing engagement with literacies. Intellectually, we must center the realities of those whom we study (McKinley, Chapter 9), as well as their sociomaterial circumstances for literacy practice (Stornaiuolo, Chapter 5). Perhaps less obvious are the interpersonal implications of innovation: Change requires us to build and sustain relationships with new collaborators, including both the communities and individuals we study and the colleagues who can help to push us methodologically (Ghiso, Chapter 13). A final call for change is intrapersonal – methodological innovation of the kind presented in this volume means that we must become comfortable with the inevitable need for flexibility as we follow literacies and their users, and with the reality that researchers inevitably must make choices in research, which should be guided by the goals of this work and a commitment to documenting and/or supporting social and structural change.

We close this volume with a call for qualitative multilingual literacy researchers to continue to innovate and to also challenge themselves to inform and educate others on how methodological innovation is interconnected with pursuing equitable and ethical research. Individual researchers cannot do this alone, however. Gatekeepers such as journal editors and funding agencies can help validate, support, and reward methodological innovations, especially those that push boundaries in challenging inequities in education and centering ethical approaches to research. Mentors can also push themselves to innovate and pursue innovative methodologies with their mentees at different levels. With literacies and literacy researchers on the move, such profession-wide changes are necessary to create the space and flexibility for new approaches to develop and flourish.

References

Alcoff, L. M. (2022). Extractivist epistemologies. *Tapuya: Latin American Science, Technology and Society*, 5(1), 1–23.

Cinaglia, C., Rabie-Ahmed, A., & De Costa, P. I. (2024). Introduction. In P. I. De Costa, A. Rabie-Ahmed, & C. Cinaglia (Eds.), *Ethical issues in applied linguistics scholarship* (pp. 1–7). John Benjamins.

De Costa, P. I., Lee, J., Rawal, H., & Li Wei. (2019). Ethics in Applied Linguistics research. In J. McKinley & H. Rose (Eds.), *The Routledge handbook of research methods in Applied Linguistics* (pp. 122–130). Routledge.

Index